# A Cultural History of Jewish Dress

**Dress, Body, Culture**

Series Editor: **Joanne B. Eicher**, *Regents' Professor, University of Minnesota*

Advisory Board:
**Ruth Barnes**, *Ashmolean Museum, University of Oxford*
**James Hall**, *University of Illinois at Chicago*
**Ted Polhemus**, *Curator, "Street Style" Exhibition, Victoria and Albert Museum*
**Griselda Pollock**, *University of Leeds*
**Valerie Steele**, *The Museum at the Fashion Institute of Technology*
**Lou Taylor**, *University of Brighton*
**John Wright**, *University of Minnesota*

Books in this provocative series seek to articulate the connections between culture and dress, defined here in its broadest possible sense as any modification or supplement to the body. Interdisciplinary in its approach, the series highlights the dialogue between identity and dress, cosmetics, coiffure, and body alterations as manifested in practices as varied as plastic surgery, tattooing, and ritual scarification. The series aims, in particular, to analyze the meaning of dress in relation to popular culture and gender issues and will include works grounded in anthropology, sociology, history, art history, literature, and folklore.

ISSN: 1360–466X

Previously published in the Series

**Helen Bradley Foster**, *"New Raiments of Self": African American Clothing in the Antebellum South*
**Claudine Griggs**, *S/he: Changing Sex and Changing Clothes*
**Michaele Thurgood Haynes**, *Dressing Up Debutantes: Pageantry and Glitz in Texas*
**Anne Brydon and Sandra Niessen**, *Consuming Fashion: Adorning the Transnational Body*
**Dani Cavallaro and Alexandra Warwick**, *Fashioning the Frame: Boundaries, Dress and the Body*
**Judith Perani and Norma H. Wolff**, *Cloth, Dress and Art Patronage in Africa*
**Linda B. Arthur**, *Religion, Dress and the Body*
**Paul Jobling**, *Fashion Spreads: Word and Image in Fashion Photography*
**Fadwa El Guindi**, *Veil: Modesty, Privacy and Resistance*
**Thomas S. Abler**, *Hinterland Warriors and Military Dress: European Empires and Exotic Uniforms*
**Linda Welters**, *Folk Dress in Europe and Anatolia: Beliefs about Protection and Fertility*
**Kim K.P. Johnson and Sharron J. Lennon**, *Appearance and Power*
**Barbara Burman**, *The Culture of Sewing*
**Annette Lynch**, *Dress, Gender and Cultural Change*
**Antonia Young**, *Women Who Become Men*
**David Muggleton**, *Inside Subculture: The Postmodern Meaning of Style*
**Nicola White**, *Reconstructing Italian Fashion: America and the Development of the Italian Fashion Industry*
**Brian J. McVeigh**, *Wearing Ideology: The Uniformity of Self-Presentation in Japan*
**Shaun Cole**, *Don We Now Our Gay Apparel: Gay Men's Dress in the Twentieth Century*
**Kate Ince**, *Orlan: Millennial Female*
**Nicola White and Ian Griffiths**, *The Fashion Business: Theory, Practice, Image*
**Ali Guy, Eileen Green, and Maura Banim**, *Through the Wardrobe: Women's Relationships with their Clothes*
**Linda B. Arthur**, *Undressing Religion: Commitment and Conversion from a Cross-Cultural Perspective*
**William J.F. Keenan**, *Dressed to Impress: Looking the Part*
**Joanne Entwistle and Elizabeth Wilson**, *Body Dressing*
**Leigh Summers**, *Bound to Please: A History of the Victorian Corset*
**Paul Hodkinson**, *Goth: Identity, Style and Subculture*
**Leslie W. Rabine**, *The Global Circulation of African Fashion*
**Michael Carter**, *Fashion Classics from Carlyle to Barthes*
**Sandra Niessen, Ann Marie Leshkowich, and Carla Jones**, *Re-Orienting Fashion: The Globalization of Asian Dress*
**Kim K.P. Johnson, Susan J. Torntore, and Joanne B. Eicher**, *Fashion Foundations: Early Writings on Fashion and Dress*
**Helen Bradley Foster and Donald Clay Johnson**, *Wedding Dress Across Cultures*
**Eugenia Paulicelli**, *Fashion under Fascism: Beyond the Black Shirt*
**Charlotte Suthrell**, *Unzipping Gender: Sex, Cross-Dressing and Culture*
**Irene Guenther**, *Nazi Chic? Fashioning Women in the Third Reich*
**Yuniya Kawamura**, *The Japanese Revolution in Paris Fashion*
**Patricia Calefato**, *The Clothed Body*
**Ruth Barcan**, *Nudity: A Cultural Anatomy*
**Samantha Holland**, *Alternative Femininities: Body, Age and Identity*
**Alexandra Palmer and Hazel Clark**, *Old Clothes, New Looks: Second Hand Fashion*
**Yuniya Kawamura**, *Fashion-ology: An Introduction to Fashion Studies*
**Regina A. Root**, *The Latin American Fashion Reader*
**Linda Welters and Patricia A. Cunningham**, *Twentieth-Century American Fashion*
**Jennifer Craik**, *Uniforms Exposed: From Conformity to Transgression*
**Alison L. Goodrum**, *The National Fabric: Fashion, Britishness, Globalization*
**Annette Lynch and Mitchell D. Strauss**, *Changing Fashion: A Critical Introduction to Trend Analysis and Meaning*
**Catherine M. Roach**, *Stripping, Sex and Popular Culture*
**Marybeth C. Stalp**, *Quilting: The Fabric of Everyday Life*
**Jonathan S. Marion**, *Ballroom: Culture and Costume in Competitive Dance*
**Dunja Brill**, *Goth Culture: Gender, Sexuality and Style*
**Joanne Entwistle**, *The Aesthetic Economy of Fashion: Markets and Value in Clothing and Modelling*
**Juanjuan Wu**, *Chinese Fashion: From Mao to Now*
**Brent Luvaas**, *DIY Style: Fashion, Music and Global Cultures*
**Jianhua Zhao**, *The Chinese Fashion Industry*

# A Cultural History of Jewish Dress

Eric Silverman

B L O O M S B U R Y

LONDON • NEW DELHI • NEW YORK • SYDNEY

**Bloomsbury Academic**
An imprint of Bloomsbury Publishing Plc

50 Bedford Square      175 Fifth Avenue
London      New York
WC1B 3DP      NY 10010
UK      USA

www.bloomsbury.com

First published 2013

**British Library Cataloguing-in-Publication Data**
A catalogue record for this book is available from the British Library.

ISBN    978 1 84520 513 3 (Cloth)
978 1 84788 286 8 (Paper)
e-ISBN    978 0 85785 210 6 (epub)
978 0 85785 209 0 (ePDF)

**Library of Congress Cataloging-in-Publication Data**
A catalog record for this book is available from the Library of Congress.

Typeset by Apex CoVantage, LLC, Madison, WI, USA
Printed and bound in Great Britain

**For Andrea, from whom I learn so much.**
**And for Sam and Zoe, who tell me how little I know . . .**

# Contents

# List of Illustrations

# Acknowledgments

This book has been many years in the making. Along the way, I garnered considerable intellectual and ethical debts to the kindness of various people—academic colleagues, online vendors, shopkeepers, yarmulke manufacturers, students, rabbis, and others. I cannot possibly name you all. For this, I am sorry.

I gratefully acknowledge financial support for various aspects of this research from Wheelock College. I salute my many students who commented upon countless photos of yarmulkes and t-shirts. And I also tip my proverbial hat to colleagues for their conversation, wit, and intellect. Wheelock is a wonderful college, fully embracing of diversity, and I hope this book contributes in some small measure to that noble effort.

I extend enormous thanks to the Women's Studies Research Center at Brandeis University, and especially to Shula Reinharz, the director. My affiliation with the WSRC is always a source of inspiration.

I appreciated the opportunity to present aspects of this work at various conferences, including the Annual Meeting of the Modern Language Association (2004); an Anthropology Department Colloquium at Brandeis University (2007); the Women's Studies Research Center at Brandeis University (2008); a visit to Virginia Tech University sponsored by ASPECT (Alliance for Social, Political, Ethical, and Cultural Thought), the Department of History, Multicultural Programs and Services, and the Women and Minority Artist and Scholar Lecture Series (1999); and, most recently, the wonderful Twenty-Fourth Annual Klutznick-Harris Symposium, "Fashioning Jews: Clothing, Culture and Commerce," at Creighton University. I benefited greatly from these audiences.

Among the many people I would like personally to thank are the proprietors of A1 Skullcap and Brucha Yarmulkes, the kind folks at Judaica Place, Daniel Levine of Levine Judaica, Tom Ewing and Amy Nelson for their hospitality and assistance with historical material on Russia, the many men at the Chabad-Lubavitcher headquarters at 770 Eastern Parkway who tolerated my camera flash (as did innocent bystanders minding their own business in Boro Park and Crown Heights), congregants at Beth El (Sudbury, Massachusetts), Debbie Samuels-Peretz (and her father) for translations, Juli Granat for the sandals, Kerry Wallach (a young and brilliant scholar), Gail Dines and David Levy for lively dinners and conversations about Israel, various kin for anecdotes, my grandparents for their unknowing inspiration, and Mike and Janet Harvey for "reality checks." I am also, of course, keenly indebted to all the folks and institutions who kindly allowed me to use their photographs and garments, and who often provided invaluable comments. I also wish to toss a biscuit to Patch, who offered neither complaints nor complements but constantly kept me company and loved everything I wrote. Despite all this assistance, I accept full responsibility for the text.

Several people at Berg Publishers (now Bloomsbury) graciously tolerated my many delays and helped shepherd this work through to completion. Thank you to Kathryn Earle for initial discussions, Joanne Eicher for encouragement and comments, Emily Roessler for last-minute matters, and my wonderfully helpful editors Hannah Shakespeare, Julia Hall, and Anna Wright. I also want to thank Emily Johnson of Apex Publishing, and especially two anonymous reviewers for their persistent, but always helpful, recommendations.

Last, as always, I must single out my family—the entire *mishpacha*, including my parents and in-laws. I spend far too much time writing at the computer and googling this or that topic. But Andrea, Sam, and Zoe remain forever my moral and existential center.

# Introduction

A family of Jewish immigrants, dressed for a life of prosperity in the New World, poses for a portrait (Figure 1). The small child—cropped hair, leather boots, awkward stance—is my grandmother, Rebecca Grody (née Gorodnetsky), born about 1900 in Novgorod-Volynsk, Ukraine. Rebecca is surrounded by her mother, Ida, and several other regrettably now nameless relatives. Equally unknown is the location of the photographer's studio. The United States, shortly after Rebecca and her kin disembarked? Or Russia, just prior to their departure? I wish I knew more. They look sad, proud, guarded.

My grandmother posed for this portrait at a pivotal moment in history. At the turn of the century, most Jews discarded their old-fashioned garb and conventions and eagerly took up the values and ideals of a new era. Jew and non-Jew alike were swept up in momentous moral, social, and economic transformations. The modern world enshrined the novel principles of citizenship, free choice, social mobility, and consumerism. Modernity promised heretofore unknown prosperity. But in a world untethered to tradition, it was easy to lose one's self, as many did, in modern desires. You could dress like anybody, or nobody.

Long before my grandmother came ashore in New York City, a twelfth-century synod decreed the first of many edicts requiring Jews to don peculiar garb. These outfits marked Jews as Otherly—to be shunned, despised, and sometimes murdered. This marginal dress befitted a people guilty of betraying the Savior. From this angle, Jews dressed differently as God's outcasts. But Jews also dressed differently in premodern Europe because their rabbis understood any emulation of non-Jews as a violation of the divine Law as revealed by God to Moses atop Mount Sinai. The Five Books of Moses, after all, together called the Torah, clearly specify that Jews must adhere to a particular dress code—modesty, for example, and fringes. The very structure of the cosmos demanded nothing less. Clothing, too, served as a "fence" that protected Jews from the profanities and pollutions of the non-Jewish societies in which they dwelled. From this angle, Jews dressed distinctively as God's elect.

But then something happened on the eve of modernity. Jews were encouraged, and in some countries required, to doff their distinctive attire and to pull on the same garments as everybody else. No longer were Jews defined

**Figure 1**  A family of Jewish immigrants poses for a portrait. The author's grandmother (second from the left), circa 1905.

primarily *as* Jews. For the first time in over a millennium, the wider society welcomed, or at least tolerated, Jews as full citizens. And most Jews, my grandmother included, welcomed the opportunity to dress the part. They remained Jewish, to be sure, but not exclusively so. Thus they dressed to participate fully in the wider society. Most Jews, then, beginning in the late nineteenth century, dressed neither for Judaism nor for assimilation but for a delicate balance between ethnicity and citizenship. Yet religious Jews refused to upgrade their wardrobes. They invested their now traditional clothing with mystical and theological significance, never mind a deep emotional connection to their religious worldview. To change suits was tantamount to apostasy.

My grandmother, then, stood at the confluence of far-reaching historical changes to Jewish identity. Jews were suddenly pulled in different directions, each signified by clothing. Jews aspiring to societal integration and individualism tossed aside their old costumes and reached for new, modern, off-the-rack garments. But ultra-Orthodox Jews clutched their traditional attire as a sign of communal identity, difference, and all-encompassing piousness that resisted the very modern values that drove other Jews to yearn for the latest styles. In 1900, all Jews dressed, even if unaware, either to welcome the future or to bemoan it.

My grandmother and her family also portray the middle class they and most Jews hoped to enter, and eventually did. We see jewelry, a stately demeanor, proper posture, clean clothing, and fashionable hairstyles, all amid a faux parlor setting. We also glimpse no garments that bespeak an unmistakable Jewish identity—no head coverings, for example, or prayer shawls. This family dresses for citizenship, yet its members are modestly attired in high necklines, long sleeves, and dark dresses with muted embellishment. Above all else, my grandmother and her kin dress between two worlds, Old and New, Jewish and secular. They dress for passages real and metaphoric.

This book is not about my grandmother. But it is about the clothing choices and constraints she and other Jews, from the ancient Israelites to the New Jew Cool, experienced throughout history. I do not, however, catalog Jewish costumes. Rather, I explore the symbolism, meanings, and messages of both Jewish garments and clothing merely worn by Jews. My argument is that Jewish clothing materializes a series of ongoing, irresolvable conversations about identity. This argument has three general trajectories.

First, I contend that Jewish clothing encodes a conversation concerning the roles and privileges accorded to men and women in both the streets and the pews. Second, I propose that Jewish garments display a conflict between authority and practice, or ideology and social life. In some contexts, this conflict pertained to dress codes imposed by non-Jewish authorities; in other settings, the Jewish public resisted its very own rabbis and communal leaders. Folk wear, we might say, clashed with formal wear. Last, I argue that Jewish clothing symbolizes a wide-ranging tension between what I call ethnic particularism and acculturation—between dressing for a distinctively Jewish identity and dressing like ordinary citizens.

## HIGH HOLIDAYS AND HAUTE COUTURE

To illustrate how clothing communicates the tension between ethnicity and citizenship, let me pose a seemingly straightforward question: What is appropriate attire for the synagogue? As it turns out, Jews have passionately debated this matter for over a century.

In the 1970s, my family and I attended a Conservative synagogue in a suburb of New York City. (The term "Conservative" here, as I discuss shortly, refers to a particular denomination of modern Judaism, not a political outlook.) Traditionally, male Jews over the age of thirteen pray in a devotional shawl or scarf, called a *tallit*, ornamented with knotted fringes called *tzitzit*. Most men in the congregation, I recall, wore the scarves, normally stacked by the dozens in wooden bins located just outside the sanctuary doors. My male peers and I, draped in these inexpensive, black-and-white, mass-produced ritual garments, sat in the pews and mischievously unraveled the fringes.

Some men, however, wore something altogether different. They conspicuously enwrapped themselves in large, often colorful shawls that conveyed a stylish sense of piety. Size *did* matter. These men were not necessarily more devout than other congregants. But they aimed to make a fashion statement that expressed the value of American individualism even as they dressed for a traditional communal ritual.

Competitive piety in the synagogue is not restricted to prayer shawls. In the United States, Jews have long associated the autumnal High Holy Days of Rosh Hashanah (New Year) and Yom Kippur (Day of Atonement) with displays of the newest seasonal fashions, particularly in affluent communities. In fact, clothiers first advertised new High Holy Day outfits over a century ago. Since then, congregants and clergy have annually bemoaned this "synagogue chic." Still, how better to exhibit respect for the Almighty, never mind show off your worldly accomplishments, than to pray in the latest styles?

As far back as 1898, *The New York Times* reported on the "gaudy attire" worn on Rosh Hashanah.[1] A few years later, Rabbi Maurice Harris of Manhattan was so appalled by this opulence that he penned what might be the first of innumerable American High Holy Day sermons on the topic. But more was at stake than reverence. In the early twentieth century, Jews faced enormous pressure from themselves and others to dress in accordance with the proper dictates of taste and etiquette befitting an upstanding citizen. These concerns highlighted the precarious position of Jews in American society (Prell 1999). African Americans confronted a similar repertoire of fashion dos and don'ts. Both groups, finally freed from old constraints, self-consciously strove to dress for a proper role in a modern consumerist society (Heinze 1990: 30; Joselit 2001: 37). For Jews, especially on Rosh Hashanah and Yom Kippur, clothing communicated the place and role of the community in a pluralistic democracy.

Let us move forward a century. In 2006, the *Jewish Daily Forward* published a tongue-in-cheek interview with Isaac Mizrahi, the Jewish "superstar fashion designer," on proper High Holiday attire.[2] "I say go over the top," advised Mizrahi: fur trim for Rosh Hashanah (a "classic") and, on Yom Kippur, "A Day-Glo pink dress might not be the best idea. But a pale, fleshy pink one might be divine (especially with pearls)." As for non-leather shoes, traditionally worn on Yom Kippur, "What about a divine pair of satin Prada platform clogs? Or velvet clogs from Marc Jacobs with socks? That's a sin anyone could atone for." But not all Jews see the High Holy Days as an occasion for competitive dressing. In a plea for simplicity, Rabbi Moti Rieber bewailed an old chestnut that pokes fun at such impious sartorial sumptuousness. "What did the mink say to the fox? See you on Rosh Hashanah" (2005). The classic rabbis of old rejected impoverishment and exhorted Jews to dress nicely for God. But the rabbis also valued moderation. What we often see in the pews today is an effort to dress as much as stylish Americans as praying Jews—to uphold tradition while embracing secular consumerism.

Devotional boasting on the High Holy Days extends even to shoes, but not in the well-heeled sense suggested by Isaac Mizrahi. On Yom Kippur, devout Jews "afflict" and "humble" their souls, as per Leviticus 23:27, by shunning work, food, drink, bathing, sex, and sandals.[3] Traditional authorities extended the ban to all leather garments since comfort and luxury, in their view, foil any sincere repentance. Moreover, some modern Jews find it difficult to beg for divine compassion while standing, as they say, in a dead animal. In consequence, many Jews today pray in canvas sneakers on Yom Kippur. But the conspicuous appearance of bright, white, athletic footwear, while true to the letter of the law, often seems to violate the humble spirit of the day by hinting at immodest piety.[4] Some Jews during Yom Kippur, too, now slip on colorful plastic Crocs, thus adding another stylish, hence acculturated, touch to the traditional prohibition on leather. In response, an ultra-Orthodox or *Haredi* rabbi in Israel recently judged Crocs "inadvisable" on the High Holy Days. His reasoning? They are too comfortable.[5]

Not long ago, the High Holy Days called for formal attire, including evening gowns and top hats. Garments akin to sneakers and Crocs were beyond the pale. Not so by the 1970s, when casual garb increasingly appeared in the pews. Thus an article in the *United Synagogue Review* berated female congregants in 1972 for attending services in "hot pants," "micromini skirts," and "pants suits or slacks."[6] The synagogue was no place for unseemly garments that heightened sexual differences or hid them altogether. The same essay scolded men for abandoning suits and neckties. Sabbath morning services now pitifully resembled "the first link on the golf course." American Jews increasingly dressed their days of holiness in the garb of secular holidays.

I offer these comments on High Holy Day attire to illustrate how one can "read" clothing for insights into wider debates and tensions about Jewish identity. My approach to the meaning of garments arises from the interpretive tradition of American symbolic anthropology. I thus see clothing as unconsciously or unintentionally sewn from a broad worldview consisting of historical complexity, gendered nuance, and competing visions of morality (see, e.g., Banerjee and Miller 2008; Barnes and Eicher 1993; Eicher 1999, 2000; Hansen 2004; Were and Küchler 2005). At the same time, I understand men and women deliberately to pull on clothing, much as they use many items of material culture, to display authority, voice discontent, and manipulate social life. Clothing is irreducibly multitextured.

This is not the first scholarly book on Jewish clothing. In 1967, Alfred Rubens published *A History of Jewish Costume*.[7] I seek, however, neither to replace nor to invalidate Rubens's compendium. Rather, in a sense, I aim to enlarge and update, and thus to complement, his and other prior studies. I do so in several ways. First, I include garments lacking from earlier works, specifically religious and ritual items such as prayer shawls and yarmulkes.

Second, I address contemporary garments and debates and include a much broader, up-to-date range of scholarship and sources. Third, I offer an anthropological perspective. As such, to repeat, I do not catalog or describe garments. This book is not a laundry list. Rather, I interpret clothing for symbolic messages. This brings me to the fourth and final way this book complements earlier studies. I explicitly argue that Jewish clothing expresses unresolved conversations about Jewish identity.

## A BRIEF HISTORY

To provide a necessary context, I need briefly to sketch the history of Judaism, beginning with ancient Israel. The Hebrew Bible, as I detail in Chapter 1, is a massive anthology of myth, legend, and law—perhaps even some bona fide history—reflecting the worldview of the ancient Israelites. The Israelites entered the land of Canaan from Egypt around 1200 B.C.E., shortly before the collapse of the great Bronze Age civilizations. They organized into tribes, built agricultural settlements and towns, warred with their neighbors and among themselves, and established a monarchy around 1020 B.C.E. The crown passed from Saul to David, thence to Solomon, who initiated construction of the First Temple in Jerusalem sometime in the mid-tenth century B.C.E. Upon Solomon's death, the monarchy split into two kingdoms. The Assyrians conquered the north, then Babylon invaded the southern kingdom in 586 B.C.E., razing the Temple and casting the Israelites into exile. Ancient Israel ceased to exist.

Not long thereafter, Babylon fell to Persia. Cyrus the Great allowed the Jews to rebuild their nation and sanctuary in 538 B.C.E., thus inaugurating the Second Temple period, also called Early Judaism. This era included the finalization of the Torah, the spread of Greek culture into the eastern Mediterranean and the subsequent Maccabean revolt in the second century B.C.E., and the rise of early Christianity. The period came to a calamitous end with several failed Jewish revolts and the Roman destruction of the Second Temple in the year 70. The biblical era was over.

The loss of the Temple was a decisive, catastrophic moment in Jewish history. Even today, despite the establishment of the modern nation of Israel, many devout Jews dwell in a state of spiritual exile that will cease only, in their view, with the messianic anointing of a new sanctuary. The razing of the Temple made impossible the fulfillment of many biblical commandments and denied Judaism a central place in the world. But this calamity also gave birth to Judaism as we know it today: a postbiblical, worldwide religion of rabbis leading their congregants in prayer and study at local synagogues rather than hereditary priests officiating over animal sacrifices in Jerusalem.

After the destruction of the Second Temple, two great centers of rabbinic thought arose in Palestine and Babylon. The task of these "classic rabbis," as I call them, was to fine-tune and especially update the divine Law, as given in the Torah, to fit a nonbiblical reality. The first great codification of rabbinic legislation was the Mishnah, a lengthy series of legal conversations dating to the early third century and a generation of scholars called the Tannaim. In Jewish tradition, however, the ultimate authorship of the Mishnah was none other than the Almighty. In this view, God presented *two* revelations to Moses, the Written Law, more commonly known as the Five Books of Moses or the Torah, and the Oral Law, which served as a legal commentary on the Torah. The Oral Law was transmitted by word of mouth from Moses to Joshua, thence to the prophets, and eventually to the early rabbis, who finally put these commentaries to parchment. This text and tradition has no place in Christianity. But traditional Jews see the conversations of the Oral Law as the authoritative foundation of Judaism—conversations that continue today, thus clarifying the translation of divine will into the practicalities of everyday life.

The second wave of rabbinic sages, the Amoraim of the third to sixth centuries, composed two enormous commentaries on the Mishnah, the Jerusalem Talmud and the more commanding Babylonian Talmud. Both versions of the Talmud include legends, biblical expositions, lore, and legal answers (*responsa*) to practical questions. The Mishnah and Talmud served, until the modern era, as the authoritative moral center and ideal vision of Jewish life.[8]

For centuries, the rabbis dressed and steered their communities in accordance with traditional Jewish law, called *halacha*, which they codified in massive tomes. The study of halacha was the prerogative of a learned male elite. But Jews did not only live under the authority of their rabbis. They also dwelled and dressed beneath the stern, often brutal gaze of church and state. Indeed, from the fourth century onward, the overwhelming fact of Jewish life in Europe was the official dominance of Christianity, which viewed Jews as a despised minority. For most Jews, the official warp and waft of everyday life consisted of rabbinic legislation and Gentile law.

The hegemony of the rabbis began to fray in the eighteenth century with the rise of Hasidism. This mystical movement split from the Jewish establishment, then called the *Mitnagdim* or "opponents" for its bitter hostility to Hasidism. These two feuding sects then dominated European Jewry until the mid-nineteenth century, when Reform Judaism championed an ambitious program of religious modernization. Suddenly, Hasidim and Mitnagdim found common ground in the confrontation with modernity and acculturation. Reform Jews, flush with the promise of emancipation and citizenship, sought to weave Judaism into the fabric of the wider society. They encouraged Jews to dress like everybody else. But traditionalists opposed any such liberalism and remained committed to dressing for a life apart.

Today, Orthodox Jewry consists of two broad groups, often called ultra-Orthodox and Modern Orthodox. The former consists of Hasidim and other traditionalists who steadfastly oppose most forms of acculturation, including modern clothing. (They actually prefer the term *Haredim*; *haredi* means "fearful one"). By contrast, Modern Orthodox Jews strive to synthesize devout Judaism with contemporary life. Between Orthodoxy and Reform Jewry lies the Conservative movement, called *Masorti* in Israel. Unlike Reform Judaism, the Conservative movement values fidelity to traditional Jewish law; unlike Orthodoxy, Conservative Jews are fully integrated into modern society.

These sectarian distinctions are crucial to understanding the styles and meanings of Jewish clothing, especially after the nineteenth century. Understandably, readers unfamiliar with contemporary Judaism may initially find all this rather confusing. Scholars of Judaism may sneer at my hasty history. But, of course, my intention was not to write yet another history of the Jews. More significant, I confess to a certain tension in this book since I aim for a broad readership that includes, but is not limited to, my colleagues in the Academy. Perhaps most likely to raise scholarly hackles is the interdisciplinary scope of this study—for which I am unapologetic. Although I am a cultural anthropologist by training, this book is tethered to no single discipline. Drawing on the great literary theorist Mikhail Bakhtin (1984), I see Jewish clothing as expressive of an open-ended conversation about what it means to be Jewish (see also Lipset and Silverman 2005). This sweeping conversation resists confinement to any bounded academic discipline. It is a dialogue full of pathos and joy, tradition and modernity, men and women, authority and subversion—a conversation open always, if we listen carefully, to what Bakhtin called the "double-faced fullness of life" (1984: 62).

## CHAPTER SUMMARIES

Chapter 1 surveys ancient Israelite apparel, focusing on the Hebrew Bible. What, I ask, did Israelite clothing symbolize, both in actual social life and in the literary context of biblical narratives? I contend that ancient clothing—including shoes, gifts, veils, fringes, magical amulets, and a taboo blended textile—served as metaphors for key values and conflicts in the Israelite worldview. I also probe the enduring legacy of these garments, especially the so-called biblical or Israeli sandal, ironically invented only recently.

Chapter 2 begins by asking if Jews dressed uniquely in late antiquity, and then turns to dress regulations in classic rabbinic texts, especially the Talmud. The rabbis took little for granted. Even the most mundane matters called for deliberation and guidance. This legalistic outlook profoundly influenced dress, down to the order of tying shoes. I also show how clothing symbolized many principal dimensions of the rabbinic outlook, including gender, the duality of life and death, and the idea of a "fence" separating Jew from Gentile. This chapter, too, discusses rabbinic rules regarding the attachment of knotted fringes (tzitzit) to Jewish garments, and the small ritual boxes called *tefillin* that encase biblical passages, which Jews lash to the body during morning prayers. I end with recent debates over electric shavers, which evidence the long-standing tension between acculturation and separatism.

Chapter 3 surveys the long and shameful history of derisive dress codes imposed by church and royalty on European Jews since the thirteenth century. Actually, I begin with the Islamic world, where we find the original besmirching of Jews with contemptuous badges, hats, and other garments. The chapter ends with the revival of this terrible tradition during the Holocaust, or *Shoah* in Hebrew, and, more recently, the appearance of stars on clothing by Israelis protesting the dismantling of settlements in the occupied territories. In effect, this chapter asks how Jews were dressed by others. And did Jews heed these edicts?

Chapter 4 turns to the rise of modernity, perhaps the most consequential transition for Jewish identity and dress over the past millennium. For centuries, church and state clothed Jews in a type of anti-fashion. But on the eve of modernity, Europe switched suit and ordered Jews to dress like ordinary citizens. In the same era, Reform Judaism embarked on its widespread, if not radical, program of religious modernization. Most Jews eventually attuned their wardrobes to the values of individualism, citizenship, style, and consumerism. In contrast, religious Jews increasingly appeared to dress in anachronistic attire. This chapter, then, explores the clash between the secular allure of acculturation and the religious mandate of ethnic distinctiveness.

Chapter 4 also discusses premodern efforts by Jewish leaders to constrain lavish clothing. These regulations were yet another attempt by Jewish authorities to shore up various "fences" protecting the community and social order—boundaries the folk seemed intent on dismantling, often with garments. This chapter also investigates the classic era of immigration to the United States, when Jews struggled with how to look, shop, and dress like proper Americans, not distinctive Jews. In this and other chapters, it is important to note, I focus mostly on Ashkenazi Jewry—that is, Yiddish-speaking Jews from Central and Eastern Europe who eventually migrated en masse to the United States and elsewhere in the nineteenth and twentieth centuries. (Those who remained in Europe, of course, suffered near-total devastation during the Shoah.) Generally speaking, I do not discuss in detail Sephardi Jews from Spain and Portugal (expelled, I add, by King Ferdinand and Queen Isabella in 1492), nor the Jews of North Africa, India, Asia, and the Islamic world.[9]

Chapter 5 explores how the rabbinic concept of modesty, or *tzniut*, shapes and colors women's clothing, especially today. Indeed, I open with a recent conference convened by ultra-Orthodox men in Jerusalem to tackle a new fashion crisis: spandex. I then probe the rules that govern Orthodox and ultra-Orthodox women's attire, including hems, hues, necklines, and sleeves, and discuss a recent uproar that occurred when "kosher" wigs were discovered to be plaited from hair shorn at a Hindu temple in India. I also explore online retailers of modest garb, the tension between modesty and fashion, girls' dolls, legal conflicts over head coverings in the United States and Europe, and the thorny question of empowerment or encumbrance. Throughout, I often make reference to clothing worn by devout Muslim women.

In Chapter 6, I investigate the origins, symbolism, and stylistic nuances of the characteristic black hats and frocks that adorn Hasidic and ultra-Orthodox or Haredi men. In this chapter, too, I discuss modern aspects of the biblical taboo on wool and linen blends (*sha'atnez*), including "laboratories" that test garments since off-the-rack coats advertised as 100 percent wool might also contain some linen fibers and thus violate divine law. Last, I show that certain aspects of Hasidic consumerism bespeak the very allure of secular tastes that Haredi Jews must also reject.

Chapter 7 begins with an exploration of the rules and symbolism of tefillin, the black boxes and straps Jewish men traditionally don each morning for prayer. I then turn to recent renditions of these ritual items that the rabbis of old surely never imagined, including "tefillin dates," a Tefillin Barbie doll, and vegan tefillin. (Incidentally, a Jewish teenager attempting to pray in tefillin on a US Airways flight from New York City to Kentucky in January 2010 caused such a fright that the captain diverted the plane to Philadelphia.[10]) Moreover, I extensively discuss different forms of the tallit or prayer shawl, especially nontraditional designs tailored for women who, until recently, never wore these garments. Here, again, we see a complex interweaving of tradition and modernity, or religious distinctiveness and acculturation.

In Chapter 7, too, I explore the tzitzit fringes that adorn prayer shawls and Orthodox men's undershirts. According to the Torah, these fringes must contain a single blue thread. The Talmud derives this hue from an animal called a *chilazon*. But centuries ago, Jews remarkably forgot the identity of this creature, and so most Jews today are familiar only with white tassels. Recently, however, several devout organizations identified competing candidates for the enigmatic animal, and so some Jews once again wear blue threads. The chapter concludes by asking, What do you carry in your tallit bag? This question might seem humorous. But it reveals both interesting gender differences and a fascinating blend of sacred and profane.

Chapter 8 investigates the origin and history of what is perhaps the most distinctive and public of all Jewish garments: the small round cap or yarmulke. However much this item is seen as traditional, I trace its canonical status to the first half of the twentieth century and the decline of hats in men's fashion. This quintessentially Jewish garment, in other words, largely became Jewish in re-sponse to secular society. I also discuss the denominational symbolism of different types of yarmulkes, and the recent efflorescence of what I call the pop culture yarmulke. Today, Jews delight in decorating their yarmulkes with sports logos, rock-and-roll iconography, television characters, superheroes, and insignia that synthesize tradition with individualism and religious particularism with generic citizenship.

The final chapter examines the latest controversy in Jewish clothing. Over the past decade, young Jews have creatively endeavored to reinvent Judaism by resisting the terms of Jewishness established by mainstream institutions and authorities, never mind their own parents. Variously called Hipster Jews, New Jews, and Heebsters, they reject both traditional Jewish identities and ethnic invisibility. Instead, the New Jew Cool proudly expresses a hip-hop style of Jewishness—and its adherents do so, it turns out, on their t-shirts, panties, boxer shorts, and thongs. This controversial movement is simply the latest voice, as I summarize in the conclusion to this book, in an ongoing, ir-resolvable debate over Jewish identity—a conversation spoken through cloth.

# –1–

# (Un)Dressing the Israelites

And the Lord God made skin coats for the human and his wife, and He clothed them.

Genesis 3:21

The mythic events in Eden establish the importance of clothing. Originally, the first two humans walked "naked," lacking both garments and "shame" (Genesis 2:25). In Hebrew, this nudity ('*arummim*) foreshadows the "shrewd" ('*arum*) serpent that suggested an infamous snack, resulting in humanity's expulsion from Paradise. The consumption of the forbidden (literally, "lustful") fruit opened human eyes to "good and evil" as well as to bare licentiousness. This awakening necessitated fig leaf loincloths, then heavenly tailored "cloaks of skins" (Genesis 3:7, 21). Theologians have long debated whether this divine outfit represented forgiveness or punishment (e.g., Oden 1987: 96–97). Actually, the question is misguided. Dress in this and other biblical tales, I maintain, resists any unitary or simple meaning.

This chapter surveys biblical clothing and adornments. I discuss specific items such as veils, hems, and shoes. But I am especially keen to show that biblical garb, both real and metaphoric, conveyed symbolic messages concerning power, gender, and identity.

## READING THE BIBLE

What can the Hebrew Bible accurately tell us about Israelite garb—or any aspect of the ancient world? To traditionalists, the Torah records the words of God. Its facticity lies beyond question. But scholars approach the Torah as a complex tapestry of myth, legend, and law, largely irreducible to self-evident or singular messages. As Gruenwald writes in regard to the rabbinic exegetical tradition known as *midrash*, "the text is realized in being interpreted" (1993: 11–12).

So how, then, should we read the Hebrew Bible? As a transparent window through which to view ancient society? Surely not. Biblical stories and legal codes, Niditch shows, reflect the emerging outlook and self-identity of a small tribe of people dwelling at the crossroads of clashing global powers from the late Bronze Age through the sixth century B.C.E. (2008, chapter 1). And like all societies, whether in the Near East or New Guinea, the Israelites saw themselves as not just different from their neighbors, but as better than them. Biblical texts do not record history. Rather, they encode a worldview.

Modern scholars generally parse the Torah into distinct source documents composed in different historical eras (see Friedman 1987). Each literary stratum displays characteristic traits. Thus the creation myth in Genesis 1 is typically attributed to the Priestly source dating from around the time of the Babylonian exile (597/586–538 B.C.E.). This source, for example, habitually used the term *Elohim* to refer to God. But the drama in Eden is traced to a much earlier source, the Yahwist, dating to the tenth century B.C.E. As the narrative moves forward in time, in this sense, it actually moves backward.

The different oral or literary strands were eventually edited, occasionally annotated, and woven together during the Second Temple period, or perhaps earlier, during the exile. Of course, the Hebrew Bible contains far more than the Five Books of Moses. We must also consider the twenty-one books of the Prophets (*Nevi'im*) and the thirteen additional compositions called the Writings (*Kethuvim*). The canonization of these two compilations postdated that of the Torah, but they contain earlier texts. The linear progression of the Hebrew Bible we know so well today—the "story" if you will—belies a complex editorial and historical process that unfolded, almost like a palimpsest, over centuries.

In reading the Hebrew Bible, I am suggesting, interpretive nuance is everything. Rarely does the Hebrew convey an unambiguous meaning. When telling the story of the Creation, to cite a famous example, different translations evoke a world "unformed and void," "astonishingly empty," and "wild and waste." Darkness spread over the "surface of the deep"—or perhaps the "face of Ocean." And what issued forth from God just prior to the appearance of light: "wind," "Divine Presence," "breath," or "rushing-spirit"? These differences, depending on what you are reading for, might very well make a difference.

All this suggests that one can read the Hebrew Bible in many ways and for many purposes. You can take the entire text as a unified whole, given by the redactors, and probe for narrative and thematic continuities—or explore gaps and contradictions. You can read the text as literature, focusing on plot, drama, and character—or situate discrete passages in their historical contexts. You can revel in ambiguity—or strive for precision. You can read the lines—or between them. I prefer a pluralistic method that, invoking the eminent anthropologist Clifford Geertz (1973), approaches the text as an Israelite reading of Israelite experience, a story Israelites told themselves about themselves. And often, I will now show, this story was woven into clothing.

## A WARDROBE OF UNCERTAINTY

Before I turn to the symbolism of Israelite attire, I need first say something about fabrics. Here, I focus mainly on vocabulary and assume, however mindful of the interpretive pitfalls, that oft-mentioned words—at least those we can easily understand—afford some glimpse of the ancient material world.

Several biblical passages refer to animal pelts or tanned hides. But the earliest Israelites, like most pastoral peoples, probably dressed in wool (*zemer*) sheared from dark goats and light sheep (e.g., Psalm 147:16; Song of Songs 1:5).[1] After the Israelites established agricultural settlements, they could also dress in coarse, off-white linen (*pishta*, *peshet*). The wealthy enjoyed more sumptuous textiles such as byssus, or "sea silk," spun from fibers secreted by mollusks. The Torah records two types of this fabric, both imports: Egyptian *šēš* and Levantine *bûs*. Elites dressed well. They also required, in one regal or fanciful instance, a "keeper of the wardrobe" (2 Kings 22:14).

Priests dressed in distinctive outfits made from a plain, perhaps white, linen called *bad*. This textile conveyed, as I discuss later, an aura of ritual purity. But purity did not imply impoverishment. Priestly linen, while not as rich as royal fabrics, still exceeded anything worn by commoners. We would expect nothing less in an ancient society that so highly valued rank and privilege.

Cotton (*chuwr*) arrived rather late in the Near East, long after the eras that pertain to most biblical tales. Cotton appears only in the book of Esther (1:6; 8:15). True silk (*meshi*) receives a single reference (Ezekiel 16:10). Based on linguistic evidence, then, most Israelites dressed in wool and linen. Commoners also likely dressed in shades of black and white. Any other hues required additional, costly processing.

Natural dyes adhere poorly to plant cellulose. The ancients therefore dyed wool, not linen (Milgrom 1983). Three colors predominated: worm-scarlet or crimson (*shani towla*), purple (*argaman*), and blue (*tekhelet*). The latter two dyes, laboriously manufactured by the Phoenicians and other coastal peoples, fetched enormous sums, and thus symbolized, like gold trim and precious stones, wealth and royalty (e.g., Jeremiah 10:9; Proverbs 31). The Israelites themselves extracted crimson from dried scale insects.[2] Crimson also signified affluence. But most Israelites enjoyed no such luxury. They dressed in unadorned, practical garb befitting the everyday toil of premodern agriculture and husbandry.

But what types of garments did the Israelites wear? The answer is unclear. Scattered throughout the Hebrew Bible is a sizable catalog of clothing and fashion accessories. Ancient inscriptions, Egyptian temple paintings, and Babylonian stelae offer additional insights. All these sources, however, generally aimed to convey symbolic messages, if not outright propaganda.

Nonetheless, let us assume some actual correspondence between the vocabulary of the Hebrew Bible and the garments hung in ancient wardrobes.
What can we learn?

Actually, the metaphor of the wardrobe is entirely misleading. The ancients
filled their world with far fewer things than do we moderns. In biblical Israel,
as in premodern Europe, all clothing was precious, and thus offered as payment, collateral, and pledges (e.g., Amos 2:8; Proverbs 20:16). Only with the
rise of the industrial revolution and mass production, not much earlier than a
century ago, could the average person acquire an extensive closet.

That said, what did the Israelites wear? Unfortunately, most of the relevant
Hebrew terms lack specificity. They appear, moreover, in a wide range of narrative contexts, often with considerable literary innuendo. Most words for
clothing conjure multiple possibilities. For example, the Hebrew Bible often
dresses Israelite men, and sometimes women, in a basic article variously
understood as a girdle, apron, or loincloth (*chagor*). Sometimes this garment served as military armor (2 Samuel 18:11). It was fashioned from linen
(Jeremiah 13:10), leather (2 Kings 1:8), and, in one prophetic fantasy, gold
(Daniel 10:5). A fig leaf version covered Adam and Eve. In Isaiah 3:24, the
*chagor* evoked opulence in contrast to a servile, rope-like belt (*niqpah*). Yet
most biblical passages refer to the *chagor* as a mundane article.

Other garments evidence the same linguistic slipperiness. The word *simlah* refers to an outer cloak (e.g., Exodus 12:34), but also to generic clothing
and, more chillingly, to a bed sheet that, when bloodied, attested to bridal
virginity (Deuteronomy 22:17). Another cloak, the *salmah*, seemingly resembled the *simlah* and may differ only through a scribal error that reversed two
Hebrew letters. Several other biblical words refer to nondescript clothing,
such as the cognates *lebush* and *malbush*, as well as *kesût*.[3] The latter term,
too, specifies a wife's garments (Exodus 21:10), warm garb (Job 24:7), and
a blanket or nightshirt (Exodus 22:27). The word *mad* also refers to clothing in general (Leviticus 6:10) as well as a saddle blanket (Judges 5:10) and
armor (1 Samuel 17:38, 39). Clearly, the variety of ancient clothing exceeded
the available lexicon. It is a bit like asking someone today to plainly describe
a shirt.

Another frequently mentioned outer garment is the *kětonet* tunic or coat
(e.g., Song of Songs 5:3). Both commoners and priests wore the *kětonet*,
the latter woven from the linen called *bad* I mentioned earlier. Women, too,
dressed in the *kětonet* as well as the *simlah*. Both men and women also
wore a skirt or robe called a *shuwl*. (In Isaiah 6:1, God's *shuwl* filled the entire temple!) Yet Israelite clothing also differentiated gender. Thus Isaiah 3
registers several female fashion accessories, including headbands or sashes
(*kišurîm*). But the same passage mentions a purse or scribal bag (*ḥarîtîm*)
also carried by men (2 Kings 5:23). Here, again, we see the futility of trying

to assign each word for Israelite clothing to specific garments. With the exception of priestly attire, which I discuss later, the Torah provides no sewing patterns. As I stressed in the introduction, I am little interested, however, in tabulating an ancient laundry list. Perhaps it is best to conclude that the Hebrew Bible uses a relatively small lexicon to refer to a broad range of often indeterminate garments. Of far greater importance to both myself and the Israelites is the symbolism of biblical clothing.

## CLOTHING AS METAPHOR

The prophet Isaiah clothed ancient loins in righteousness (11:5). Other passages garb the Israelites in strength, splendor, justice, and horror (Proverbs 31:25; Isaiah 52:1; Job 29:14; Psalm 55:6). While God is "robed in grandeur" (Psalm 93:1), the wicked are "clothed in a curse" (Psalm 109:28–29). Clothing also represented divine reward for humility—a turban instead of ashes, a mantle of praise rather than a heavy spirit (Isaiah 61:3). Even time is likened to clothing. God endures eternally, said the Psalmist, but we humans depressingly "shall wear out like a garment" (102:27). Israelite clothing, I am suggesting, was not just material. It was also pervasively, profoundly metaphoric.

Clothing symbolized politics. Men of rank carried an identifying seal or signet, perhaps a special ring attached to an ornamental cord (see Genesis 38). Men also toted a staff or scepter (*matteh*, *shevet*). The same two words also denoted "tribe" (e.g., Genesis 49:16), thus materializing the relationship between manhood, social order, and leadership. Clothing, too, betokened prophetic authority and divine potency. When the prophet Elijah dropped his cloak ('*adderet*) while ascending to heaven in a fiery chariot, his successor, Elisha, retrieved the garment and placed it on the Jordan River. The waters miraculously parted (2 Kings 2:13). In this and many biblical tales, clothing communicated messages about a person's place in society.

We can also discern the symbolic use of biblical clothing in regard to sandals or shoes, called *na'al* (Chinitz 2007; Prouser 2008). Of particular importance was the removal of footwear. Shoelessness, especially on holy ground, expressed humility (Exodus 3:5; Joshua 5:15). Even today, some Jews pray barefoot in the synagogue during the High Holy Days. Biblical barefootedness also signified grief (2 Samuel 15:30) and, like nakedness in general, captivity (Isaiah 20:4).

The most famous reference to symbolic shoes in the Hebrew Bible is also the most vexing. In ancient Israel, as in many societies, sons inherited their fathers' wealth and renown. The death of an heirless man was therefore no trivial matter. To redress this patrilineal tragedy, the Israelites practiced the levirate,

whereby a widow married a brother of her deceased husband. Their firstborn—
ideally a son, for that was the point—was the legal heir of the dead man.

But what if the surviving brother refused this obligation? In Genesis 38,
God killed a man named Onan who declined to sire "seed" for his deceased
brother. Deuteronomy provides a more humane alternative: the *chalitzah*
ceremony (25:5–10). A man wanting legal exemption from his leviratic duty
stated his intention before the city elders. The widow then publicly removed
his shoe, spat in his face, and proclaimed: "So shall be done to the man who
will not build his brother's house." He was henceforth called something akin
to "the House of the Slipped-off Shoe."

The public removal of the shoe, writes Hezser, symbolically reduced the
brother to undignified, unshod impoverishment (2008: 49). But sometimes a
shoe, to playfully invoke Freud, is not just a shoe. In the Hebrew Bible, "feet"
and "legs" often euphemistically referred to the genitals (e.g., 1 Samuel
24:3). (Skeptical readers might ponder an ancient Israelite's difficulty with
trying to understand literally such idioms as "powder one's nose," "visit the
restroom," and "sanitary napkin.") From this angle, the widow shamed her
reluctant brother-in-law by expectorating—that is, by symbolically ejaculat-
ing—into his face. If we see the shoe as phallic, moreover, then the widow
additionally emasculated her brother-in-law, thus responding in kind to his re-
fusal to impregnate her with his "shoe." But if we take the shoe as a female
symbol, then the widow removed a representation of her own body from the
brother-in-law's "foot," again answering in kind his chaste rejection of the leviratic obligation. In the biblical *chalitzah* ceremony, the widow publicly did
to her brother-in-law what he refused to do privately with her. The Hebrew
Bible thus reverses a key motif in the Cinderella tale: shoes are removed by
women, not fitted by men, to signify the absence of marital intercourse.[4]

## VEILING, UNVEILING, AND DISROBING

Another garment rich with symbolism is the veil (*tsa'iyph*). But scholars disagree on the function of this garment (see van der Toorn 1995). In fact, no
biblical passage or divine decree mandates veiling. In Genesis 24, Rebekah
put on a veil to "cover herself" upon meeting Isaac, her future husband. But
why? Did Rebekah do so as a feminine greeting? Was an unveiled appearance undignified (e.g., Song of Songs 5:7)? Did the veil, as Isaiah 47:1–3 implies, symbolically protect virginity? Or signal wealth and prominence (Isaiah
3:23)? We can discern no plain or stable answer.

The veil is central to the narrative of Genesis 38. God inexplicably kills
the husband of a childless woman named Tamar. Following leviratic custom,
the deceased's father, Judah, sent his second-born son, Onan, to Tamar in

marriage. But Onan refused, as I just mentioned, "knowing that the seed would not count as his." For this infamous act of coitus interruptus, to repeat, God smote Onan. Judah then pledged his last-born son to Tamar. But he never made good on his promise. Tamar, now publically humiliated, removed her mourning garb, donned a veil, and waited at a crossroads to seduce, and so disgrace, her father-in-law.

To some readers, this passage implies that biblical veils identified prostitutes. But recent scholars see Tamar's veil as a typical item of feminine attire, removed as a sign of grief. Tamar's veil represented only the cessation of mourning. Prostitutes announced their trade by loitering at specific locations, not by wearing distinctive clothing (Huddlestun 2001). At the very least, Tamar's veil helped establish the dénouement of the plot. It is noteworthy, in this regard, that a common biblical word for generic clothing, *beged*, linguistically resembles the Hebrew word for deceit, or *bagad*. In the Joseph tales, in fact, *beged* garments appear precisely during moments of betrayal (Navon 2004). Tamar's veil took on a similar, although not exclusive, meaning.

Many centuries after the biblical era, Jewish grooms veiled their brides to symbolically enclose them within male authority. (Many Jews still practice this rite, called *bedekin*.) No such custom exists in the Bible. But a biblical suitor enacted a similar gesture during betrothal to signal his right to intercourse: he covered his intended with the hem of his garment (e.g., Ezekiel 16:8). Thus Ruth, seeking to wed a distant kinsman named Boaz, uncovered his "feet," then bid Boaz to spread his robe over her body (Ruth 3:4–9). Like Tamar's veil, this practice illustrated the value, encoded in clothing, placed on the concealment and exposure of women.

The same nuance explains the idiom of a father's "skirt" (*kanaph*). Deuteronomy 22:30 declares: "A man shall not wed his father's wife, and he shall not uncover his father's skirt." (Among the polygynous Israelites, I note, a father's wife was not necessarily one's birth mother.) Wives, like the clothing they received in marriage, were a husband's legal property. He alone could uncover the "skirt." The biblical veil similarly represented the right of certain men to cloak and reveal female bodies.

This symbolism even pertained to God. The prophetic literature likened sinful Israelites—women *and* men—to an unfaithful, defiled wife. In Lamentations 1:9, for example, Israel's robe reeks with the same ritual pollution (*tumah*) associated with menstruation (e.g., Leviticus 15). When Israel morally strays in Jeremiah 13:26, God threatens to lift the community's skirt, shamefully exposing Israel's female genitals. As a biblical literary device, I am suggesting, episodes of covering and uncovering conveyed messages about power, sexuality, and privilege.

Even Moses veiled his face. So powerful was his encounter with God atop Mount Sinai that Moses descended not solely with the tablets of the Law.

He also carried an otherworldly radiance, perhaps horns, a condition Moses normally veiled except when speaking with God (Exodus 34:33–35).[5] The word that refers to Moses's facial covering (*masveh*) only occurs once, so its precise meaning is vague. Nevertheless, I suggest that Moses dressed as much to conceal his identity, like women, as to display it.

Moses's veil also implied his marriage to God since an ancient husband, as I intimated a moment ago, provisioned his wife "to cover her nakedness" (Hosea 2:11). The obligation to clothe a woman, however, also entailed the right to undress her, and not merely for intimacy. Husbands in several Near Eastern societies initiated divorce by snipping their wives' hems (Kruger 1984). Perhaps they also took a cue from God's shocking behavior in Ezekiel 16:39 and disrobed their ex-wives in public. Both gestures materialized a husband's entitlement to strip a spouse of her status and shelter (van der Toorn 1995: 336–37). The very man who once clothed a woman now displayed her nakedness for all to see and scorn. But Israelite law permitted wives no such privilege. Here, again, we see the role of clothing in expressing power and gender.

Forceful disrobing in the ancient Near East commonly humiliated warfare captives (2 Samuel 10:4). An unclothed person, symbolically attired in no social conventions, shamefully lacked a legitimate position in society. Nakedness also signified madness and poverty (e.g., Job 12:17, 19). Similarly, rent clothing signaled contrition and grief (e.g., Genesis 44:13; Job 2:12; Joel 2:13). For a similar reason, I propose, women removed their veils during mourning. After suffering rape by a half-brother, the daughter of King David, also named Tamar, tore her coat to represent her violently torn body and psyche (2 Samuel 13:18; McKay 1996: 194–96). One prophet foretold the dissolution of the twelve Israelite tribes by splitting his robe into a dozen pieces (1 King 11:29–31). All told, the ancients shredded clothing to represent holes in their souls, bodies, and society.

Not surprising, disrobing also conveyed erotic intent. To "see" someone in biblical tales was often tantamount to "knowing" them sexually and often illicitly. One thinks immediately of the shame of Adam and Eve upon consuming naked self-awareness. Likewise, Noah disembarked from his ark, planted a vineyard, imbibed wine, and passed out naked and drunk in his tent. Noah's son, Ham, "saw" his father's unclad, stupefied body. For this, Noah cursed his grandson "to be the lowest of slaves" (Genesis 9). What did Ham see?

Actually, the appropriate question is, what did Ham do? The biblical verb "to uncover" often appears in connection with incestuous and adulterous "nakedness." Thus Leviticus 20:11 warns, "If a man lies with his father's wife, it is the nakedness of his father that he has uncovered; the two shall be put to death." Ham did not literally "see" his father. Rather, Ham slept with his mother's co-wife. This explanation also accounts for why Noah cursed his grandson: the boy was the offspring of Ham's unlawful encounter.[6]

While the Torah censures real and metaphoric "nakedness," God nonetheless requires adult men to undress infant boys and perform circumcision (Silverman 2006). Similarly, junior men swore oaths of allegiance by clasping the penis or "thigh" of their elders (e.g., Genesis 24:2). This gesture, in fact, was still practiced not long ago in the Middle East (Patai 1959: 167–68). Even God ambiguously "revealed" himself (Genesis 35:7). Biblical undressing, I am arguing, symbolically sustained or subverted society and personhood.

To this, we need again add a gendered nuance. Public nakedness, we saw, generally conveyed disgrace—say, when cutting a man's gown to expose his buttocks (2 Samuel 10:4). In one memorable episode, King David so rapturously danced upon bringing the Ark of the Covenant to Jerusalem that he despicably revealed himself (2 Samuel 6:12–20). The Law even forbade the Israelites from ascending a staircase to the altar, "that your nakedness not be exposed upon it" (Exodus 20:26). Clearly, God wished no glimpse of male genitals outside the circumcision ritual. And humans were generally forbidden from glancing at the divine countenance (Exodus 3:6; 33:20). But God registered no such qualms about peeking at the female body.

Several biblical tales, in fact, pivot on the display of naked women for male enjoyment. When King David, strolling atop his palace one evening, famously caught sight of Bathsheba bathing, he sent his couriers to fetch her for an adulterous tryst (2 Samuel). In the opening scene of the book of Esther, the besotted king of Persia orders his queen, wearing little more than her crown, to strut before his banqueting guests. She refuses, resulting in exile.

Biblical acts of undressing conveyed messages about power and gender. In most instances, disrobing stripped away a person's identity and status while affirming the authority of the superior (see Kruger 1984: 79). In a few all-male settings, however, masculine nudity served social order. Giving garments, I now show, conveyed a similar political symbolism.

## GIFTING GARB

Gifts of clothing, we saw, placed women within a husband's legal control. By contrast, clothing transacted between men, particularly the generic garment called a *ketonet*, often represented the bestowal of authority and rank (e.g., 2 Kings 9:13; Huddlestun 2002; Oden 1987: 100–1). Both types of gifts defined the recipient's social role. In fact, God gave a *ketonet* to the premier humans in Eden (Genesis 3:21), thus signaling our special status in Creation. Of all the *ketonet* garments mentioned in the Hebrew Bible, Joseph's colorful coat is surely the most famous. But was his cloak truly so adorned?

The Hebrew word that describes Joseph's coat is the plural of an uncertain term (*passim*) that only occurs in two biblical tales (Genesis 37; 2 Samuel 13). Nowhere does the Torah outright characterize Joseph's coat as multicolored. Yet the Greek translation of the Bible, called the Septuagint and dating roughly to the third century B.C.E., colors the garment. The Latin and King James translations, based on the Greek, follow suit. Did the Greek translators err, or read a lost Hebrew text? We do not know. Perhaps, then, the outstanding feature of the coat had nothing to do with color.

The fashion statement made by Joseph's outfit likely pertained to cuffs, not colors. Some classic rabbis parsed the word *passim* after an Aramaic cognate referring to the soles of the feet and the palms of the hands (see Matthews 1995: 30). Only the leisured elite could enjoy a long-sleeved or long-hemmed garment. The common folk, as noted earlier, dressed for labor amid the fields and flocks. A lengthy garment thus clothed Joseph, the favored son among his hard-working brothers, for relaxation. The coat, too, represented a gift of rank—albeit a gift that ruptured the solidarity of an Israelite kin group.

Joseph's resentful brothers, of course, grab the cloak, toss Joseph into a pit, and rip apart the garment, dipping the scraps into blood. They sell Joseph to a caravan, then present the stained and tattered tunic to their father, Jacob. The elder patriarch sobs, thinking his favorite son the victim of a wild beast. The long coat offered Joseph no shelter from sibling rivalry. Similarly, the lengthy sleeves and hems of the same type of garment (*ketonet*) failed to protect feminine chastity in the horrible tale recorded in 2 Samuel 13, which I mentioned earlier. Instead, Tamar was brutally raped by a sibling. In both tales, a cloak representing honor and privilege is violently stripped away to signify the shredding of a family and a body.

Eventually, Joseph arrives in Egypt to serve as a houseboy. One day, the master's wife grabs Joseph by his cloak and begs, "lie with me" (Genesis 39:7). Joseph flees, unluckily leaving the cloak still clutched in his would-be seducer's hands. Furious at the rebuttal, the spurned lover presents the garment to her husband as evidence that Joseph tried to "play" with her. Joseph is immediately imprisoned but eventually exonerated after some deft dream interpretation for the pharaoh. Joseph then receives a new outfit and a royal appointment. Twice Joseph loses clothing and status, and twice he gains garb and prestige. A young David similarly acquires garments and political power while his rival, King Saul, suffers the loss of clothing and authority (Prouser 1996: 29–30). The book of Esther, too, slowly deprives its villain, Haman, of garments, prestige, and ultimately his life while granting the hero, Mordechai, new clothing and status (Siebert-Hommes 2002). In all these tales, transactions of clothing signify the loss and achievement of authority.

In all these tales, men alone received governmental garb. Women were generally excluded from the political system. Occasionally, however, women managed to insert themselves into politics, often by using garments to disguise their intentions. Thus Tamar, shamed by her dishonest father-in-law, veiled her identity to exact revenge. In the end, he admitted, "she is more in the right than I." Genesis 27 details another female manipulation of clothing to subvert or redirect masculine power. The chapter opens with Isaac, nearly blind and lying upon his deathbed, preparing to bestow the paternal blessing onto Esau, his hirsute firstborn son. But Rebekah, Isaac's wife, favors Jacob, their younger child. She tells the boy to dress in Esau's clothing and to slip on shaggy goat skins. The ruse works. Isaac, thinking he is stroking Esau, passes the blessing onto Jacob—the man later named Israel. In this tale, the very foundation of the Israelite nation rested on a deceitful costume—that is, on the use of clothing by women to gain a degree of political agency normally conferred only onto men.[7]

## PRIESTLY VESTMENTS

The symbolic power of biblical clothing is especially pronounced in regard to the priesthood. Israelite priests dressed in unique garments that reflected their privileged status as the intermediaries between humanity and God. According to Exodus 28:40–43, all priests dressed in the same general four garments: tunic or robe (*kětonet*), sash or girdle ('*abnět*), one of two kinds of head coverings, as I clarify momentarily, and plain linen (*bad*) breeches (*mikněsê*). Priests wore this outfit when entering the sanctuary or approaching the altar. (Incidentally, the breeches surely helped thwart any unseemly exposures, which, as I discussed earlier, offended the deity.) God enforced the priestly dress code on penalty of death. Clearly, proper attire was central to Israelite religion.

The High Priest's costume resembled the uniform of his ceremonial minions. But he enjoyed additional flourish (Exodus 28). First, the High Priest dressed in an embroidered, checkered, or plaited sash. Second, he sported a fancy turban (*mitznefet*) rather than an ordinary priestly cap (*migba'ah*).[8] Last, the High Priest generally enjoyed the finer *šēš* linen, enhanced with colorful trim and golden ornaments. Additionally, the High Priest donned four items that were his privilege alone. This costume consisted of a ritual vest or apron called the *ephod*, a breastpiece, a "robe (*me'el*) of the ephod," and a diadem, all made by skilled artisans "endowed with wisdom." Only the Tabernacle rivaled the sumptuousness of these appurtenances.[9]

The ephod was made from the finer *šēš* linen as well as gold and, perhaps most significant, blue, indigo, and worm-scarlet threads—a tripartite color scheme, we will see later, reserved for holy persons and the Tabernacle.[10] The shoulder straps contained two carnelian or onyx stones sheathed in gold filigree and engraved with the names of the twelve Israelite tribes. A "breastpiece of judgment," which resembled the ephod, was lashed to the apron with golden chains and a blue cord. No other Israelite dressed in any comparable costume.

The breastpiece displayed a dozen gold-encased gems and precious stones. Each ornament bore the name of a tribe. This impressive tableau transformed the High Priest into a representation of Israelite society. The breastpiece also contained an inner pouch that concealed two occult objects, the legendary Urim and Thummim (see Numbers 27:21; 1 Samuel 28:6). These mysterious items, like the breastplate, lay atop the High Priest's heart. What were they? Scholars offer many interpretations (see Van Dam 1997). Most likely, the Urim and Thummim were oracular or divination objects, perhaps crystals, inscribed lots, or light and dark pebbles.

Several features of the "robe of the ephod"[11] uniquely represented the High Priest's elite status, including its all-blue color and tear-resistant collar. From the hem dangled golden bells and linen pomegranates dyed purple and worm-scarlet. These ornaments emanated some sort of din whenever the High Priest crossed the threshold of the sanctuary, "that he may not die." Perhaps this chime begged God to allow the High Priest safe passage into the holy sanctum, or simply announced, as ritual noises often do cross-culturally (Needham 1967), the presence of the sacred.

All priestly garb paralleled in style and material the outer court hangings of the portable sanctuary. But the weaving techniques used to fabricate the High Priest's costume also matched the decorative textiles of the inner court or Tabernacle, the terrestrial abode of God (Haran 1978: 166–68). The final item in the High Priest's exclusive wardrobe was a golden diadem engraved with the phrase "Holy to the Lord (*Yahweh*)." A blue cord lashed this tiara to a fine linen turban (*mitznefet*). Although the Israelite kings also wore crowns or diadems (*nēzer*), only the High Priest's coronet is described as "holy." All told, clothing transformed the High Priest into an embodiment of the Tabernacle, thus uniting God and humanity.

The High Priest possessed another outfit, worn solely for entering the Holy of Holies, the place of the Ark of the Covenant, to enact a sacrificial atonement for Israelite sins (Leviticus 16:4). This costume consisted of the typical priestly garments—breeches, tunic, girdle, and turban—but woven entirely from plain *bad* linen rather than the finer *šēš* fabric that normally clothed the High Priest.[12] The simplicity of this uniform, especially on a religious figurehead normally attired in opulent raiment, evoked an aura of exceptional holiness. Whether through sheer simplicity or awe-inspiring elegance, the High Priest dressed to preside over the divine realm on earth.

Curiously, the Torah never mentions priestly footwear. Biblical barefootedness, we will see later, symbolized destitution. In fact, shows Palmer, ritual references to sandaled feet across the ancient Near East represented the ownership of land (2011). Priestly shoelessness thus signified humility. Indeed, while non-priestly men claimed land, God claimed the priesthood (e.g., Joshua 13:33). In this sense, continues Palmer, priests transcended this world even as they walked upon it. To this, I add that the image of the High Priest, bedecked in his regalia yet standing upon unshod feet, powerfully united nature and culture, or terrestrial and divine.

## CHANGING AND LAUNDERING

The aphorism "cleanliness is next to godliness" aptly befits the myriad references to ritual laundering in the Torah.[13] The ancient Israelites washed garments besmirched by various pollutants, including menstrual blood, ejaculate, mildew, skin disease, and bodily discharges (Leviticus 13–17; Numbers 19). The Israelites also scrubbed their garments in preparation for the Sinaic revelation (Exodus 19:10) and upon an accidental splattering of a sin offering (Leviticus 6:20–21). The priests, too, washed clothing after performing certain ritual duties (Leviticus 16:24–28). Clean garments represented an orderly society and cosmos.

Curiously, God in Ezekiel 44 requires priests to wear linen in the inner court of the Temple, never wool or other materials likely to cause perspiration. This rule, too, I suggest, reflected the Israelite value on maintaining clean bodily boundaries. Hence, only healthy priests could sacrifice animals—and then only unblemished livestock. The Law forbade priests from entering the courtyard dressed in sweaty clothing because, to draw on Douglas, an uncontainable body signified an unruly universe (1966).

Outfit changes accompanied various purification ceremonies (e.g., Genesis 35:2; Numbers 8:7; Zechariah 3). The priests, too, removed their sacerdotal vestments after certain ritual duties to safely encounter the common folk (Ezekiel 42:14; 44:19). The High Priest's costume, as I mentioned earlier, symbolically united the universe. But all other aspects of Israelite religion and society, including clothing, scrupulously maintained the boundary between sacred and profane. But did biblical clothing serve as an ethnic boundary? Were the Israelites uniquely attired? I now attempt an answer.

## RITUAL HEADBANDS AND FRINGE BENEFITS

The Hebrew Bible records a number of head coverings, mostly on men, including cord headbands (*hăbālîm*; 1 Kings 20:31), a garland ('*anaq*; Proverbs 1:9; 4:9), and a turban (*sānîp*; e.g., Isaiah 3:23). Today, the most distinctive aspect of Jewish attire is surely the male skullcap, called a *kippah* in Hebrew and a *yarmulke* in Yiddish. Yet the Torah mentions no such garment. Orthodox head coverings, as I explain in later chapters, developed many centuries after the biblical era. They are, in many respects, modern. However, the Torah does prescribe another ritual item worn on the head—and also lashed to the hand.

Exodus 13, a list of regulations spoken by God to Moses, includes this curious statement: "And it shall serve as a sign on your hand and as a reminder between your eyes, that the teaching of the Lord shall be in your mouth; that with a strong hand the Lord freed you from Egypt." A few verses later, we learn: "It shall be for a sign upon your hand and *totafot* between your eyes, for with a mighty hand the Lord freed us from Egypt" (Exodus 13:16). Deuteronomy twice repeats this edict, with slight variation (6:8; 11:18). But none of these passages describes either the "it" or the *totafot*. What were they?

Jews today associate these objects with tefillin, or *phylacteries* in Greek. Yet contemporary tefillin—biblical inscriptions encased in black boxes and strapped to the forehead and arm, as I discuss in the next chapter—surely differ from these enigmatic ancient items. Scholars generally concur that the "it" mentioned in Exodus 13 refers to some type of amulet (see Cohn 2008, chapter 2). The *totafot* are more mysterious. Speiser proposes a double-headed figurine or a symbol of the four directions (1957). Cohon suggests a brand or tattoo (1987: 339–41). Most scholars agree with Tigay and see the *totafot* as a headband or pendant (1982). But we know little more.

Israelite religion forbade a number of bodily practices that characterized the worship of other peoples, including funerary gashing (Leviticus 19:28), idolatrous lacerations (1 Kings 18:28), and fraudulent prophetic stigmata (Zechariah 13:6). Clearly, the intent of these edicts was to set the Israelites apart from their neighbors. But the Hebrew Bible, as we just saw, also records many Israelite charms, ornaments, and corporeal markings (e.g., Ezekiel 9; Isaiah 44:5; 2 Kings 11:12). In regard to the latter, one thinks immediately of circumcision (Genesis 17) and the infamous yet protective "mark" on Cain (Genesis 4:15). Although the exact nature of the *totafot* and hand sign mentioned in Exodus 13 remains uncertain, these ritual items fit into a wider pattern of altering, adorning, and dressing the biblical body to designate membership in the covenantal community. But I know of no evidence that these two mysterious objects *uniquely* adorned the Israelites. Yet one article did seemingly serve as a national emblem: blue fringes.

In Numbers 15:37–41, God tells the "sons" of Israel to attach "fringes" or "tassels" (tzitzit) to their garments—generic garments, I add (*beged*). The deity also prescribes a thread or cord of blue (*tekhelet*). "Look at it," commands the Torah, "and recall all the commandments of the Lord and observe them, so that you do not follow your heart and eyes in your lustful urge"—or, more literally, "go whoring."

But where should the Israelites specifically affix these tassels? The plural word used in Numbers 15:38, *kanaphayim*, variously refers to corners, wings, borders, skirts, scallops, extremities, and hems. A similar command in Deuteronomy 22:12, albeit lacking mention of the blue cord, offers greater specificity by mentioning "four" *kanaphayim*. Taken together, I see these two commands as requiring the Israelites to attach tassels, including a blue thread, to the four corners of their garments. (The Deuteronomy passage also uses a generic term for clothing, *kesût*.) Centuries later, as I show in Chapter 7, Jews would translate these edicts into fringed prayer shawls and tasseled undergarments. But the original meaning was different.

The fringes, I maintain, like the *totafot* and hand sign discussed earlier, instance the cross-cultural utilization of knots to represent the binding or sealing of vows (Gandz 1930). In Proverbs, the Israelites metaphorically tied divine commandments to their necks (3:3), hearts (6:21), and fingers (7:3; see also Isaiah 8:16; Job 14:17). The fringes similarly reminded the Israelites that they were bound to the Law. Knots also figure prominently among the Iatmul people of the middle Sepik River in Papua New Guinea, among whom I have conducted anthropological fieldwork since the latter 1980s (e.g., Silverman 2001). To remember the date of a market, women traditionally untie knotted cords, one knot representing each day. Maternal uncles lash ensorcelled bands to the wrists, ankles, and necks of their nieces and nephews to promote health and fortune—to keep their sisters' children, we might say, intact. Mourners wear similar knotted twine to contain their souls, as Iatmul say, lest they fatally loose themselves in grief. More practically, mothers implore their daughters to securely tether canoes lest the vessels float downriver at night. Throughout Iatmul culture, knots and ties represent memory, permanence, and containment. The biblical fringes did likewise: bind the people to an eternal deity, Law, and community, thus serving as an existential anchor. But was this custom unique in the ancient world? Yes and no.

Many peoples throughout the Mediterranean used tassels and ornamental cords as regal and ritual insignia (Kruger 1988). Often, the hem was the most ornate part of a garment, symbolizing rank and authority. Fascinatingly, clay imprints of hems served as ancient legal signatures (Stephen 1931: 63–64). Mesopotamian texts report on the cutting of hems in exorcisms and divorces. The Babylonians seized the fringes of their deities in acts of supplication (Stephens 1931). They also grasped hems during business negotiations. In Israel, King Saul botched a similar gesture after unsuccessfully begging forgiveness from Samuel for violating a divine decree (1 Samuel 15). As the prophet turned to leave, Saul grabbed Samuel's hem, tearing the garment. The significance of this insult was not lost on Samuel. "The Lord has this day," he responded to Saul, "torn the kingship over Israel away from you." Later, when Saul entered a cave to "cover his feet" or defecate, his rival, David, whom the king wanted dead, stealthily snipped Saul's hem (1 Samuel 24). Symbolically, David castrated the king while foreshadowing his ascension to the throne (Paul 1985). He also avenged Saul's prior assault on Samuel's hem.

The biblical symbolism of hems and fringes was hardly unique in the ancient world. Yet why adorn the hems of *every* Israelite—or every Israelite *man*? Why not embellish only the garb of the wealthy and powerful, like other Near Eastern societies? Because, answers Milgrom, the ubiquitous presence of fringes marked *all* Israelites, even the poor, as divinely chosen royalty (1983). This message, but not the tassel, seems unique in the ancient world. The blue thread supports this interpretation. In the biblical era, as I elaborate in Chapter 7, only elites could afford to dress in blue clothing. Yet all Israelites were so adorned, at least with a single thread, and thus the entire Israelite community again appeared regal. Together, the fringes and blue cord tethered all Israelites to the Law and signaled the divine election of Israel above all other peoples.

## ETHNIC BLENDS AND BOUNDARIES

The Black Obelisk, a stele from northern Iraq dating to the ninth century B.C.E. and now on display in the British Museum, shows vanquished Israelites presenting tribute to the Assyrian king Shalmaneser III. The captives, including the prostrating Israelite king, Jehu, wear undergarment tunics and tasseled cloaks. These bas-relief depictions suggest that dress denoted ancient ethnicity. The Torah offers some corroboration. In the early seventh century, the prophet Zephaniah thundered against Israelites who, among other transgressions, "don a foreign garment (*malbush*)" (1:8). This rebuke was perhaps narrowly directed at vestments worn for the worship of Baal (see 2 Kings 10:22). But Zephaniah's rant might also suggest the presence of a national costume or style.

The book of Leviticus supports this interpretation. In Hebrew, the linguistic root of "holy" means "keep apart." Ordinarily, the biblical worldview construed mixtures as polluting, and thus many religious rules aimed to separate categories. Leviticus 19, for example, forbids the Israelites from cross-breeding domestic animals and from sowing their fields with different kinds of seeds. The same chapter includes this curious stricture: "Nor shall a garment of different kinds of thread (*sha'atnez*) come upon you." Characteristically, the Torah offers no clarification. The word *sha'atnez* is neither Hebrew nor Semitic but a loanword, perhaps Egyptian. The word appears again in Deuteronomy 22:11: "Thou shall not wear *sha'atnez*, wool and linen together." But why?

The guidelines of daily comportment in ancient Israel stressed boundaries and separations. The Temple, however, represented divine unity. Accordingly, argues Hamel, priests encountered mixtures largely forbidden to other Israelites (2001). Recall that ancient technology could only dye woolen fibers, not flax. The High Priest's robe, therefore, as well as regular priestly sashes and certain Tabernacle curtains, conspicuously blended wool and linen. These textiles symbolized the creation of worldly order from originary cosmic disorder. These fabrics, too, inverted the everyday dress code of commoners to visually highlight the prominence of the Law. Of course, the commandment to wear a blue thread necessarily dressed all Israelites in the taboo blend, thus tethering the entire community to the priesthood. But that was the limit of ancient egalitarianism. Regular folk were permitted no further garments spun from the sacred mixture. In short, the *sha'atnez* prohibition reflected social and cosmic order and attired the Israelites apart from other peoples.

The Torah forbids one additional vestimentary mixture or mix-up: "There shall not be a man's gear on a woman, and a man shall not wear a woman's garment, for whoever does all these is abhorrent to the Lord your God" (Deuteronomy 22:5). The word for clothing here is generic (*simlah*); the term for "gear" (*keli*) often refers to military armor. The edict thus seemingly bans women from outfitting themselves for battle and forbids men from dressing like women.

But while the rule addresses a generic woman (*ishah*), it does not refer to just any man. Rather, the decree speaks about an elite man called a *geber*, known for exceptional religious and military skills. The law bars these men, and *only* these men, from wearing women's clothing lest they compromise, argues Vedeler, their manhood (2008). Other men could seemingly dress as they pleased. At the same time, the decree prohibits all women from taking up the emblem or weapon of these privileged men.

Many scholars also suggest that this rule censured ritual transvestitism, thus again separating the Israelites from their neighbors. The prohibition was narrowly cultic, however, not broadly ethical. Since everyday transvestitism was nowhere socially acceptable in the ancient Near East, contends Vedeler, biblical authorities had little reason to address the issue. The rule did not concern erotic or everyday cross-dressing among ordinary men, or among women in general. The edict simply protected the privileged status of elite men while banning transvestitism from Israelite religion. The rule, in other words, sought to accomplish the same goal as several other Israelite dress codes: to make visible the boundaries of social order and ethnicity.

## HAIRDOS AND DON'TS

Hair in the Hebrew Bible often communicated similar messages as clothing. For example, Leviticus 21:5 bars priests from paring the corners or sides of their beards. On them, writes Niditch, a "whole" head of hair, like their white attire, symbolized bodily and ritual wholeness (2008: 106–7).

Israelite hair, too, again like clothing, signaled national identity. Thus Jeremiah described certain non-Israelites as "them [that are] in the utmost corners" (9:25)—that is, people with clipped side locks. Other passages ban funerary tonsures (Deuteronomy 14:1; Leviticus 21:5) and forbid grieving priests from shaving their pates or yanking out their hair (Ezekiel 44:20; Leviticus 10:6). Both laws set the Israelites apart from neighboring mourners. Indeed, the prophetic literature often refers to mortuary shaving as a sign of remorse for violating the Law (e.g., Ezekiel 7:18; Jeremiah 16:6). But these declarations did not reflect actual social practice. Rather, the prophets sought to besmirch immoral Israelites with a disgusting, alien custom (see Niditch 2008, chapter 5). Appearance, once again, symbolized an Israelite's position in the social order—or outside it.

Women's hair receives enormous attention in biblical texts. An Israelite warrior desiring a "beautiful" captive first granted his prisoner a month of grieving for her parents (Deuteronomy 21:10–13). She also trimmed her nails, shed her captivity cloak, and shaved her head. The new outfit, manicure, and coiffure symbolized the captive's transition from a foreign war spoil to an Israelite wife. She was made to dress for a new status.

A far more terrifying expression of power and sexuality was the *sotah* ordeal (Numbers 5:11–31; Niditch 2008, chapter 6). A husband suspecting his wife of infidelity, but lacking proof or witness, brought her to a priest. While she stood before God, the priest shaved or, more likely, unfurled her hair, then made the suspected adulteress or *sotah* drink "the waters of bitterness." If she was guilty, the concoction brought about infertility. Her belly would swell, in the biblical idiom, and her thigh drop and waste away. She was henceforth deemed a "curse upon her people." But if the *sotah* was innocent, "she shall be unharmed and able to retain seed."

The brutal and public seizure of women's hair during the *sotah* ordeal, in my view, dramatized men's efforts to control female desire and fertility. A wife unwilling to contain her sexuality within her husband's authority, thereby disordering his house, suffered the consequent disordering of her hair and body. In this context, hair doubled for clothing. The disheveling of the woman's locks was tantamount to a forced undressing. Israelite wives, I add, lacked any comparable recourse when suspecting their husbands of betrayal.

Priests and women reproduced Israelite society, priests through ritual and sacrifice and women through uterine fertility. On both, unkempt hair symbolically threatened social order (Margalit 1995). Only devotional ascetics called Nazarites, such as Sampson, could legitimately grow wild tresses (Numbers 6). The Torah says little about what Nazarites actually did. But we know what they could not do: sip wine, touch corpses, and trim their locks. Nazarites polluted by cadavers re-consecrated their hair and status partly by shaving their heads to grow new hair. They ended their vows by burning their locks. This flowing mane signified exceptional religious devotion and, in Sampson's case, celibate potency (Judges 13–16). Yet Sampson failed to heed his mop.[14] He lost his hair and his brawn "on the knees" of a Philistine woman, Delilah, and subsequently lost his life. Symbolically, we might say, Delilah did to Sampson what Israelite men regularly did to women—only in this case, it proved a national tragedy.

## BEJEWELING SIN AND SOCIAL ORDER

The Hebrew Bible catalogs an impressive trove of jewelry. Yet the exact identification of many ornaments remains, as in the case of clothing, unclear. Of far greater interest is the symbolism of jewelry. Did Israelite adornments, like clothing, communicate messages about identity and social order? The prophet Isaiah (3:18–23) berated the aristocracy, personified as the bejeweled "daughters of Zion," for vainly strutting, "heads thrown back," in tinkling anklets, bangles, rings, drop pendants, nose rings, snake charms, armlets, moon ornaments, "soul house" talismans, and sun disk pendants (Platt 1979). It seems unlikely that any Israelite actually possessed such opulence. Rather, the idea of feminine ornamentation symbolized immoral decadence. Indeed, the stern prophets, all of them men, often pinned Israelite sins on women's apparel. When Israel strays from the Law in Ezekiel 16, for example, the nation is stripped of its jewels and garments, then stoned and skewered with swords.

Adornments frequently connote sinfulness, most famously when the Hebrews melted their baubles into the golden calf (Exodus 32:2–4). Biblical texts also call attention to jewelry when disparaging other societies (Judges 8:24). But I see no evidence in the Hebrew Bible suggesting that the Israelites adorned themselves distinctively. Moreover, embellishment did not always challenge the official religious system—to wit, the luxurious appearance of the High Priest and the sanctuary. In fact, the fringes attached to Israelite garments, no less than the ritual items affixed to Israelite hands and foreheads, resembled nothing if not prominent ornaments. Biblical jewelry, then, like clothing, conveyed purposes both moral and taboo, thus sustaining or subverting the social order—or both.

## BIBLICAL DRESS TODAY

The classic era of the Israelites as recorded in the Torah faded some twenty-five centuries ago. But the allure of biblical clothing endures. Israelite garb is much beloved and fantasized by the directors of Hollywood epics (Llewellyn-Jones 2005). Costume designers for church dramas, too, sew imaginative, albeit rather more modest, visions of biblical outfits. The appearance of biblical dress in modern settings sometimes conveys controversial sentiments. The Torah mentions that non-priestly Israelites donned sackcloth during mourning (e.g., Leviticus 21:10). Ultra-Orthodox or Haredi rabbis in downtown Jerusalem did likewise in 2006 while protesting a gay pride parade (Figure 2).

**Figure 2**   Israeli rabbis dressed in sackcloth protest gay pride parade. Getty Images.

Many evangelical Christians and ultra-Orthodox Jews remain especially enthralled by the High Priest's costume. Online retailers offer replica ephod
necklaces (e.g., www.jerusalem-gifts.com). The quasi-scholarly messianic
Temple Institute took this fascination one step further by painstakingly rec-
reating the High Priest's costume in preparation for the immanent rebuilding
of the Temple (www.templeinstitute.org). Another such Jewish organization,
Beged Ivri, sells "beautiful biblical garments for the modern Israelite" (www.
begedivri.com). Both fundamentalist groups show that ancient garb, at least
for some, is not so ancient at all.

Ironically, perhaps the most widespread modern item plucked from the biblical wardrobe is also somewhat fictitious. We do not know precisely how the
Israelites shod their soles. The biblical word for footwear (*na'al*) could equally
refer to shoes and to sandals. By the Talmudic era, however, the word clearly
specified shoes. The rabbis referred to sandals with the same Greek loanword used by English speakers today, *sandalon*, only spelled in Hebrew. There
is reason, then, to contend that the ancient Israelites walked in shoes. But
sandals, of course, predominate in film, drama, and Israeli souvenir shops
(Figure 3). Sandals, too, form part of the Zionist national costume.

Contemporary Israeli sandals display a wide range of fashions. Israel-
Catalog.com, for example, sells "trendy Biblical-style sandals . . . Feel the soft
leather lining and flexible sole, the Biblical experience at its best." With names
like Galilee, Golan, and Negev, these sandals roam the landscape of biblical
and modern Israel. Christian retailers offer their own theological topography

**Figure 3**    Israeli sandals: the invention of a biblical tradition. Photo by author.

of sandals, including the Bethlehem and Nazareth styles (www.israeli-gifts. com). Amazon.com even sells "Unisex Water Buffalo Hippie Jesus Sandals." And Christians unable in person to visit the Holy Land can purchase Walking in Their Sandals 2.0, a multimedia CD-ROM of biblical events and places. Clearly, the sandal today conveys a powerful image of the Holy Land.

Yet "biblical sandals" are an invented tradition, dating to the generation of Russian Jewish émigrés who arrived in Palestine in the early twentieth century (Ben-Meir 2008; Oz 2000: 213). The sandals were created entirely by chance when two members of an agricultural cooperative or *kibbutz*, ordinarily engaged in repairing shoes, tinkered with a new type of footwear. Initially, these sandals materialized the socialist ideal of rustic frugality. They were originally known as *khugistic* sandals (Ben-Meir 2008), since they helped define the attire of the Zionist "circle" (*khug*). The sandals were affordable, thus democratic, as well as durable and gender neutral—that is, untainted by bourgeois luxury (Ben-Meir 2008: 80). *Khugistic* sandals made possible a key initiation rite required of many early Jewish settlers in Palestine: walking the land.

*Khugistic* sandals—two straps affixed to a thin leather sole, worn without socks—rapidly grew in popularity. By the 1950s, this now-characteristic style of Israeli footwear gained a new moniker: "Nimrod" sandals. The name may have derived from a Jewish shoe business in the Netherlands that relocated to Tel Aviv on the eve of World War II (Ben-Meir 2008: 83). This sandal combined tough asceticism with a biblical aura. In the 1960s, the "biblical sandal" attained its current status as a genuine ethnic custom.

The sandal legitimated the modern state of Israel by tethering Zionism to ancient authenticity.

The early Jewish settlers keenly understood the symbolic importance of costume (Raz 1999). Baron Edmond Benjamin de Rothschild, an ardent Zionist and scion of a French Jewish banking family, purchased several hundred Middle Eastern cloaks, or *abbayas*, for the new arrivals. Rothschild believed that Jews living in Palestine should dress like their non-Jewish neighbors. But affluent and urban settlers favored the latest European fashions from Beirut and Paris, while agricultural workers pulled on the humble garb of the Middle Eastern peasantry.

Eventually, the settlers took up European-looking clothing which, like the sandals, visualized an ethic of unadorned, largely masculine, utilitarianism (Helman 2008). The early Zionists in Palestine mainly dressed in austere blues, whites, and khakis (Ben-Meir 2008: 81). They worked in shorts and dark boots or sandals, often going barefoot afterward, and three types of headgear: kerchiefs, straw hats, and the now iconic *tembel* or conical fabric hat (Raz 2008). To some settlers, this outfit served as a de facto national dress code. Indeed, pre-state newspapers often raised the question of a national costume. The Levant Fair of 1936 sponsored a contest for an outfit blending Eastern, Western, and Jewish elements. After statehood, the issue again surfaced in regard to the appropriate attire for overseas bureaucrats (Raz 1999). No official costume ever emerged. Secular Israelis came to prefer European fashions. But they also remained bound to the sandals that evoke, however fictitiously, ancient roots. Clothing in Israel thus came to differentiate Jew from non-Jew while tying the country to both modern Europe and biblical antiquity.

All ideologies, like clothing and shoes, eventually wear thin. "There was a time," tells a recent article in *The Jerusalem Post*, "when you could spot an Israeli abroad by his shoes, generally leather sandals with two tough straps . . . For better or worse, the image of the sabra [native-born Israeli] began and ended with the biblical sandal."[15] But no longer. Younger Israelis today find little support for their nationalism or arches from the "biblical sandal." Instead, they prefer a more recent, global fashion: plastic Crocs.


## CONCLUSION

Traditional Judaism is often cast as an artless religion, trapped by the Second Commandment of the Decalogue that forbids "graven images" (Exodus 20:4). Yet the aniconic edict specifically refers to cultic images that depict deities other than Yahweh. The Torah never prohibits image making itself. Indeed, every repetition of the Second Commandment specifically mentions idolatry (e.g., Exodus 34:17; Leviticus 26:1). The aniconic imperative dramatically clashed with the centrality of bodily and visual experience in Israelite religion.

The Hebrew Bible describes in rich detail the appearance of the Tabernacle and Temple as well as sacerdotal objects, priestly attire, ritual performances, and fringes. Indeed, the efficacy of Israelite worship entailed a visual experience. Even God's existence became known through dramatic spectacles such as pillars of smoke and a burning bush. The deity could savor sacrifices, sniff incense, walk, sit, shout, and insist that no human but Moses peek at the divine countenance. God, too, took a keen interest in the bodies of men and women—in hair, menstruation, food, sexuality, circumcision, and, of course, clothing. For a disembodied deity, as Eilberg-Schwartz stresses, the Israelites thought about God in remarkably corporeal ways (1994). Israelite religion enshrined display.

In the postbiblical era, Jewish art renounced the human form. But Judaism still highlighted the body. Jews ate certain foods, rested on the Sabbath, removed foreskins, and dressed in ritual garb. In the eyes of medieval Christians, moreover, Jews exhibited grotesque disfigurements, such as tails and bloody exudations, in punishment for betraying Christ (Silverman 2006, chapter 8). To Jew and non-Jew alike, the Jewish body was the central feature of Jewish identity. But Judaism construes the body as neither good nor bad. What matters is what you *do* with your body. And in Judaism, the best way to ensure that you do right by the body is to dress properly. Just how the rabbis imagined this costume is the topic of the next chapter.

# –2–

# The Fashion of the Rabbis

Who is rich? He who is happy with his lot.

Rabbi Ben Zoma, *Sayings of the Fathers*, chapter 4

Despite efforts by biblical authorities to dress the Israelites apart from their neighbors, subsequent ancient writers mention nary a word about Jewish attire. No ancient Greek or Latin text, writes Shaye Cohen, "says that Jews are distinctive because of their clothing" (1993). Especially remarkable is the absence of derogatory remarks. After all, ancient authors mocked virtually every aspect of Judaism. But while the Romans ridiculed Celtic and German clothing, and the Greeks laughed at Persian garb, Jewish threads passed unnoticed.

I begin this chapter by surveying the evidence for distinctive Jewish attire in the centuries following the closure of the Hebrew Bible. The bulk of the chapter, however, focuses on the classic rabbis and the authoritative vision of Jewish dress that still shapes devout wardrobes. How did the rabbis think about dress? Did everyday Jews listen? And what values and conflicts did clothing materialize in rabbinic culture?

## DRESSING AT THE MILLENNIUM

To start, let us examine Jewish attire in the immediate postbiblical period. What do we know? As it turns out, very little. But the absence of information might actually tell us a great deal about how Jews did *not* dress. And this, I will argue, is of crucial importance.

A text from the second century B.C.E. called the Letter of Aristeas mentions the presence of "a distinguishing mark as a reminder" on Jewish clothing (Knowles 2004: 16). Presumably, the author referred to fringes. But few other ancient texts comment on the same feature. Perhaps the "mark" was so obviously Jewish that it hardly warranted comment. Or maybe the mark was not, in fact, evident at all.

The Maccabean literature offers further hints about Jewish clothing in the same era. These texts detail the brutal occupation of Palestine by the Seleucid Greeks and the triumphant Jewish revolt celebrated annually on Chanukah.

The Maccabees routed the Greeks. They also slaughtered Jews who embraced Hellenistic culture—say, by wearing a hat typical of Greek youth (2 Maccabees 4:12). But the tale says nothing about Jewish caps. Still, the Maccabees prevailed, and so we would expect that subsequent Jews in antiquity dressed distinctively. But the evidence suggests otherwise.

Another text from the Second Temple Period mentions that Jewish women favored colorful garments and ornaments (1 Enoch 98:2). But preference is not prescription. These women perhaps dressed distinctly—but not distinctly Jewish. The same composition chided the wealthy for wearing extravagant outfits, especially men who exceeded "what is proper for their sex and status." Flavious Josephus, writing in the first century, similarly ridiculed Jewish warriors for dressing in female attire to sneak up on the Romans, drawing "their swords from under their finely dyed cloaks" (*Jewish War* 4: 561–65). But neither text speaks to an ethnic costume.

Josephus also remarked that the Essenes, an itinerant group of ascetic Jews living in Palestine at the turn of the millennium, dressed in plain, white, often tattered clothing, perhaps modeled after the suits of the biblical priesthood. This costume expressed a fundamentalist approach to the Law and also likely served to critique the lavishly attired rich (Tigchelaar 2003). Josephus likewise commented that the Levites, a biblical tribe of religious functionaries, appealed to Herod Agrippa II for the right to dress in priestly vestments (*Antiquities of the Jews* 20: 216–18). But Josephus favored no such innovation. For him, Jewish society could only properly function with a stable dress code (Edwards 1994: 157). Yet Josephus nowhere indicates that the Israelites dressed apart from the Romans—that distinctive garb, in other words, was essential to the self-definition of Judaism.

The New Testament mentions that the Great Sanhedrin, the supreme assembly of early Judaism, dressed in white (Acts 23:1–3). Matthew (23:5–6) criticized both Jewish scribes and the Pharisees, another first-century sect, for flaunting oversized phylacteries and fringes (Knowles 2004: 161–62). Although neither the Gospels nor Jesus spoke about a distinctive Jewish attire, the well-known parable of the Good Samaritan suggests that one existed (Luke 10:30–37). In this story, a priest and a Levite disregard a naked man, stripped and beaten by thieves, lying in the road. The Good Samaritan, of course, famously offers aid. But why did the priest and the Levite ignore the victim? One possibility is that, taking the victim for dead, these religious authorities simply wished to avoid the ritual defilement associated with corpses. Yet most readers of the parable see the priest and the Levite in a rather more unfavorable light. The tale implies that the victim was Jewish. The parable also suggests, more crucially, that clothing communicated ethnic and religious identity (Knowles 2004). But the thieves pilfered the victim's garments and so passersby had no way of discerning his Jewishness.

The mugging brutally rendered the victim anonymous in an era lacking any widespread commitment to universal humanism. An unknown person was a non-person. The Samaritan was "good" precisely because he showed compassion to a man lacking clothing, hence, a clear identity. Unfortunately for our purposes, Luke never mentions what precise garments would have signaled the victim's Jewishness.

But perhaps *no* costume would have done so. Luke seemingly erred. New Testament Jews, like all Roman citizens, dressed in standard Greek garb—including the *himation* outer garment (Mark 13:16) and the *chiton* shirt (Matthew 5:4). Archaeological excavations reveal that Jew and non-Jew both favored tunics with purple bands, called *clavus* in Latin and *'imrah* in Hebrew, that often denoted age, gender, and rank (Knowles 2004: 158–59). Mediterranean Jews also adorned their garments with the same L-shaped fabric attachments that appear in early Christian mosaics (Welch and Foley 1996). The meaning of these patterns remains unknown. But they surely did not tag Jews.

Second-century Jews living near the Dead Sea, unlike the Greeks and Romans, dressed in two-piece tunics (Roussin 1994: 183–84). In fact, the Mishnah endorsed this style as economical (M. Negim 11:9). Should the garment incur some impurity, the owner might fortunately need only replace half his shirt. But no other ancient author comments on this feature. It was a difference that did not evidently make a difference.

What about hair? Jewish women in late antiquity generally braided, twisted, and pinned their locks (Thompson 1988). But there is no evidence for distinct Jewish hairdos. And while the Talmud proclaimed beards the "adornment of the face" (B. Shabbat 152a), other ancient sources remain silent on Jewish facial hair and earlocks (Thompson 1988: 104). Jews groomed like everybody else.

In sum, Jewish clothing in late antiquity was not very Jewish at all. Any effort by the Torah or Israelite authorities to institutionalize an ethnic dress code failed. Nonetheless, as I now show, the classic rabbis invested dress with considerable significance.

## GOD IS IN THE DETAILS

Traditional Judaism is a legalistic religion. Ritual regulations govern almost all aspects of human existence. Devout Jews attribute these laws to divine revelation as recorded by the Torah. In the thirteenth century, Moses ben Maimon, better known as Maimonides, identified a total of 613 biblical commandments. (Numerous versions are posted on the Internet.) To religious Jews, these laws remain eternally binding.

But biblical commandments, as we saw in Chapter 1, consistently lack practical guidelines. As a result, religious Jews ascribe enormous importance to historical conversations among noted rabbis and sages seeking to translate the broad precepts of the Torah into precise rituals and mundane practices. Jewish religious law or halacha, like the common law systems of many modern nation-states, largely builds on cases and precedents—dating back, as I mentioned in the introduction, to the third century (see Elon 1994). The law is not mandated by an infallible authority, as in the papacy, or by a legislative body. Nor is it left up to individual whim. Rather, halacha is continuously debated by communal leaders charged with interpretive authority. Although the classic rabbis tended to agree on the basic, broad premises of Judaism, they nonetheless frequently differed in regard to the details, sometimes resulting in competing and dissenting rulings.

Early Christianity saw Christ as culminating and therefore annulling much of the Torah. Indeed, the church read most Mosaic laws not as codes of conduct but as allegories alluding to Jesus. The Apostle Paul and, later, the church, indignantly accused Jews of doggedly adhering to meaningless rules or "works" to the exclusion of genuine spirituality or "faith." But this canard grossly misunderstands Judaism. It ignores the fact that traditional Judaism contains a core set of theological precepts, which Maimonides codified as the "13 Principles of Faith." The rabbis and religious Jews formulated these rules not in the absence of belief, but in the simple desire to avoid transgressing God's design for humanity. This outlook profoundly colored Jewish dress.

Rabbinic legal decisors, called *poskim*, reaffirmed the biblical dress code. The Torah contains both positive or performative and negative or prohibitive decrees. The former, as compiled by Maimonides, include tefillin, fringes, philanthropic generosity, the *chalitzah* shoe removal ceremony, and the ritual cleansing of defiled garments. Prohibitions include wool and linen blends, cross-dressing, idolatrous garb, and denying clothing to a spouse or ex-wife. The rabbis also censored opulent attire and immodest apparel.[1]

An excellent example of rabbinic logic in regard to clothing pertains to the Sabbath ban on work (e.g., Exodus 31:12–17). What exactly constitutes "work"? Mindful that any ambiguity might result in the unintended violation of God's will, the early rabbis identified thirty-nine specific categories of prohibited Sabbath labor, including sorting, weaving, tearing, writing, lighting, and hammering (B. Shabbath). To prevent carrying, another Sabbath taboo, some medieval Jews sewed shut a sleeve on their ritual gowns (Pollack 1971: 161). For the same reason, the rabbis counseled against wearing new, tattered, or ill-fitting footwear on the Sabbath or wading across a stream lest a sandal accidentally float to the surface (B. Shabbath 141b; B. Yoma 78a). Jews in early modern Europe even appealed to a Polish rabbi for advice on whether the unusual weight of a novel cape, adopted from the non-Jews of Nuremburg (itself a potential transgression), violated the Sabbath ban on carrying (Daxelmüller 1995: 42). It did.

The rabbis also prohibited certain kinds of tying on the Sabbath, mainly permanent knots (B. Berachoth 111b–112a). They permitted hair ribbons, blouse straps, and shoelaces. But what if a lace snaps? Can one replace a broken shoelace on the Sabbath? No, ruled the central Jewish legal code, the *Shulhan Arukh*, collated in the sixteenth century. The insertion of the new lace effectively completes a "container." Alternatively, the act "creates" the shoe. Since both vessel making and creating are prohibited Sabbath activities, one instead threads a new lace through only a few eyelets or ties together the broken strap with a temporary knot.[2]

The early rabbis also prohibited laundering on the Sabbath—no soaking, scrubbing, squeezing, shaking, plucking lint, or even folding clothing along the original creases. Why the latter? Because folding "finishes" the garment, another forbidden Sabbath labor. At best, one lightly wipes or scrapes a garment on the Sabbath. Many readers today might view these rules as pica-yune or byzantine. But they served the function of transforming the littlest detail into an affirmation of God, thus clothing religious Jews at all times in the Law.

We can also see the juridical and totalizing aspects of traditional Judaism in regard to tefillin. These objects, as noted in Chapter 1, derived from the ambiguous headband and "hand sign" mentioned in Exodus and Deuteron-omy. A set of tefillin consists of two leather cases attached to straps. Each case contains biblical verses. Devout Jews—until recently, as I discuss in Chapter 7, only men—wind or "lay" tefillin around an arm and the forehead for weekday morning prayers (Figure 4). Despite biblical roots, tefillin are postbiblical. The earliest archaeological remnants date to the second century B.C.E. and served as amulets promising long life (Cohn 2008). After some variation in shape and textual content, tefillin were formalized in the third or fourth century commentary, *Mekhilta de Rabbi Ishmael*. This source set the four passages as Exodus 13:9–10, Exodus 13:11–16, Deuteronomy 6:4–9, and Deuteronomy 11:13–21.

The rabbis regulated virtually every aspect of tefillin: preparing the parch-ment, stitching the cases, arranging the texts, the type of ink, the square shape and black color, whether to attach the head or arm piece first, the use of the writing hand to wind the strap, and so forth (e.g., B. Menachoth 34b–37b). They prohibited the wearing of tefillin in the bathroom, while sleeping, and during intimacy (e.g., B. Sukkah 26a). The rabbis also rejected red tefillin since the color evoked Egyptian amulets (Cohon 1987: 346). This tint, too, conjured feminine licentiousness and blood. Indeed, red might give the im-pression that a man engaged in intimacy with a menstruating woman while wearing his tefillin (B. Menachoth 35a).[3]

**Figure 4**   Hasidic man wearing a tallit and tefillin. Photo by author.

At one time, some Jews may have worn tefillin throughout the day (Cohn 2008: 132). But the practice eventually shifted to the daytime, perhaps to avoid association with nocturnal magic, and then to morning prayers (Cohon 1987: 344). But not every morning. The Torah describes the precursors of tefillin as a divine "sign" (*ot*). The same word refers to the Sabbath and major holidays (e.g., Exodus 31:13). To avoid ritual redundancy, Jews do not lay tefillin on these religious occasions.

Rabbinic law prohibits the selling of tefillin and fringes to Gentiles lest non-Jewish swindlers try to pass as Jews (e.g., B. Menachoth 43a). Perhaps these edicts also suggest that people of all religions once desired tefillin for use as charms. In fact, the rabbis rejected circular tefillin precisely to avoid similarity with pagan talismans (Cohn 2008: 151–54). Yet Jews themselves often used tefillin for magical purposes. In one tale, a Jew named Elisha heroically defies Rome by walking the street in his tefillin (B. Shabbat 49a). When seen, Elisha flees, untying his tefillin as he runs. He is eventually snagged by Roman officials and asked to identify the objects concealed in his hand. "The wings of a dove," Elisha replies, opening his palm. And so it was.

## FRINGE BENEFITS

The rabbis were equally particular about the fringes (tzitzit). The Torah commands the Israelites to *look* at the fringes (Numbers 15:39). Accordingly, rabbinic law affixes tassels only on daytime garments (B. Shabbath 25b). Even the blind must wear fringes for the benefit of the seeing (B. Shabbath 27b). Valid tzitzit may not be woven from the garment itself but must be attached as separate threads made specifically to fulfill the commandment (B. Sukkah 9a). Proper intentionality is crucial. For this reason, many Orthodox Jews reject machine-made tzitzit and wear instead only hand-spun fringes. Others require only that the machine operator consciously ponder the commandment while pushing the button.

The Torah, recall, prohibits wool and linen blends (*sha'atnez*). But the Torah also requires the attachment of blue threads to Israelite fringes—woolen threads, as I discussed in Chapter 1. To avoid any contradiction, the early rabbis exempted the fringes from the law of *sha'atnez*. The rabbis, too, addressed all sorts of minute matters concerning the fringes (B. Menachoth 37b–44a). Which thread does one first insert into the garment, blue or white?

**Figure 5**   Hasidic man, bending over his prayer book, draped in a tallit. Photo by author.

**Figure 6**  Hasidic boys in tzitzit fringes, black velvet yarmulkes, and Air Jordan sneakers selling soda on a sidewalk in Brooklyn. Photo by author.

How long are the fringes? What is the minimum size of a fringe-worthy garment? And so forth.

In the Middle Ages, Jews devised a fringed undergarment, worn throughout the day, called a *tallit katan* ("small tallit") or *arba kanfot* ("four corners"). The larger garment, now worn only for prayer, became known as a *tallit gadol* or "large tallit" (Figure 5). The smaller article perhaps allowed Jews to follow the Law without attracting hostile notice (Cohon 1987: 363). But it may also evidence the pull of acculturation (Figure 6). Some Hasidic sects reserve the large tallit, called *tallis* in Yiddish, for married men. (The plural is *tallitot* or *talleisim*.) But in most communities today, any man past the age of thirteen— the year of his bar mitzvah (Figure 7)—may, and in some denominations must, wear the tallit for prayer. Women, too, now increasingly take up the garment, as I detail in Chapter 7.

A legitimate ritual fringe consists of four strings, one slightly longer (called the *shamesh* or "assistant"), all doubled over to make eight strands. The bundle

**Figure 7**   The author posing in his prayer shawl (tallit) on the morning of his bar mitzvah in 1975. Photo by P. Silverman.

is tied into five double knots, each separating a precise number of loops wound from the longer strand. A valid fringe, too, as opposed to an insignificant thread or an ornamental tassel, must measure at least twelve Talmudic "fingers" in length. (One Talmudic "finger," or *agudel*, equals the width of an average thumb.) At least four "fingers" of the fringe must consist of the knots and windings. I will say much more on the symbolism of the fringes in Chapter 7. For now, I want only to mention one interpretation.

The rabbis of the Talmud understood the fringes to represent all 613 commandments of the Torah (B. Menachoth 43b; B. Nedarim 25a). The logic of this symbolism arises from the use of Hebrew letters to represent numerals. By assigning arithmetic values to words and phrases, rabbinic numerology (*gematria*) seeks to discern hidden meanings in religious precepts and biblical passages—to peer beneath the actual words and narratives, called the "garments of the Torah" (see Wolfson 2004). The letters of the word *tzitzit* total 600. This sum, when added to the eight threads and five knots on each fringe, equals 613, or the precise number of laws in the Torah. The rabbis thus saw the fringes as a protective garment of holiness, a vestimentary fence, that also bound Jews, as noted in Chapter 1, to the Law.

## STITCHING A FENCE AND BLURRING BOUNDARIES

The classic rabbis often elaborated on biblical edicts. They created this religious "fence" (*seyag*) to protect Jews from inadvertent transgressions. The concept is crucial to understanding religious Judaism, especially rabbinic remonstrations against acculturation. Indeed, this taboo was known as *chukkat ha-goy*, to "walk in the ways of the other nations" (e.g., Deuteronomy 12:30; Jeremiah 10:2; Leviticus 18:3; 20:23). Proper attire, the rabbis hoped, would serve as a hedge against any such acculturation. Indeed, Jews should suffer martyrdom, declared the Talmud, rather than renounce the slightest commandment or custom, even "changing the strap of one's shoe" (B. Sanhedrin 74a–74b). A fourteenth-century father was quite clear on this point in his ethical will: "you must not adopt non-Jewish fashions of dress . . . Never change the fashions of your fathers" (Abrahams 1891: 463).

But what exactly constitutes forbidden attire? A garment made by Gentiles? Or a style that originated with non-Jews, even if the item itself was manufactured by a Jew? Even today, the answer remains somewhat unclear. Some rabbis banned clothing that conveyed non-Jewish values such as arrogance, idolatry, and immodesty (Stern 1994: 191–92). Others allowed Gentile garb so long as the intent was not to pass as a non-Jew, or if a Jew simply wished to avoid embarrassment when interacting with Gentile officials (B. Baba Kama 83a). The Law clearly forbade Jews from imitating Gentiles. But the rabbis struggled to translate this ethical mandate into practical guidelines.

In fifteenth-century Italy, for example, a potential fashion faux pas for Jewish physicians was a red hooded robe (Woolf 2000–1). The rabbis generally disapproved of red clothing since the color evoked, as I mentioned in regard to tefillin, non-Jewish lust. Moreover, the gown unquestionably derived from Gentile tastes. But Rabbi Colon permitted the robe so long as Jewish physicians intended neither to pass as non-Jews nor to swagger but only to advertise their medical knowledge to potential patients. Under these specific conditions, the gown violated no divine decree. In fact, observed Rabbi Colon, most Italian Jews dressed like non-Jews. If the Torah prohibited any garment deriving from Gentile tailors or styles, then the entire Jewish community of Italy was guilty of sin—a patently absurd conclusion. As long as Jews abided by Jewish values, Rabbi Colon ruled, they could enjoy local fashions.

Rabbi Colon's acceptance of the red gown did not amount to an endorsement of assimilation. Far from it. Nonetheless, many of Colon's contemporaries rejected any vestimentary liberalism (Woolf 2000–1: 54). They forbade Gentile garments *tout court*. But these efforts were more rhetorical than real since premodern Europe tolerated little blurring (or little official blurring) of religious boundaries (Bonfil 1994: 111). Unofficially, Jews thoroughly participated in non-Jewish forms of popular culture (Daxelmüller 1995).

Jewish attire was no less localized. That the rabbis thought it urgent to re-peatedly renew their dress codes suggests that most Jews yearned to dress like their neighbors.

The Talmud specifies the proper order for putting on shoes—right then left—to separate Jew from non-Jew (B. Shabbat 61a; Jacobson 2002). But I see little evidence that everyday Jews listened. Indeed, almost all garments mentioned in the Talmud were plucked from the standard Greek and Roman wardrobe and lexicon (e.g., B. Shabbath 120a; Roussin 1994: 183; Rubens 1967: 21–22). In the classic period of rabbinic thought, to repeat, Jews dressed like everybody else.

Documents detailing Jewish life in medieval Egypt support this contention (Stillman 1974, 1976). Trousseaux lists, for example, mention an astonish-ing range of garments: bathrobes, sleeved dresses, Sicilian robes, scarves, turbans, sashes, gowns ornamented with coins, and an impressive variety of jewelry. We read mention of over sixty different fabrics, including a dozen silks, and a spectacular feast of colors ranging from pistachio, saffron, and pomegranate to apricot, pear, and chickpea. All this clothing and finery re-flected socioeconomic class, however, not ethnicity or religion.

In Europe, illuminated Hebrew manuscripts from the latter Middle Ages simi-larly display no particularly Jewish necklines, sleeve shapes, headgear, shoes, colors, or decorations (Metzger and Metzger 1982). In these illustrations, every-day clothing reflected a Jew's wealth, gender, occupation, region, and historical era but not his or her Jewishness. These pictures—all inked by Jews, I stress—may reflect social reality, that is, how Jews actually dressed. More likely, they portray a particular ideology—how Jews wished to be seen, at least by them-selves. Either way, the illustrations strikingly omit distinctly Jewish apparel, thus repudiating the rabbis and, as I discuss in the next chapter, the church.

It is important to note that these illustrations show no effort to erase Jewishness. Many pictures, in fact, depict religious activities. We see men, women, and children praying inside the synagogue—all bedecked, I note, with some sort of head covering. Yet many Jewish men appear hatless in public. Likewise, the illustrations show no earlocks, no consistent pattern of beards, and no Jewish haircuts. The Jews in these manuscripts act like Jews. But they fail to dress apart from the wider society.

If these illustrations reveal anything, it is that the rabbis legislated one world while their congregants dwelled, or wished to dwell, in another. But even the rabbis eventually came to dress like others. Although the Torah describes priestly attire in great detail, the classic rabbis never devised a clerical costume—in part, I maintain, because Judaism, unlike ancient Israel or the Christian church, never institutionalized a formal hierarchy. Nonethe-less, the classic rabbis wanted clothing to separate themselves and schol-ars from ordinary men (e.g., B. Shabbath 145b; Shapero 1987). The learned were held to higher standards of cleanliness—frequent laundering, spotless shoes, no grease stains (B. Berachoth 43b; B. Shabbath 114a). Scholars should dress "attractive and clean," counseled Maimonides, avoiding lavish clothing that might attract undue attention and frayed outfits that would disgrace their position (*Hilchot De'ot* 5:9). Maimonides recommended garments "of the middle range"—say, long, modest sleeves and hems. But not too long, Maimonides added, lest one dress like "the haughty."[4]

Today, many rabbis and cantors, especially on the High Holy Days, dress in formal vestments. And they do so with some irony. For while the rabbis of late antiquity and the Middle Ages railed against emulating Gentiles, their later counterparts did just that: took up the liturgical garb and styles of non-Jewish clergy. Many trace this innovation to the rise of Reform Judaism and the adoption of Catholic garb during the second half of the nineteenth century. But Asher Salah recently argued that seventeenth-century iconography shows rabbis from the Netherlands and Italy attired in a garment that resembles both a Protestant clerical cassock and a physician's robe (2011). Before that time, rabbis dressed like their congregants with the occasional exception of a large, sumptuous prayer shawl draped over the head. In Italy, many took the new rabbinic garment as evidence for the wider "Protestantization" of Italian Judaism. (Other examples of the process, also common in America today, include referring to the synagogue and rabbi as "temple" and "Reverend.") The novel rabbinic robe, too, befitted the new institutional role of the Italian rabbi as the formal head of a synagogue rather than a more diffuse leader and spiritual guide. In the eighteenth century, Italian rabbis also dressed in clerical bands and round hats. This outfit, no longer worn by others, now distinctively characterized the rabbinate. The rabbis, then, like most Jews throughout history, stitched their garments from non-Jewish fashions. They dressed to express, knowingly or not, a long-standing tension between religious particularism and acculturation.

## JEWISH JEWELRY?

Rabbinic conversations about jewelry speak to similar matters as clothing. Rabbi Akiva, we learn from the Talmud, presented his wife with a necklace or tiara ornamented with a "Jerusalem of Gold" (B. Shabbath 59a–b). But little else in rabbinic literature hints at characteristically Jewish jewelry. Some rabbis banned jewelry ornamented with heathenish images such as suns, moons, and dragons (Grossmark 2005). Other rabbis barred only costly such ornaments, assuming that worthless baubles were made for fashion, not malevolence. Another opinion tolerated pagan gems, but only after a non-Jew nullified the idolatrous intent or aura of the item by marring or spitting upon the image. These deliberations suggest, once again, that some Jews wished to dress beyond the official "fence."

The classic rabbis, as we would expect, forbade Jews from wearing garments associated with pagan worship (Grossmark 2005). Thus a cloak presented by a non-Jew to an idol as a ritual offering was categorically taboo. But if an idolater simply wore the cloak for warmth, and then slung the garment on the effigy for storage, a Jew could rightly wear it. Here, as in the case of jewelry, the rabbis sought to avoid even the mere appearance of respect for heathen deities. Still, Jews often appealed to amulets for healing, fortune, and protection (Trachtenberg 1939). Jews were no less superstitious than their neighbors.

Premodern European Jews developed one distinct genre of jewelry: a large, ornate ring featuring a three-dimensional palace, typically identified as the Jerusalem Temple. These rings often contained Hebrew or Yiddish inscriptions such as the catchall congratulations "mazel tov" (literally, "good luck"). Some rings contained a sprig of myrtle (Abrahams 1896/1969: 181–82). Scholars remain uncertain on the precise function of these items (e.g., Weinstein 2003: 204–5). But the general consensus is that Jewish communities lent these rings for betrothal or wedding ceremonies. Later, the groom presented his bride with a modest, sometimes decorated band. Of course the communal ring, used only occasionally, hardly served as a public sign of Jewishness.

Jews developed another genre of jewelry, one that could only signal Jewishness to other religious Jews. Religious law bars devout Jews from carrying anything, we have seen, including house keys, on the Sabbath. (Car keys are irrelevant since a running automobile engine violates the Sabbath ban on "kindling.") To evade this prohibition, medieval Jews attached keys to their belts as adornments (Roth 2003). Today, Judaica shops sell the Adjustable Shabbos[5] Key Belt—two nylon straps connected to a plastic buckle and interconnected metal hooks. To merely dangle keys from a hook is tantamount to "carrying," a forbidden Sabbath act. Instead, you snap each key between adjacent hooks. This way, the keys form part of the belt and thus are "worn," like clothing, but not "carried." Similarly, one can place a house key into a specially made brooch and wear it as jewelry. The Adjustable Shabbos Key Belt is a recent example of both the legalistic nature of Judaism and the desire by observant Jews to seemingly violate, within the letter of the law, the very inviolate "fence" they steadfastly defend. Although only Jews, as far as I know, resort to such rigorous circumventions of religious law (Dundes 2002), the resulting belts and brooches do not themselves, while serving a wholly Jewish function, resemble any particularly Jewish style.

## CROSS-DRESSING AND UNDRESSING

The original context and concerns of the biblical ban on cross-dressing, which I discussed in Chapter 1, had long faded by the rabbinic era. To the rabbis, this rule simply forbade men from dressing in women's clothing, and vice versa. And it did so to prevent unseemly commingling. Why else, asked Rashi, would men don female garb if not to immorally consort with women? The ban also aimed to maintain "natural" gender distinctions and to shelter Jews from paganism since the rabbis often associated cross-dressing with idolatrous heretics. Violators, said Maimonides, should be whipped.

The rabbis expanded the biblical edict and barred men from all sorts of female activities, including plucking grey hairs, using mirrors, applying cosmetics, and dressing in multicolored clothing. The rabbis similarly pressed women to avoid male garb (see B. Nazir 59a; B. Shabbat 94b; Rosenthal 2001; Satlow 1995). Rabbi Nathan ben Joseph advised women to wear colorful dresses to hide their menstrual stains and also to please their husbands (B. Nidah 61b; B. Pesachim 109a).[6] In the rabbinic imagination, clothing should separate men from women as much as Jews from Gentiles.

Many rabbis permitted Jews to dress according to local customs—provided, of course, they sought to pass neither as non-Jews nor the other gender. Today, for example, Jewish men can don kilts in Scotland—but not in Boston, where such attire would appear feminine. Conversely, some Orthodox women now wear feminine-styled pants (see Chapter 5). But they could never pull on trousers cut in a masculine style. The Talmud reports that Rabbi Judah and his wife both wore the same embroidered cloak, albeit for different activities (B. Nedarim 49b). But this arrangement, perhaps symptomatic of poverty, diverged from all other rabbinic statements affirming the importance of segregated wardrobes.

The rabbis contemplated not just clothing but also nudity. They looked upon male nakedness, especially the penis, as an affront to God. The rabbis forbade naked prayer, minimally requiring a belt to symbolically divide, following Isaiah 11:5, the intellect from bodily passion and filth (B. Megilah 24b). In fact, the rabbis mocked the Greeks and Romans for erecting statues of their gods in places frequented by naked men, such as gymnasia (Satlow 1997: 434–35). Some sages even boasted of never glancing at their own genitals (B. Shabbat 118b). The rabbis also abhorred the idea of a superior man undressing before his juniors.

But no Jewish man, thought the rabbis, even when naked, truly lacks clothing. The rabbis construed circumcision as an indelible, mystical garment of holiness that perfects the male body and protects against the unseemly urges of unrestrained, natural humanity—albeit a "garment" that must always appear clothed in public (Silverman 2006: 130). Circumcision, too, separated Jewish masculinity from Greco-Roman and, later, Christian manhood.

In all, male nudity was a sordid, non-Jewish custom that violated the boundaries between man and God, Jew and non-Jew, humanity and nature, and social categories. The rabbis viewed female nakedness rather differently: as a distraction to men. Women should only appear naked before their husbands. Even a small amount of uncovered female flesh—no more than a handbreadth, it turns out—might distract men from their religious duties. The rabbis even exempted women from the punishment of stoning lest the victim's clothing shred, thus arousing the stone throwers (B. Sanhedrin 44b–45a). The same Talmudic passage voiced concern with the biblical interrogation of suspected adulteresses during the *sotah* ordeal (Chapter 1). The early rabbis abolished the rite. They also understood the ancient priest to expose both the woman's hair and her breasts (M. Sotah 1:5)—but not if she was beautiful, lest the priest succumb to lust.

Rabbinic concerns with female flesh might suggest a puritanical theme in rabbinic Judaism. Not so. The rabbis understood the divine command in Genesis 1:28 to "be fruitful and multiply" as stipulating reproduction. Exodus 21:10 mandated something entirely different. This passage forbids male divorcees from denying food, clothing, and "marital rights" to ex-wives. The rabbis understood the latter phrase as referring to pleasurable sexuality, and in consequence required husbands to regularly pleasure their spouses (see B. Ketuboth 61b–62b; Boyarin 1993, chapter 5; Satlow 1995, chapter 7). In rabbinic culture, clothing domesticated human desire. Dress did not deny sexuality altogether.

But the effort to dress sexuality in legitimacy hardy proved egalitarian. The concept of modesty or tzniut mandates all-encompassing restraint (e.g., B. Sukkah 49b). Jews should neither intrude in the world nor allow for worldly intrusions (Stern 1994: 223–45). The rabbis anchored this value to an exhortation by the prophet Micah "to walk modestly with your God" (6:8). Predictably, this charge conveys little specificity. It certainly makes no reference to dress. Indeed, the Torah never overtly speaks about modest clothing. But the rabbis understood a proper wardrobe to restrain vanity and desire and to shield Jews from the polluting, often illicit dangers of the non-Jewish world. All this holds true regardless of gender.

But the experience and rationale for modest garb differs significantly between men and women. In biblical culture, as we saw in Chapter 1, the concept of "nakedness" (*ervah*) violated divine order. But while the Torah generally construed "nakedness" as genital, the Talmud rephrased the concept as *any* exposure of *female* skin in excess, to repeat, of a handbreadth (B. Berachot 24a). To be sure, the rabbis repeatedly counseled men, especially during prayer, to disregard a woman's voice, hair, legs, "even . . . her small finger" (B. Berachot 24a; B. Kiddushin 70a). But the real solution in rabbinic culture to the male libido was not for men to police their own behavior. It was for women, as I elaborate in Chapter 5, to cover their bodies with ample clothing. Women were thus made accountable for their own conduct *as well as* the behavior of men who might cave at the merest sight of female flesh.

Men appear in public more frequently than women, said the rabbis, and so must assume the weighty responsibility for maintaining the outward appearance of Judaism (Stern 1994: 242–43). But in practice, the ethic of modesty confines women within far more rigorous rules—partly, declared the Talmud, as punishment for Eve's sin (B. Eiruvin 100b).

## CLOTHING LIFE AND DEATH

The rabbis generally favored a somber dress code as befitting their conservative outlook. They found red particularly troubling, as I mentioned earlier, especially on women. The color evoked menstrual blood and non-Jewish licentiousness (see B. Berachoth 20a). Even today, many Orthodox and ultra-Orthodox women avoid red garments. The official avoidance of red, too, I suggest, pertained to the prominence of dualisms in rabbinic culture—a binary code often communicated through a white-black color scheme.

Rabbinic culture generally associated black with mourning and sometimes sin. White colored weddings, festivals, the New Year, scholars, humility, and holiness (Shapero 1987). Officially, the rabbis dressed themselves and the cosmos in black and white (see also Roth 2003: 174). But most Jews, as I showed, dressed as colorfully as their Christian neighbors.

Although black was the color of mourning, Jews devised a white burial garment called a *kittel* (Figure 8). This robe is woven from white cotton, linen, or, today, polyester, tied with a white belt or *gartel*, and often embellished with simple lace or embroidery. Men also traditionally wear the *kittel* for the Passover feast (*seder*), their own weddings, and especially the Day of Atonement (Yom Kippur), when Jews contemplate their transgressions and beg divine compassion. The whiteness, after Isaiah 1:18, signifies purity. The early twentieth-century author S. N. Behrman, however, looked upon the white *kittel* on Yom Kippur as a "macabre and scary" reminder of God's "life-and-death verdicts" (1954: 95). The *kittel* should never contain gold, writes Rabbi Kitov, lest the gown conjure the idolatrous golden calf. But silver is fine, resembling white and thus "purity and mercy" (1968: 78–79). White *kittels*, too, comments Heilman, signify the rebirthing theme of so many Jewish rites of passage (2001: 60). Mourners don black to signify the darkness of death and earthly interment. But the white garb of the corpse, I suggest, points the way to a heavenly destination.

In Germany, Jewish brides once dressed in fur-trimmed mourning dresses with a white cotton gown (Abrahams 1896/1969: 187, 204–5; Pollack

**Figure 8**   Ritual *kittel* gowns in a Judaica shop. Photo by author.

1971: 37; Roth 2005: 47). This outfit was intended to dampen matrimonial merriment by evoking the destruction of the Temple. The groom similarly dressed in a white mourning cowl, sometimes sprinkled with ashes. But the wedding party wore festive attire. Here, again, we see a tension between the official dress code, which aimed to convey a white-black moral universe, and popular sentiments.

The white burial gown democratized death. But not all Jews went to their graves in simple garb. Burial once occurred in ornate dress (Bonfil 1994: 266). But most Jews eventually adopted modest burial attire. Today, Orthodox Jews often dress corpses in *kittel* gowns wrapped in white belts (Heilman 2001: 60–61). The sash is knotted thirteen times, partly to signify the Thirteen Attributes of Divine Mercy (Exodus 34:6–7), then thrice looped to form the Hebrew letter *shin*, an abbreviation of the divine name *Shaddai*. Men are also buried in trousers and tunic undershirts. Orthodox women receive similar burial garb with the addition of a veil and long apron. In death, as in life, official rabbinic dress codes aimed to separate men from women and Jews from Gentiles.

Men are also traditionally buried in their prayer shawls. Ashkenazi Jews untie or snip one of the deceased's fringes to de-sanctify the garment for burial, especially to signal his release from all ritual obligations. Alternatively, Jews may dress the deceased in a fringeless *tallit katan*. In fact, Jewish burial clothes generally lack buttons and knots (Heilman 2001: 59, 110). This way, no garment will tether the soul to earth, denying its final passage to heaven.

The Talmud extensively discusses mourning customs and garb (e.g., B. Mo'ed Katan 22b–26b). Mourners abstain from leather shoes, sexual intercourse, bathing, laundering, normal greetings, cosmetics, and the study of the Torah, among other things. A key Jewish mourning symbol is called *kriah* (Leviticus 10:6). Survivors rend a garment, then wear the tattered article for thirty days.

The specifics of *kriah* are considerable, and evidence yet again the legal fastidiousness of rabbinic culture as well as the importance of symbolism. Mourners should rip a garment while standing in a flush of grief—yet not on the Sabbath and certain festivals, when Jewish law prohibits "tearing." One may not further cleave a preexisting tear nor purchase a garment, such as an inexpensive shirt, specifically for this purpose. A valid funerary rip is substantial and noticeable, ideally running from breast to navel—within the bounds of modesty, of course. Normally, only close kin practice *kriah*. Upon the death of a Torah scholar, however, or when witnessing a person's final moment, all Jews should rend clothing.

Mourners shred the right side of a garment or, when grieving a parent, the left side, over the heart. You can use any implement—but only your hands when, again, mourning a parent. You may not rip a seam, lest the gesture appear accidental. And you must shred an outer garment normally worn indoors, which excludes overcoats, undergarments, mittens, lingerie, and pajamas. Later, one can mend the garment, but the mourning symbol for a parent must always remain discernible. The rabbis, however, mindful of Deuteronomy 20:19, "Thou shalt not destroy," censured any excessive mourning.

Jews should also rend their garments upon hearing blasphemy or terrible news, such as the desecration of a Torah scroll, and when beholding the remnants of the Holy Land, especially the Jerusalem Temple. Today, many Jews practice *kriah* at the Western Wall. Recently, religious Zionists performed *kriah* when the Israeli army dismantled settlements in the West Bank. At least one *frum* or strictly observant summer program in Israel recommends packing an old t-shirt for the performance of *kriah* in Jerusalem, thus ironically violating, as I just noted, long-standing rabbinic law.[7] Yet many rabbis void this particular genre of *kriah* since Jews now exercise political sovereignty over Jerusalem. On the Internet, I came upon two other alternatives to performing *kriah* at the Temple Mount: visit the Western Wall on the Sabbath, when "tearing" is prohibited, or make use of the ban on shredding borrowed garments by ritually "selling" your clothing to another Jew prior to visiting the Holy City. Upon your return, buy back your wardrobe.[8]

Most contemporary Jews practice mourning *kriah* formulaically, just prior to the funeral. They also tear black ribbons, pinned to their shirts and blouses, provided by Jewish funeral homes. But "how shallow, how disappointing, how pitiably trivial," writes Lamm in his widely read book, *The Jewish Way in Death and Mourning*, to symbolize grief "not by an act of historic and religious significance, but by the little black ribbon or button—invented by enterprising American undertakers . . . a meaningless and impersonal strip of cloth pinned on us by a stranger" (2000: 45). (*Kriah* ribbons are widely available on the Internet: $12.99 on sale for a gross.) Some readers may bemoan this practice as an untoward intrusion of modern consumerism into traditional ritual. But the vestimentary effort to balance Jewish symbolism with wider, non-Jewish trends and fashions is as much a time-honored tradition, I have argued in this chapter, as the *kriah* gesture itself.

## SHOE SYMBOLISM

Many themes outlined in this chapter—legalism, gender, symbolism, and the endurance of rabbinic law—come together in the form of a special shoe made exclusively for the *chalitzah* rite. This biblical ceremony, recall from Chapter 1, released a man from his levirate duty to sire "seed" on behalf of a deceased heirless brother—his duty, that is, to marry the widow (see also Hezser 2008). The ceremony also severed the widow from her brother-in-law so she could freely wed anew. The ancient Israelites, like almost all tribal societies, practiced polygyny. Men could marry multiple wives. But women were restricted to a single husband. Thus an Israelite widow not freed from her brother-in-law was unable to remarry. The brother, however, suffered no such restriction. The decision was entirely his.

The Torah offers few guidelines on the performance of the *chalitzah* rite. We learn only that the widow publicly unshod her brother-in-law, then uttered a brief statement. But the rabbis, tolerating little ambiguity, posed myriad questions (e.g., B. Kiddushin 14a–b; B. Yevamoth 101a–106b). Which foot? What type of shoe? Could it be placed on an artificial leg? And what exactly *is* a shoe? Despite seeking resolution to these and other uncertainties concerning the *chalitzah* rite, the rabbis of old never addressed the legal disadvantage of the widow. A cruel man could thus condemn his brother's widow to a lifetime of solitary misery or, more likely, extort a sizable sum in exchange for the ceremony.[9]

Today, acculturated Jews confine the ceremony to the medieval past. They see the shoe, if at all, only in museums. But religious Jews still practice the rite. In general, however, a religious prenuptial agreement now supersedes the ceremony. Still, many Orthodox communities possess a special

**Figure 9**  *Chalitzah* shoe. Courtesy of the Bata Shoe Museum, Toronto, ©.

*chalitzah* shoe (Figure 9). Only one brother-in-law need perform the rite, which takes place before a rabbinical legal court (*beth din*) consisting of at least three male officiants. The *chalitzah* shoe is sewn from two pieces of leather and secured with straps (three at the front, two in the back), all cut from the hides of kosher animals. The brother-in-law washes his right foot, straps on the shoe, and walks four cubits, or about two meters. The widow recites in Hebrew, "My brother-in-law refuses to raise unto his brother a name in Israel; he will not marry me." In turn, the brother-in-law responds, "I do not wish to take her." The widow then uses her right hand to untie the shoe and toss it a short distance. She spits on the ground, and thrice repeats the biblical phrase "So shall be done to that man who will not build his brother's house, and his name shall be called in Israel, 'the house of the slipped-off shoe.'" The court repeats this phrase three times, and the rite concludes.

Reform Judaism formally abandoned the *chalitzah* ceremony during two of its foundational forums, the Philadelphia conference (1869) and the Augsburg synod (1871). In practice, Conservative Judaism also discarded the rite although the procedure remains valid in the Conservative legal code (Hezser 2008: 58–59). Many Orthodox Jews, to repeat, continue the ceremony. In Israel, as the United States embassy advises, the rite is mandatory.[10]

Today, Jews enthralled by medieval mysticism or Kabbalah, including certain Hasidim, see the right side of the body as representing "the power to give, be outward and expressive."[11] The left side symbolizes "the power to hold back, be inward and restrained." Right is kindness and assertion; left, discipline and submission. Psychological wholeness requires balance. But the dominant side of our body, or "giving," should triumph over the weaker side, or "holding back." This symbolism extends to footwear:

> Putting on a shoe is an act of giving (to your foot), so you put the shoe on your stronger foot first. You then tie the lace on the weaker foot, as tying is an act of restraint. However, untying a shoe is releasing and letting go, so when you are untying shoelaces the stronger foot takes precedence. Removing your shoe is taking away, an act of discipline, so for that the weaker comes first. It all symbolizes the same point—discipline is important, but kindness should dominate.

For some Jews, dressing in the lowliest of shoes provides an opportunity to reflect on a moral worldview.

Sometimes, the removal of footwear is an important sign of humility. God, after all, ordered Moses to stand barefoot upon the "holy ground" before the burning bush (Exodus 3:5). Jews should similarly remove their shoes when treading on the Temple Mount in Jerusalem (B. Berachoth 54a). Some Hasidim also remove footwear before approaching the gravesite of a *tzaddik* or holy person. These shoeless moments aside, footwear became the norm for prayer and synagogues.

Jewish shoes also serve a memorial function. At Holocaust museums and monuments, enormous heaps of discarded footwear, removed from victims, powerfully silence visitors (Feldman 2008). Jews themselves traditionally put shoes to a more tender memorial use: a distraught son, unable to accept his father's death, may slip a lace from the man's right shoe into his own left shoe (Heilman 2001: 144). Henceforth, the son walks in his father's memory.

## NEITHER POVERTY NOR FLAMBOYANCE

Clothing, we have seen, symbolized key values in rabbinic culture, including modesty, the Law, protective fences, and life and death. Clothing also displays deference and compassion. Early Christianity debased the body and shunned this world so the soul may enter the next. Thus the church urged poverty as a path to God. Yet otherworldly penury often amounted to the same boastful piety the Apostle Paul bitterly attributed to Jews. Many monastic orders reveled in competitive wretchedness—wearing rags, refusing to launder, picking through refuse.

The rabbis rejected monasticism and asceticism. They saw Judaism as an embodied religion. Pleasant attire betokened reverence (Schwartz 2004). As a fourteenth-century father put it, "always to wear nice and clean clothes, that God and men may love and honor you" (Abrahams 1891: 463). Neat and tidy garments also upheld the ideal of purity so vital to biblical religion. The Sabbath in particular called for special outfits (B. Shabbath 113a). Not only did ragged garb dishonor God and the sanctity of the Sabbath, but tattered clothing might expose immodest flesh and thus prevent a Jew from praying before the Torah scrolls (B. Megilah 24b). To the rabbis, poverty was tragic, not divine.

Indeed, the rabbis saw footwear as the minimal condition of human dignity, second only to food (B. Shabbath 129a, 152a). Nonetheless, the rabbis loathed conspicuous consumption and endorsed thrift (B. Baba Metzia 29b; B. Shabbath 140b). Ostentation leads to arrogance, envy, and anti-Semitism. Lavish apparel, too, preached Rabbi Saul ha-Levi Morteira in seventeenth-century Amsterdam, seemed outright unseemly for a people living in exile (Saperstein 1989: 270–85). Jewish authorities also valued moderation to prevent the wealthy from shaming the underprivileged (B. Shevu'oth 31a; M. Taanith 4:8). This moral concern applied even in death. Jews, we saw earlier, traditionally bury the dead in plain white gowns. The Talmud attributes this innovation to Rabbi Gamliel in the first century (B. Kethuboth 8b). The rabbi wished to end the custom of dressing the dead in fancy attire, which magnified the burden of bereavement.

The rabbis viewed ragged garments, like hunger, as a sign of impoverishment calling for communal assistance. Medieval Jews practiced various forms of public aid, including synagogue distributions of food and clothing (e.g., B. Baba Bathra 8a; Cohen 2005). Jews also tithed and dropped coins into charity boxes after weekday prayers. Parents implored their children to donate to the poor (see Abrahams 1896/1969, chapter 17). Jewish legal codes make clear the obligation of individuals and communities to translate the value of compassion into real action by clothing other Jews in proper attire.

## CONCLUSION

The Hebrew Bible twice forbade Israelite men from paring their beards. The rabbis, ever sensitive to biblical nuances, pondered this doubled injunction. Leviticus 19:27 mentions "destroying" hair. Leviticus 21:5 speaks about "shaving." Why the distinction? After extensive debate, the rabbis concluded that "destroying" referred to the total removal of hair, down to the surface of the skin, or just below, at the roots. By contrast, "shaving" specified the use of a single blade to both slice and "destroy" hair. The upshot is that men may remove or "destroy" facial hair but not by "shaving" (B. Kiddushin 35b–36a; B. Makkoth 201–21a). Instead, Jews may use tweezers, dissolving creams, modern electrolysis, and scissors.

What about electric shavers? Many rabbis, ever wary of change, outright reject these modern appliances. But some authorities permit electric shavers with a thin screen that separates the blades from direct contact with the skin (see Broyde 1997). This way, the blades seem to snip, like scissors, rather than slice and "destroy" in the manner of a straight razor.

Actually, the matter of electric shavers is rather more complex, as one can read on the website www.koshershaver.org (see also www.star-k.org/kashrus/kk-mitzvos-shavers.htm). The same source provides instructions on how to mechanically modify new "lift and cut" electric razors in accordance with rabbinic law. Or you can simply mail your razor to Koshershaver in Lakewood, New Jersey. They will perform the koshering adjustment as a free service.

Modern Jews might find this miniscule attention to electric shavers rather silly. But devout Jews see the world through a lens hewn by a firm commitment to abide by the letter of the Law. The fuss over electric razors, too, illustrates the desire to remain scrupulously observant yet thoroughly immersed in a modern consumerist society—the very society Orthodox Jews must, in order to remain Orthodox, also reject. This way, Orthodox Jews appear to both breach and rebuild their religious "fence." Indeed, the classic rabbis, I showed, saw clothing as a crucial hedge against the dilution of a traditional religious identity. But the overwhelming evidence suggests that this fence existed far more in the minds of the learned elite than in the minds of the common folk. Most Jews, I showed, did not, as it were, kosher their razors, nor did they care to do so. The rabbis were not pleased.

I also showed that Jewish clothing—or, more precisely, clothing worn by Jews—displayed a rich symbolism as well as, more important, a twofold tension. On one hand, the religious requirement of ethnic particularism clashed with the desire for acculturation. On the other hand, the rabbis found it necessary, again and again, to reassert their authority against the folk who seemed intent on dressing as they pleased, typically to display their worldly successes.

This chapter focused on conversations about clothing within the Jewish community. But Jews lived as minorities in a world dominated by the church. And the church was no more pleased with conventional Jewish attire than were the rabbis. Ironically, both the rabbis and the church wanted Jews to dress apart. The rabbis did so to preserve the moral integrity of Judaism. By contrast, as I now show, the church dressed Jews in rather different attire.

# Bitter Bonnets and Badges

Each Jew, after he is seven years old, shall wear a distinguishing mark on his outer garment, that is to say, in the form of two Tablets joined, of yellow felt of the length of six inches and of the breadth of three inches.

*The Statute of the Jewry*, King Edward I of England, 1275

In 1213, Pope Innocent III, seeking to codify Catholicism, summoned the Fourth Lateran Council, an enormous conclave of bishops, patriarchs, abbots, and other ecumenical figures from across Europe. Canon sixty-eight would have a long-lasting effect on the lives of European Jews:

In some provinces a difference in dress distinguishes the Jews or Saracens [Muslims] from the Christians, but in certain others such a confusion has grown up that they cannot be distinguished by any difference. Thus it happens at times that through error Christians have relations with the women of Jews or Saracens, and Jews and Saracens with Christian women. Therefore, that they may not, under pretext of error of this sort, excuse themselves in the future for the excesses of such prohibited intercourse, we decree that such Jews and Saracens of both sexes in every Christian province and at all times shall be marked off in the eyes of the public from other peoples through the character of their dress.[1]

Jewish clothing, as Kisch remarks, suddenly became an international problem (1942: 105).

## DRESSING THE INFIDEL

The "problem" of Jewish dress was initially Muslim, not European. The first Islamic ruler to impose dress requirements on non-Muslims is generally said to be Abbasid Caliph al-Mutawakkil in the mid-ninth century. Jews and Christians were classed as protected yet subservient subjects known as *dhimmis*. The caliph required the dhimmis to dress distinctively to avoid any confusion with Muslims. Jews were assigned "honey-colored" garments, unique buttons on their caps, and a pair of patches atop their sleeves.

No premodern polity in the Islamic world or Europe amounted to a liberal democracy. The great Enlightenment values of individualism and free choice,

never mind modern multiculturalism, would not become enshrined for centuries. It was official policy everywhere that minorities suffer indignities. Such
was the fact of life. There could be little hope for "civil rights" in a milieu
where both civility and rights were inextricably tied to religious affiliation.

But there was a key difference between the fate of the Jews in medieval
Christendom and in the classical world of Islam (Cohen 1994). In Europe,
the church sought to banish Jews to the margins of society—to prevent intercourse, social and otherwise, between Jew and Christian. The church, moreover, anchored these regulations to a worldview in which Jews betrayed Christ
and thus deserved nothing less than abject debasement. From the onset,
this religious hatred was singular and vicious.

By contrast, the Islamic world was far more multiethnic than Europe. Jews
were not the sole embodiment of difference. Other prominent minorities included Christians and Zoroastrians. Moreover, Islamic dress codes were
not fueled by religious hatred. Rather, Muslim rulers aimed to "sharpen the
boundaries" between conquered peoples and the minority Arab rulers in order
to maintain "the proper functioning of an interethnic etiquette in an inherently hierarchical society" (Cohen 1994: 63–64). While Christian abhorrence
of Jews was visceral, totalizing, and fathomless, Middle Eastern and North
African Muslims married Jewish women, ate Jewish food, and admitted Jews
into almost all occupations (Cohen 1994: 114). They feared mainly the loss
of social order and power. Still, classical Islam fostered no Jewish utopia.
Dress codes make this point amply clear, especially after the thirteenth century, when the general decline of the golden age of Islam fostered a surge of
anti-Judaism.

In 1198, the Almohad amir of Spain and North Africa, Abū Yūsuf Ya'qub al-
Mansūr, ordered Jews to don conspicuous, dark blue garb. This outfit included
absurdly wide sleeves and "headgear of a grotesque shape" that resembled
a pack saddle rather than the dignified Muslim turban (Shinar 2000; Ye'or
1985: 189). The amir's son changed the color of this derisive costume to yellow, thereby perhaps influencing the future Lateran Council.

Evidence exists for an even earlier besmirching of Jews and Christians in
the Muslim world. A seventh-century letter by Umar ibn al-Khattab mentions
metal neck seals affixed to the dhimmis, removed only upon payment of an
annual tax (Robinson 2005). The same communiqué refers to a range of garments intended to demarcate the dhimmis, including special belts, quilted
bonnets, and twisted shoe laces (Lichtenstadter 1943). In the same century, the Pact of Umar banned Christians from taking up Muslim-styled clothing, haircuts, verbal expressions, surnames, and weaponry. Marcus assumes
that these regulations applied to all "conquered peoples, including the Jews"
(1999: 14). Sometime in the ninth century, reports Stillman, Ahmad ibn Talib,
an Islamic judge or *qadi* in Tunisia, ordered the dhimmis to sew a patch on

the shoulder of each outer garment—a pig for Christians, an ape for Jews (2003: 105).

In Egypt, the caliph al-Hâkim bi-Amr Allâh (996–1020) assigned Jews necklaces with large wooden cows that alluded to the idolatrous golden calf (Roth 2003). The caliph also prohibited Jews from placing rings on their right hands. In the public baths, foreskins identified Christian men. But Jews and Muslims both practice circumcision. To prevent any confusion, the caliph required bathing Jews to wear lockets shaped like chicken claws. Al-Hâkim also ordered Jewish and Christian women to walk in yellow boots with mismatched gaiters. Later, Jews wore bells (Ye'or 1985: 205). It was hardly a flattering dress code.

For several centuries, Jews could only pass through the Muslim quarter of Fez in straw footwear (Stillman 2003: 115). In the twelfth century, a Jewish philosopher, Ibn Aqnin, fled the city to live as a crypto-Jew in Barcelona because the "loathsome" North African dress code "allows our blood to be spilled with impunity" and "make[s] us resemble the inferior state of women" in Islam (Ye'or 1985: 346–51). In 1301, the Mamluks of Egypt color coded non-Muslims (Stillman 2003: 111). Jews were assigned yellow turbans and dismissed from administrative positions. A decade later, the dhimmis collectively offered to pay the vast sum of seven hundred thousand dinars simply for the privilege of wearing white turbans (Stillman 2003: 111). They even offered to sew distinct patches on the hats. The offer was refused. Indeed, "the *dhimmis*," wrote Ibn Qayyim al-Jawziyya in the fourteenth century, "are the most disobedient of His command and contrary to His word; consequently it befits them to be . . . humiliated, belittled, and rendered abominable so that the sign of contempt is manifest upon them . . . it is necessary to impose upon the *dhimmis* a special garb so that they can be recognized" (Ye'or 1985:197). Proper attire would prevent Muslims from ever treating Jews and Christians as legitimate persons.

Did Jews obey these regulations? Surely some did, rightly fearing the consequences of noncompliance. But the fabrics, styles, and colors worn by medieval Jews in Egypt, which I discussed in the previous chapter, suggest both flexibility and lax enforcement. Moreover, the constant efforts by Islamic authorities to renew and enforce dress codes, I suggest, speaks to persistent efforts by Jews and other minorities to evade regulations. But evasion, we will see momentarily, had its limits.

An interesting footnote to this long saga of ethnic marking concerns shoes and prayer. Muslim clerics once forbade the faithful from praying shoeless, like Jews (Kister 1989). Eventually, Jews retained their shoes for prayer while Muslims, perhaps emulating a former Jewish custom, now remove their soles in the mosque.[2] In the fifteenth century, Rabbi Shelomoh Duran, known as the Rashbash, issued a *responsum*, or rabbinic legal decision, allowing Jews in

Muslim countries to pray shoeless (Finkel 1990: 38). In Christian communities, however, synagogue etiquette generally requires footwear.

Shoes in North Africa often proved far from trivial. In the early nineteenth
century, English diplomat Percival Barton Lord witnessed Jews in Algeria and
Morocco compelled "to take off their slippers on passing a mosque, or the
house of the *cady*, or even of some of the principle Mussulmans, though
in some cities, such as Fez, and particularly Saffy, where there are numerous sanctuaries, they are compelled to go altogether barefoot" (Ye'or 1985:
295). By this time, the Islamic world was no longer content merely with maintaining hierarchy. Jews were now thoroughly loathed. Islamic authorities in
Tunisia made Jews drop to their knees upon passing the *kasbah*, "and then
to walk with lowered head." The authorities also required Jews to remove
their slippers when passing mosques (von Hesse-Wartegg 1882: 118). In
Marrakesh, reported J. Halévy in an 1877 issue of the *Bulletin of the Alliance
Israélite Universelle*, Jews were:

> Prohibited to wear a turban, which is the only sure protection for the head against
> the rays of the tropical sun, and who cannot, thanks to a cruel refinement, even
> wear shoes outside of their quarters . . . It is impossible to imagine the suffer-
> ings of these wretches, who, amid the jeerings of the Muslim population along
> the road, jump and cringe with pain, their feet torn and their nails crushed by the
> stone. (cited in Ye'or 1985: 316–17)

Lord also reported that the emperor of Morocco, after mistaking a finely
dressed Jew for a person of importance, wrathfully ordered the man stripped,
clothed in "coarse black burnoose," spat upon, and beaten (Ye'or 1985:
298). In 1788, the Ottoman ruler or *dey* of Algiers ordered the flogging of any
Jew who dressed in Muslim attire. They were lucky. In 1758, the sultan ex-
ecuted a Jew in Constantinople for dressing in forbidden garb. In 1823, the
wrong hat worn by a Jew proved equally fatal in Tunisia.

In 1900, Shah Nasr-ad-Din imposed wide-ranging restrictions on Iranian
Jews. To protect Muslim purity from the flow of infidel filth, he confined Jews to
their homes during rain or snow. Nasr-ad-Din also required Jewish women to
dress like prostitutes. He banned Jewish men from wearing finery or matching
shoes, and made Jews sew red patches on their outfits (Ye'or 1985: 336).
Jews, too, could only carry—never wear—their coats in public.

In Yemen, reported the director of the Alliance Israélite Universelle school
in 1910, the Jew was "despised." He was "not allowed to wear white or colored garments outside his quarter . . . he must wear a ridiculously short
garment that does not cover his legs, and he must walk barefooted and
wear on his head a little black cap" (Ye'or 1985: 343). In the mid-1940s,
writes Ye'or, Yemenite Jews were still forbidden from publicly walking in shoes
(1985: 380). Even as late as the 1960s, authorities in southern Iran banned

Jewish women from veiling in public (Loeb 1977: 18–19). This restriction might appeal to contemporary sensibilities. But it dreadfully exposed Jewish women to scrutiny, accusations of immorality, and continuous harassment by Muslim men.

We must also, as I did in the last chapter, consider the symbolism of color. North African Muslims generally dressed in white, red, and green. These tones locally evoke life, purity, and fertility (Shinar 2000). Jews wore black, the shade of misfortune, demons, slavery, and death. Jews also dressed in blue, a hue "alien and sinister," as well as yellow, which tarnished traitors, liars, and other miscreants. Jews, too, donned purple, the tint normally worn for mourning. In both cut and color, the Islamic world dressed Jews for ostracism. These regulations did far more than merely reinforce a sociopolitical hierarchy. They amounted to a form of violence. Church and state in Europe, as I now show, were no less cruel.

## A BADGE OF SHAME

What prompted Pope Innocent III in 1213 to impose a dress code on European Jews? In one view, the pope's edict materialized a pervasive dread of any sustained interaction between Jews and Christians, especially sex and miscegenation (Vincent 1994/96). Plainly put, distinctive Jewish clothing would protect Christian virtue. A second explanation pertains to the end times. Innocent III ardently believed in the Second Coming, and even timed the event for 1284. But the apocalypse required Muslim conversion to Christianity, and so the pope called for the Fifth Crusade to seize Jerusalem. Once victorious, the crusaders would need to identify the conquered. And since Innocent III, like many Europeans, viewed Jews as an Islamic fifth column, they, too, would need suitable marking. In short, the regulation of Jewish clothing would hasten the return of Christ (Cutler 1970). The Fifth Crusade failed in the Nile Delta, and the Second Coming obviously never arrived. But Innocent III's effort to clothe Jews in derisive garb would last over five centuries.[3]

England swiftly heeded the call. In 1218, King Henry III and the archbishop of Canterbury ordered Jews to wear "two white tablets made of white linen or parchment so that, by a sign of this kind, Jews can be patently distinguished from Christians." A few years later, the Council of Oxford stipulated that the badge must measure two fingers in length by four.[4] The shape of the English badge (Figure 10) was likely intended to invoke the stone tablets of the Mosaic Law.[5]

In France, Canon Three of the 1227 Synod of Narbonne declared: "That Jews may be distinguished from others, we decree and emphatically command

**Figure 10**   Medieval Jewish badge shaped like the Tablets of the Law (from the Cott.Nero.D.II. Folio No: 183v, British Library). HIP/Art Resource.

that in the center of the breast (of their garments) they shall wear an oval badge, the measure of one finger in width and one half a palm in height." In 1269, Louis IX required Jews to affix a patch of yellow felt or linen, a palm long and four fingers wide, on both sides of their outer garments. Jews who refused suffered the forfeiture of the garment, no small burden in premodern eras, or a hefty fine. King John in 1363 changed the patch to red and white, lowered the age of display to adolescence, and imposed a veil on women. Philip IV literally made Jews pay for this shame, then expelled them entirely from France in 1306.

The shape of the circular badge was not incidental. The disk referred to the treachery of Judas Iscariot, the very embodiment of Israel (Matthew 27:9), who betrayed Jesus in the Gospels of Matthew, Mark, and Luke for thirty coins of silver. You cannot serve, declares the New Testament, both God and mammon. The circular badge evidenced that Jews chose wrongly.

The oval badge, too, argued Trachtenberg, represented the round wafer or host consumed by Catholics during Holy Communion (1943). The patch served as a visual reminder that Jews continued to refuse the sacrament, thus condemning themselves to eternal damnation. The badge also pointed to the persistent yet fraudulent belief that Jews maliciously stabbed, stomped, burned, slashed, insulted, and otherwise desecrated the sacramental bread. The round patch also identified the killers of Christ, thus connecting Jews to Cain, the biblical scoundrel who murdered his own brother and was subsequently marked by God (see Mellinkoff 1981).[6] The patch, like the crime of deicide it signified, would blight Jews until they finally submit to the purifying waters of baptism. Followers of the church required no mark in European society: they were the norm. Jews were tagged as different.

Recently, Flora Cassen offered a new and fascinating interpretation of the symbolism of the round badge in Italy (2011). Italian documents never referred to the badge with descriptive terms—say, the word "round." Instead, Italian sources graphically represented the badge with a circle or O. According to an early sixteenth-century source, the O represented the number zero to signify that the Jew was a "nonentity among men" who "got much out of nothing" through usury. The O connected Jews to a fearful sense of nothingness, a godless and heretical void.

In the thirteenth century, Jews in Sicily, France, Germany, Poland, and elsewhere in Europe were assigned patches and further clothing restrictions. In 1228, for example, James I required the Jews of Aragon (Spain) to wear yellow badges and round capes. Medieval society throughout Europe often marked social pariahs, including prostitutes, lepers, insolvent debtors, and the concubines of celibate Catholic clergy, with yellow garb (Kisch 1942: 116–17).[7] Dress codes ensured that Jews would keep similar company. Forty years later, *Las siete partidas*, the Seven-Part Code enacted in Spain by Alfonso X, nicknamed *El Sabio* or "The Wise," decreed:

> Many crimes and outrageous things occur between Christians and Jews because they live together in cities, and dress alike; and in order to avoid the offenses and evils which take place for this reason, We deem it proper, and we order that all Jews, male and female, living In our dominions shall bear some distinguishing mark upon their heads so that people may plainly recognize a Jew, or a Jewess. (Marcus 1999: 43–44)

Violators were fined or lashed. Many Spanish Jews in 1219–20, writes Vincent, fled new clothing restrictions, ironically seeking refuge with Muslim Moors—the very people whose ancestors devised the idea of marking Jews (1994/96: 210).

In the fourteenth century, similar patches and decrees occurred in Granada, Castile, Portugal, Rome, Barcelona, Aragon, and elsewhere. Venetian Jews attached a yellow circle, about the size of a loaf of bread, on their garments. The patch cost four denarii (Ravid 1992). Over the next two centuries, this edict underwent several, increasingly stringent revisions (Wisch 2003: 148). In the early fifteenth century, Cologne specified in minute detail the acceptable parameters of Jewish attire, including fabrics, lengths, sleeve widths, and trimmings (see Rubens 1967: 91). Legislation in Valladolid, Spain, did likewise and also forbade Jews from dressing in the national costume (Rubens 1967: 89–90). In 1415, Pope Benedict XIII issued a "searching and cruel" papal bull (*Etsi doctoribus gentium*) designed, writes Lea, "to reduce the Jews to the lowest depths of poverty and despair" (1906: 118). This letter included a requirement that Jews wear a yellow and red badge. Over the next two centuries, comparable edicts appeared in Salzburg, Hungary, Poland, Austria, and Lithuania, among other locales.

In 1488, a letter by Italian rabbi Obadiah Bertinoro describes the Jews of Palermo as "poverty-stricken artisans . . . despised by the Christians . . . obliged to wear a piece of red cloth, about the size of a gold coin, fastened to the breast" (Marcus 1999: 453). Another badge also blotted Italian Jews: earrings. By the fifteenth century, Christian women abandoned these once popular ornaments. Earrings, especially hoops, now besmirched prostitutes, Moors, the snouts of pigs and cattle, and Jews (Hughes 1986). For a period, earrings also marked Jews in Flemish art, including Hieronymus Bosch's 1515–16 painting *Christ Carrying the Cross* (Jolly 2002). In the sixteenth century, when gold hoops again adorned respectable Christian women, they were barred to Jews.

The *Imperial Statute Book*, or *Reichspolizeiordnung*, in Germany demanded in 1530 that Jews "always and publicly" wear a yellow ring on their coats or caps. Michelangelo painted one such patch on the sleeve of Aminadab, an ancestor of Christ, in the Sistine Chapel (Wisch 2003). In 1555, Pope Paul IV decreed that Jews, "so they be identified everywhere as Jews . . . wear in full view a hat or some obvious marking, both to be yellow in color, in such a way that they may not be concealed or hidden." To be sure, as Kisch stresses, medieval law favored the spectacle of public humiliation (1942). A fascinating exploration of this cultural theme is Merback's study of the iconography of the two thieves who flanked Christ during the Crucifixion, their limbs shattered by the brutal method of execution known as the wheel (1998). Second only to hanging, this form of punishment laid the condemned across wooden slats, then smashed the arms and legs with a large cartwheel. The victim's fractured limbs were "braided" through the spokes of another wheel, which was hoisted aloft on a pole. The corpse, perhaps still alive, was picked upon by birds. Indeed, one wonders if the circular patch did not also allude to this torture. At any rate, Jewish dress codes befitted this medieval outlook: they sought to expose a vile otherness for all to see and scorn. The betrayal of Christ, and the horror of interfaith intercourse, called for nothing less than a relentless effort to debase Jews with distinctive clothing.

Historians of the Jewish badge fail to mention another reason for making Jewishness visible. Medieval Christendom, as I detail elsewhere (Silverman 2006, chapter 8), obsessed about circumcision. Theologians, in fact, even debated the status of Christ's own foreskin, removed on the eighth day after His birth, in accordance with Mosaic law (Luke 2:21). Did the Holy Prepuce remain on earth after the Resurrection or ascend to heaven with Him? An earth-bound prepuce would attest to Christ's humanation and show the Jews the brother they rejected. The alternative, however, calmed anxieties about incomplete resurrections and further proved Christ's victory over death.

Several churches, in fact, boasted the display of relics from Christ's circumcision. In the end times, moreover, it was feared that the Jewish antichrist would force circumcision onto Christians. The Church Fathers, no less than their unlearned parishioners, repeatedly demonized Jews as mutilated and mutilating—that is, as circumcised and circumcising monsters.

At the same time, popular wisdom held that Jews suffered all sorts of bodily ailments and disfigurements as punishment for snubbing Christ—bloody splotches, fetid odor (*foetor Judaicus*), tails, horns, even male menstruation (e.g., Trachtenberg 1943). Clothing, of course, can readily conceal abnormal appendages, exudations, and other bodily maladies, especially the indelible mark on the Jewish penis. Consequently, the Jewish badge and other dress codes served to remind Jew and Christian alike that the wicked race could never blend with normal European society. Jews might aspire to outfit themselves in decent fashions. But they were outcasts, and so must be reminded, again and again, to dress the part. As long as Jews refused to admit Christ into their hearts, they would wear their contemptible stubbornness on their garments.

## JEWISH HATS

In 1267, a provincial synod in Breslau, Germany, enacted a typical array of anti-Jewish legislation. The council banned fraternization between Jews and Christians, ordered the construction of ditches and fences around Jewish homes, and restricted Jewish food merchants to avoid the poisoning of Christians. The synod also required Jews to don a once popular but now unfashionable "horned hat" (*pileus cornutus*)—a soft, tapering, relatively squat cap, often bent forward at the top to resemble a peak or a horn (Kisch 1942). Thereafter, one style or another of this "Jewish hat," also called a Phrygian cap, would serve for centuries as a key marker of Jewish identity (Mellinkoff 1993; Strickland 2003). The hat amplified the message of the badge. But unlike the patch, which marked only outsiders, the hat was not inherently derogatory.

There is some debate about the earliest appearance of the peaked Jewish hat or *Judenhut*. Rubens traces the cap to the year 1097 and the Stavelot Bible, inked in a Benedictine abbey in Flemish Belgium (1967: 106). But Mellinkoff discerns an earlier style of Jewish hat in the *Old English Hexateuch*, a translation of the Hebrew Bible dating to 1025–70 (1973). This round cap, sometimes displaying a wide brim or a knot at the top, predominated in England and Flanders. It was the earliest iconographical motif to clearly designate Jews in European art. The more typical "horned" cap emerged later, as I just mentioned, in the thirteenth century.

The horned cap somewhat resembled the headgear of various Christian clerics. Any confusion, as we might expect, enflamed local anti-Judaism, resulting in further restrictions on Jewish dress. The two hats, argues Straus, share common roots in late Roman fashion (1942). The clerical cap originally passed from Asia Minor to republican Rome, then to the church. The Jewish hat evolved from a long hooded cape called a *cucullus*, originating in Gaul. In the Carolingian period from the mid-eighth through the eleventh centuries, migrating Jews carried this cap, now devoid of its cowl, to other regions of Europe. This way, the hat gained its Jewish association. By the thirteenth century or thereabouts, the old-fashioned appearance of the general "horned hat" style elicited two different non-Jewish responses (Straus 1942: 68–69). Atop Catholic clerics, the outdated cap, now in the form of a noble mitre, commanded respect. But on Jews, the anachronistic hat appeared ludicrous.

Lipton proposes a different history that traces the two pointed caps to the "peaked crowns on Persian potentates" (2008: 146). In the early twelfth century, the bishop's cap underwent a stylistic transformation. The older hat now characterized only Jews. In Christian art, this "Jewish hat" ironically first appeared on the wise men from the East bearing gifts for the infant Jesus. These caps conveyed not Jewishness but ancient, Oriental exoticism. Later, however, the hat represented Judaism as an archaic, alien religion superseded by Christianity.

In the 1220s, so it seems, Jews were allotted another cap, the tall funnel-shaped hat widely depicted in medieval art (Figure 11). This cap, too, like the "horned hat," originally lacked moral derision. It was simply a fashion trend. But the hat gained pejorative nuance after it faded from Christian popularity, and was subsequently assigned to Jews. A southern German legal code dating to the latter thirteenth century, the *Schwabenspiegel*, also forced this hat on Christian women guilty of trysts with Jewish men (Kisch 1942). A fifteenth-century Hungarian edict did likewise to conjurers, sorcerers, and witches (Trachtenberg 1943: 67). Hats, then, like the yellow color of so many imposed badges, aimed to associate Jews with undesirable others.

For most of European history, I have stressed, Jews required, on account of their Jewishness, distinctive clothing. But *all* Europeans, Jew and non-Jew alike, donned hats as a normal item of everyday attire. Caps signaled gender, occupation, class, religion, and regional ethnicity—the essential coordinates of premodern identity. Only recently, in fact, did hats fade from male fashions, a shift, we will see in Chapter 8, crucial for understanding the rise of the yarmulke. For medieval Europeans, then, hats were not innately derogatory. Moreover, almost all hats and garments assigned to Jews were once worn by Christians (Metzger and Metzger 1982). Certain articles only gained

**Figure 11**   Medieval Jewish "funnel" hat (from the fourteenth-century Codex Manesse). Bildarchiv Preussischer Kulterbesitz/ Art Resource, NY.

a Jewish identity through the vagaries of fashion combined with a persistent anti-Judaism.

Jews everywhere detested the patch. Badges marked outsiders. But the hat was more complex. To us, the conical hat appears shameful and comical. Not so in the Middle Ages (Kisch 1942; Metzger and Metzger 1982). In fact, Jews themselves proudly displayed this hat in their family crests (see Rubens 1967: 93). When King Charles IV granted Jews permission to select a communal banner in fourteenth-century Prague, the community drew a Jewish hat inside a Star of David. By this time, Jews incorporated the hat into their own sense of Jewishness as a legitimate ethnic marker. Unlike the badge, which conveyed a universal and singularly loathsome message, the moral status of the hat lay in the eye of the beholder. Together, the hat and the badge speak to a doubled tension in Jewish ethnicity: the push of separation, both self-selected and imposed, and the pull of acculturation.

## REPRESENTATION VERSUS PRACTICE

Did Jews comply with compulsory dress codes? The question is not easily answered. What we know is that enforcement varied in accordance with local economic conditions and the political concerns of ruling elites (Hughes 1986; Killerby 1994). The *idea* of branding Jews with peculiar clothing remained an important part of European culture until the eve of modernity. But the translation of this ideal into *practice* was hardly uniform. It seems likely that many Jews simply pulled on what they owned and what they could afford, not what they were legislated. They dressed in local fashions.

In thirteenth-century England, many Jews purchased dispensations (Vincent 1994/96). In fact, the pope accused Spanish bishops of imposing Jewish dress codes solely for the purpose of extorting money. In 1496, Venice assigned Jews a yellow cap or *baretta*, later called a *cappello*. Yet some professional Jews, as Ravid details, successfully applied for exemptions (1992). Occupation sometimes trumped Jewishness. Other Venetian Jews challenged the assigned dress code more slyly by darkening the yellow color, affixing various adornments, or simply toting the hat under their cloaks. Not surprising, the Venetian Council greeted each new subterfuge with additional enforcement and policies. Jews seemingly contested dress codes whenever possible, regardless of who imposed them, Gentiles or rabbis.

In the seventeenth century, the Jewish hat in Venice changed color to red. No documents offer an explanation. But Ravid proposes that Jews themselves initiated this modification to avoid the now odious connotations of yellow (1992). The color of one's hat was no trivial matter in medieval and early modern Europe. Everyday privileges often hinged on the hue and style of one's clothing. Venetian authorities refused, for example, to allow yellow caps to exit the ghetto at night. In a society where dress denoted position, a change in the color of one's hat could open locked gates. Jews, knowing full well the politics of clothing, surely labored whenever possible to change their attire.

What about pictorial evidence? What do medieval illustrations suggest about Jewish compliance with dress codes? In earlier chapters, I discussed the difficulties with assuming that premodern records accurately or wholly depict social reality. Still, these sources merit consideration. For much of European history, we saw, manuscript illustrations failed to portray Jews in distinctive garments. Even the infamous badge rarely appeared in Jewish manuscripts (Metzger and Metzger 1982). Maybe Jews understandably wished to erase this slight. But Christian artists portrayed the badge with no greater frequency. Indeed, the most common sign of Jewish identity in Christian and Jewish manuscripts was the funnel-shaped cap. But in reality, suggests Lipton, Jews wore this hat with far less regularity than illustrations suggest (1999: 17). Why, then, do we so commonly see the hat?

The answer, it seems, is that no other garment so consistently signaled religious ethnicity. For, as Lipton observes in the famous thirteenth-century *Bible moralisée*, medieval illustrations generally dressed Jews and Christians alike. Only their hats differ. In Christian texts, Jewish caps were intended to evoke obedience and wretchedness. Jews, however, saw the hat as betokening self-identity, not degrading otherness (Lipton 1999: 18). The same hat conveyed two divergent visions of Jewish difference, depending on context or perspective.

We must also consider the role of gender in regard to medieval illustrations. In the High Middle Ages, argues Lipton, Christian artists devised a distinctive appearance for Jewish men—pointed hat, swarthy complexion, hooked nose, beard—but not for Jewish women (2008). The visual context identified a Jewess, as she was called, not any specific symbolic grammar. In the "clerical imagination," Lipton continues, "the true faith was most perfectly enshrined in the Christian male." In consequence, Christian artists depicted Jews as unmistakably Jewish. The Jewess was just a woman. I propose another reason for the artistic highlighting of male Jewishness. The male Jew's body was the body of the Antichrist, the circumcised circumciser, and the potential violator of Christian women. Male Jews, in other words, powerfully threatened the chaste integrity of Christendom, and so were assigned, in art if not in reality, a distinctive cap.

## SUMPTUOUS CURTAILMENTS

Throughout premodern Europe, governing elites and religious authorities protected their privileges by regulating consumption and display, especially luxuries. These edicts, called sumptuary legislation, targeted all factions, not just Jews. Sumptuary laws generally sustained the status quo and sought to quell a rising middle class or any other group aspiring to political and economic enhancement (Hughes 1983). Everybody, in this conservative vision of social order, needed to dress for their proper position—a position defined, of course, by those in power. In times of rapid social and commercial change, writes Hunt, sumptuary laws limited the ability of individuals to mobilize newly achieved "cultural capital," such as costly clothing, to gain notice (1996).

Jewish communities also restricted luxury. These ordinances promoted the traditional value of modesty but also aimed to stem non-Jewish envy, which resulted in higher taxes or worse (Bonfil 1994; Marcus 1999; Pollack 1971: 86–88; Rubens 1967: 184–99). In 1418, for example, Jewish delegates from across Italy gathered in Forlì to regulate dress "with a view to bending hearts to behave humbly and not to attract the attention of the Gentiles."

The assembly forbade "arrogant" garb such as velvet jackets, open sleeves, silk dresses, and sable linings.

Similarly, the Jews of Metz in the latter seventeenth century restricted fur, ostrich feathers,[8] pearls, gold threads, and Gentile-made clothing. The community also scolded men who sought to "pass" by tucking their fringes inside their trousers and wearing "tiny phylacteries hidden under their wigs" (Berkovitz 1991: 19). In early eighteenth-century France, reports Roth, Jewish leaders in Carpentras policed ruffles, lace, periwig ribbons, embroidered button holes, silver buckles, and velvet trim, among other accessories, mainly to curb Gentile envy but also to restrain resentment by less affluent Jews (1928).

In the seventeenth century, Rabbi Saul ha-Levi Morteira pinned the very solidarity of the Jewish community on modest attire. He preached against "grandiose and splendid raiments, for those who begin will eventually seek their accustomed pleasures, and failing to find them, they will steal and worship false gods and turn their backs on the God of Israel" (Saperstein 1989). Since fine clothing, moreover, increasingly garnered honor and prestige, "those who refrain from such dress will be called misers. No one will think highly of them. They will be hated and scorned." Rabbi Morteira preached thrift. But no appeals to prudence, persecution, or religion persuaded Jews to renounce lavish apparel. Despite the rabbis shouting themselves hoarse, wrote Abrahams, "all the efforts of Jewish moralists were powerless against the contagion" of non-Jewish fashion (1896/1969: 292).

Rabbi Shlomo ibn Virga reported an amusing anecdote about sumptuary legislation in his 1492 book *Shabat Yehuda* (Abrahams 1896/1969: 277). Evidently, some Jewish communities overlooked women's attire and focused instead on men. "It is not fair," allegedly remarked the king of Castile to an audience of Jewish males, "that you should go like a coalman's donkey while your wives prance about harnessed like the mule of the Pope." The king's analogy was not far from the truth. Many Jews did aspire to dress, if not exactly like the papal steed, then at least like Christians. Again and again, rabbis and Jewish communal authorities harangued against opulent garb and Gentile styles. But few Jews evidently heeded these sermons and decrees. Presumably, they also ignored the hats, patches, and dress codes imposed by church and state. As I see it, Jews increasingly dressed, long before the modern era, to be seen as full participants in the wider society.

## THE YELLOW STAR OF DEATH

Modernity, as I show in the next chapter, finally granted Jews the legal right to dress like others. But the vestimentary degradation of Judaism did not fully fade with the ascendance of the Enlightenment. Far from it. Modern bureaucratic and technical sophistication actually made possible the transformation of Europe's long-standing ambivalence toward Jews into mass extermination. The Nazis, like Pope Innocent III and the Lateran Council some 800 years earlier, forced Jews to dress in distinctive garb, specifically, the infamous yellow star.[9]

Jews since the Middle Ages enjoyed few economic opportunities in central Europe. Jews were barred from guilds and certain trades. They could not, for example, freely peddle new shoes and clothing. But in 1671, Grand Duke Frederick William, partly to alleviate shortages from the Thirty Years' War, permitted Jews to sell new outfits to Christians. From this commercial courtesy, as Guenther shows in her fascinating account of fashion during the Third Reich, Jews slowly gained economic prominence in Germany, especially in the garment industry (2004).

In the early twentieth century, Paris dominated haute couture. But Berlin was the center of the ready-to-wear or *Konfektion* industry that outfitted most Europeans and Americans (Guenther 2004). Jews dominated off-the-rack manufacturing in the city and established major department stores (see Kremer, ed. 2007). This economic niche proved enormously successful for some Jewish families. But a boon to the few eventually made all Jews targets (Kaplan 1991: 31). German nationalists soon ranted against "judaicized fashion."

The Nazis accused Jewish designers and merchants of corrupting German morals, bodies, and commerce. Jews were said to endanger the nation by outfitting German women like whores and producing shoes for profit, not to suitably carry the Aryan physique. As a result, the Nazis "purified" the national clothing industry and insisted that fashion reflect Aryan values such as work, austerity, fitness, and efficiency. Women's attire should serve the nation by emphasizing pregnancy and motherhood, not French immorality, and especially not Jewish decadence (Guenther 2004; Makela 2000). Suddenly, Jews became dangerously *un*-fashionable.

But clothing worn by Jews also become valuable. The Nazis ordered Jews to surrender their wardrobes, especially winter garments. Of course, the forced disrobing of Jews threatened to undermine Nazi ideology. For years, propagandists raged about the moral perils of depraved Jewish garb. Now the Nazis admonished Germans to take up this very immoral clothing. To veil the contradiction, the Nazis removed all identifying tags from "donated" articles. They also forced Jews into textile manufacturing—in secret, of course, lest the *volk* realize the Jewish origins of their German attire.

The Jews of Lodz, writes Guenther, produced "the finest silk ties, women's lingerie, tailored jackets, fur coats, knitwear, handsewn dresses, shoes, and purses" for German soldiers and consumers (2004: 256). And they did so while clothed in rags and suffering "squalor, disease, and immense poverty" as well as the constant threat of beatings, extraditions, and death. Tragically, many

Jews dressed in their best outfits for deportation, hoping to make a good impression on the authorities. Once in the concentration camps, however, Jews were stripped and issued blood-stained, bullet-ridden, tattered clothing. For shoes, they wore "wood slabs with leather straps." In winter, many Jews lacked coats and boots, sometimes walking barefoot in the snow. With no buttons or belts, inmates bore the constant humiliation of exposure. At Auschwitz, one fortunate woman received underwear; it was made from a prayer shawl (Guenther 2004: 257). The Nazis confiscated mountains of footwear, dresses, jackets, skirts, blouses, pullovers, and undergarments from murdered Jews, all piled in warehouses for distribution to Germans.

Of course, the Germans made certain to clothe Jews in one special garment: the yellow star. It is cruelly ironic that the first mention of the star during the Nazi era actually came from a Jewish author. In April 1933, Hitler declared a national boycott of Jewish shops, which stormtroopers tagged with yellow and black Stars of David. In response, Robert Weltsch wrote an essay for the Zionist newspaper *Juedische Rundschau*: "Wear It With Pride, The Yellow Badge."[10] Since the Nazis painted the star as a "sign of contempt," Weltsch declared, Jews should "take it up, the Shield of David, and wear it with pride!"

Several years later, the Nazi regime in occupied Poland issued various decrees requiring Jews to wear distinctive badges (Friedman 1955). In November 1939, the governor-general centralized this policy. All Jewish men and women over the age of nine "must wear on the right sleeve of their clothes, overcoats, or mantles, a white armlet not less than ten centimeters in width, bearing as a distinctive sign the Star of David." A September 1941 edict forbade Jews over the age of six "to show themselves in public without the Jew star . . . a six-pointed star, outlined in black on yellow cloth the size of the palm of one's hand," and containing the word "Jude" (Figures 12–13). Once again, European Jewry suffered from the imposition of a terrible dress code. This time, truly, Jews were dressed to kill.

As the Nazis spread through Europe, so did variations of the yellow star. In Latvia, for example, men attached the patch to their left knees. Occasionally, the manufacture of badges developed into a "thriving industry" (Friedman 1955: 47). But in other localities, the chronic wartime shortage of fabric resulted in dire panic. The law called for stars to be *sewn* onto clothing. A nineteen-year-old woman, reports Friedman, trying to make do with too few patches, merely *pinned* her star. For this crime, she was sent to a concentration camp and never seen again. When Jews in an eastern Polish town complained about the scarcity of yellow cloth, the local communal leader was shot in the head. Jews across the continent, terrified about the consequences of forgetting their stars, hastily tacked signs about their houses. "Remember the Badge!" "Have you already put on the Badge?" And simply, "The Badge!"

**Figure 12** Portrait of Rose Grinbaum wearing a Jewish badge in the Olkusz ghetto. United States Holocaust Memorial Museum. Courtesy of Rose Grinbaum Futter.

For a time, wealthy Jews in Poland preferred "artistic, hand-embroidered stars," often made from silk and satin rather than plain cotton (Freidman 1955: 54–55). Only hindsight allows us to see the tragic folly of this refinement. Many Jews wore stain-resistant badges fabricated from celluloid and plastic. In the Warsaw ghetto, early badges identified Jews by profession: physician, scrap and rag collector, bus driver, and so forth. Jews themselves partly favored these distinctions in the futile hope that certain skills might appear indispensible to the Nazis. But all such differences faded by mid-1942 with the issuance of a single badge. "No longer," wrote a teacher in the Warsaw ghetto, "are there various categories of Jews" (Friedman 1955: 58). Now "there is only one large mass of outlawed, outcast, persecuted, tormented, spat on, kicked on, insulted and murdered Jews."

Admirably, some non-Jewish Europeans famously rejected the yellow star (Friedman 1955: 66–70). In France, Holland, and Belgium, non-Jews carried yellow handkerchiefs and flowers and affixed paper stars to their clothing.

**Figure 13**   A Jewish couple wearing the yellow star poses on a street in Salonika. United States Holocaust Memorial Museum Beit Lohamei Haghetaot Beth Hatefutsoth. Courtesy of Flora Carasso Mihael Beth Hatefutsoth.

A famous tale tells that King Christian X of Denmark, wishing to proclaim solidarity with Danish Jewry in 1943, wore a yellow star during his morning horseback ride through Copenhagen. But while Danes did help ferry Jews to neutral Sweden, their king never dressed in a yellow star. This urban legend is typically traced to Leon Uris's 1958 historical novel *Exodus*. But versions of the tale appeared in the early 1940s, perhaps as an effort by the Danish-American community to refute criticism in the Allied press about feeble Danish resistance (Vilhjálmsson 2003). Most of Danish Jewry never wore the yellow badge—and neither, to repeat, did their king.

    The fable about the Danish king and the Jewish star resurfaced recently in a children's story[11] and, more intriguingly, on the floor of the United States House of Representatives. In 2001, the Taliban of Afghanistan ordered Hindus to dress distinctively—a yellow patch in some reports—allegedly to signal their exemption from Islamic *sharia* law. A New York Democrat introduced a resolution in the House condemning "the Taliban's use of Nazi tactics."[12] Passage was unanimous. Many representatives cast their vote while wearing a yellow badge. Some months later, the House of Representatives offered another rebuttal of the Taliban by honoring the king of Denmark. An Australian newspaper, *The Age*, similarly celebrated the Danish king on May 25, 2001. In this version of the tale, however, the king rode his bicycle, not a horse, and he did so around the Gestapo headquarters. My point is *not* to question the ethical intent of these gestures. Rather, I want only to underscore the enduring symbolic power of the Nazi-era yellow badge.

Today, the yellow badge persists not solely as a moral emblem and a memorial to horror. It also exists as a souvenir. Auction houses and dealers regularly put forward yellow badges from the Holocaust, called the *Shoah* or "catastrophe" in Hebrew. As I write these words, only five hours and six minutes remain until the close of an eBay auction for a yellow star from the Czech Republic. (Several months later, during revisions, I see nine other "authentic" Nazi-era fabric stars on eBay.) In 2007, the Ben-Ami-Andres auction house in Tel Aviv sold a yellow star. An outraged member of the Knesset, Israel's parliament, introduced a bill titled "Prohibition of Trade in Items Related to the Holocaust or the Nazi Regime."[13]

As an icon, the yellow badge continues to appear with various contextual modifications—always to mixed reaction. In 2002, protestors in Zurich carried large yellow stars in support of the Palestinians. Slogans on the stars included "Stop the bloodbath in the Middle East" and "Never again Shoa!" A website discussing the event posts a yellow star with the words "Jude" (note the strikethrough) and, in Hebrew, "Palestinian" (http://www.redress. btinternet.co.uk/selam.htm). Similarly, a topic on the Facebook page Jewish Voice for Peace reads "Palestinians Please Wear The Yellow Star Of David."

In January 2008, the Associated Press reported that a German website responded to new anti-smoking laws by selling black t-shirts with a yellow star containing the word *raucher* or "smoker." The shirts were swiftly removed, and the promoter issued an apology. A fringe fundamentalist church on the West Coast of the United States also makes use of this icon in its bizarre apocalyptic theology (http://sabbathlove.com). As the church states, "the yellow Jewish star keeps the thought in our mind that we will soon go with our Jewish brothers and sisters into the concentration camps! Praise god! We know this will happen and we rejoice that it will soon happen . . . and we will finally meet our true brothers and sisters who keep the Sabbath and who love God and keep his Law!" The church invites Jews to seek refuge from this immanent conflagration in a shelter sited in the Willamette Valley of Oregon by none other than Jehovah.

In 2004, controversy again erupted over the contemporary use of the star, this time by Jews. When Israeli prime minister Ariel Sharon's government dismantled Jewish settlements in the West Bank, some settlers protested by wearing orange stars (Figure 14).[14] Holocaust survivors, alongside other Jews from across the political spectrum, expressed outrage. The online edition of the Israeli newspaper *Haaretz* for January 24, 2007, requested comments on the matter—and received scores. "Very appropriate." "Shame on you!" "Settlers defile the deep pain of we Jews who remember [the Holocaust], who will never forget." "The settlers have great courage making this statement. I for one salute them."

In 2007, the star again proved controversial in Israel. When survivors of the Shoah complained about their meager stipends, the Israeli government proposed a modest, some say insulting, increase of eighty-three shekels a month. To protest this, several thousand survivors, along with their families and supporters, marched outside the parliament building, some in yellow stars. And in 2012, the star again surfaced during protests in Israel, this time by ultra-Orthodox Jews accusing the Israeli government of a "spiritual holocaust."

**Figure 14**   Ultra-Orthodox (Haredi) man in Israel wearing an orange star to protest the dismantling of settlements in the occupied territories. Getty Images.

They affixed the stars to their black coats, even on children. Most Israelis and Jews worldwide were appalled.

## CONCLUSION

The Fourth Lateran Council in the thirteenth century set in motion a long European history of blighting Jews with ignoble dress codes. Of course, clothing restrictions afflicted not only Jews. For centuries, sumptuary legislation regulated the consumption habits of all Europeans, from lords to lepers. Still, Jews consistently received the most stringent restrictions. No other group was so persistently dressed by others—others who viewed its members as a wretched minority despised by God or worthy of extinction.

Perhaps the Spanish Inquisition made this point best during the public spectacle called the *Auto de Fé*. These ceremonial "acts of faith" offered compulsory penance to heretics through a Catholic mass, a procession of the guilty, and a reading of their sentences. Often, the condemned were burned at the stake, sometimes after strangling. In July 1498, the Inquisition delighted huge crowds in Rome with a spectacular Auto de Fé for 230 Spanish *marranos*—literally, Jewish "swine"—who confessed to practicing Judaism despite their forced conversion to Catholicism (Wisch 2003: 153). The penitents stood in conical caps and red and blue *sambenito*s (coarse tunics) emblazoned with large yellow crosses, the "color of heresy." Afterward, the *sambenitos* were draped on the walls of the Basilica of Santa Maria Sopra Minerva—mute garb that served as a graphic reminder and warning of Jewish apostasy.

# –4–

# **Dressing for Enlightened Citizenship**

[A]nything was to be expected of a country where the poorest devil wore a hat and a starched collar.

Abraham Cahan, *The Rise of David Levinsky*, 1917

In the late fifteenth century, Sephardi Jews fleeing the Spanish Inquisition settled in Amsterdam and prospered. Two centuries later, the city again hosted Jewish refugees, this time from the Thirty Years' War in Germany and pogroms in Poland and Lithuania. These Jews, all of Ashkenazi descent, arrived "poor, dirty, disheveled, uncultured, begging in the streets" (Nadler 2003: 28). Both Jewish communities practiced Judaism. But they could not have dressed more differently.

In 1723, French artist Bernard Picart illustrated the Jews of Amsterdam in his book *Cérémonies et coutumes religieuses de tous les peuples du monde*. Picart attired the Sephardim in the latest, finely tailored Dutch capes, stockings, boots, and caps (Figure 15; Nadler 2003: 32). By contrast, Picart's Ashkenazim appear in bedraggled coats, odd-shaped hats, and ragged beards. They look alien, archaic, and slovenly—in a phrase, too Jewish (Baskind 2007). The message was clear: Jews wishing to thrive must cease to dress distinctively.

The Jews of Amsterdam were also famously illustrated by Rembrandt. But while Picart's etchings applaud a degree of assimilation, Rembrandt painted a different visual and temporal narrative. On his canvases, the authentic Jews appear both old-fashioned and Oriental (Baskind 2007: 4–6). Together, Rembrandt and Picart represented contrary voices, phrased as clothing, in an emerging conversation about the relationship between Jewish identity and modernization.

Other European artists in the seventeenth and eighteenth centuries, especially Romeyn de Hooghe and Jan Luyken, outfitted the Jews of Amsterdam, like Picart, in elegant but not particularly or stereotypically Jewish garb (Cohen 1998, chapter 1). Portraits of American Jewry in the Colonial and Federalist periods, too, powdered wigs and all, show no distinctly Jewish garments (Brilliant 1997; Sarna 2006). The same holds true for family paintings from eighteenth-century Germany (Kaplan 2005: 248). All these Jews resembled their non-Jewish neighbors.

**Figure 15**    "Procession with Palms," etching, Bernard Picart, 1712. Art Resource, NY.

Still, the Dutch paintings depict characteristically Jewish activities. Likewise, early American Jews lived thoroughly Jewish lives (Sarna 2006). Their Judaism, in fact, barred them from legal citizenship. These Jews made little effort to cast away their Jewishness. They sought only to toss clothing that would identify them as such. For centuries, as we saw in the previous chapter, church and state clothed Jews in a type of anti-fashion. But on the eve of modernity, Europe switched suit: Jews were now encouraged and even ordered to dress indistinctly—that is, like all other citizens.

Most Jews welcomed the new vestimentary humanism. Modern dress signaled emancipation, enlightenment, and, especially in America and Germany, the ideals of democracy, social mobility, and material plenitude. On either side of the Atlantic, Jews increasingly dressed in conformity with a wider society that demanded ethnic invisibility as the price for full citizenship. In this chapter, I discuss how clothing mediated and expressed the key Jewish conflict of modernity: the clash between the secular allure of integration and the religious mandate of ethnic distinctiveness.

## SHTETL STYLE

By and large, European Jews dressed in provincial, oftentimes dated styles. In the seventeenth-century Polish territories, for example, Jews fastened their antiquated caftans with old-fashioned hooks and eyelets rather than stylish loops. They walked the streets in obsolete overcoats, and preferred black and russet tones instead of the bright colors of Polish fashion (Turnau 1990). Jewish men wore stockings and shoes, not up-to-date boots. The retrograde appearance of Jewish clothing resulted from centuries of legislation that, as I detailed in the last chapter, sought to deny Jews the right to wear the latest fashions.

In Polish Lithuania, reported Robert Johnson in his 1815 book, *Travels Through Part of the Russian Empire and the Country of Poland; Along the Southern Shores of the Baltic*, "Jews are all dressed alike, in long tunics of black silk, with a broad silken sash" (Johnson 1815: 376). Jewish women, Johnson continued with descriptive, albeit not exactly unprejudiced, abundance:

> are clad in a most ridiculous and gaudy dress of silken rags . . . loose silk vest, and a large petticoat of the same; the arms are hid in long, loose, shirt-sleeves, terminated with a deep worked frill . . . Over their dress they wear a large silk gown, (and in some instances even *two*), the sleeves of which hang down the back; a fur cloak is suspended from the neck. All this superfluity of dress is huddled on, in the most careless manner, and the hands seem constantly employed in detailing it on the body . . . their dress seems a bundle of dirt and rags: there never was a more perfect antidote to love and the graces, than a Lithuanian Jewess.

Johnson and others also noted that the Lithuanian Jewess wore a distinctive bonnet, called a *sterntichel*, trimmed with metal threads and pearls that represented her wealth and status (see also Rubens 1967: 106; Turnau 1990: 106). The "native" Lithuanians dressed in different attire. Notwithstanding Johnson's ethnocentrism, it seems clear that Jews dressed, here and elsewhere across Europe, in a unique and unfashionably passé costume (see Frankel 1980; Pollack 1971). Jews, too, I wish to stress, dressed in regional styles that signaled only a localized sense of Jewishness. It is highly unlikely that a Jew from Lithuania could have recognized a coreligionist on the streets of Cracow. There was, moreover, nothing innately Jewish about these styles. The garments all derived from the wider community. They appeared old-fashioned, but not uniquely Jewish.

Today, many Jews harbor romanticized images of the premodern Eastern European market town or *shtetl*. Nostalgia aside, not all shtetl Jews dressed like Tevye and Golde in *Fiddler on the Roof*. A 1913 Yiddish memoir by Yekhezkel Kotik provides more realistic insights (Kotik and Assaf 2002: 314–15). Contrary to the popular imagination, Kotik mentions furs, calico, pearls, jewelry, and lots of colors. The common folk dressed in hand-me-downs that conveyed no shame and proudly commemorated deceased relatives. Shtetl Jews also wore goat's wool, "strong as steel and tough and stiff as tin . . . every crease would start rattling so noisily that your approach could be heard almost a mile away."

In preparation for the Sabbath, Eastern European women would launder fresh outfits for their families (Zborowski and Herzog 1952). Men returned home from their weekday labors, grabbed a bundle of clean clothes, and hurried to the public bathhouse. After a ritual dip, they dressed in their caftans, sashes, and Sabbath caps. Jewish marriage contracts often required husbands to provision their wives with Sabbath and holiday attire.[1] A proper celebration of Passover ideally required a new outfit. Women readied their jewelry, while men donned white sashes and *kittel* gowns (see Chapter 2), which the wealthy adorned with silver. The poor could afford only a modest upgrade— say, a new hat, scarf, or shoes.

The rich invested in portable wealth such as clothing and jewelry, which they publicly exhibited on religious holidays. These valuables included tall sable hats, silk jackets, diamond earrings, pearl necklaces with gold coins, fur-trimmed shirts, fine linen, and "aprons of colorful silk, or costly white cambric embroidered with velvet flowers and artistic patterns in gold thread lace" (Wengeroff 2000: 131, 247–52). Wealthy women, too, lavished enormous attention on the headdress. This black velvet scarf and smooth-fitting cap was adorned with ribbons, netting, flowers, pearls, and diamonds. Rich and poor alike, whether by choice or fate, dressed as much for their class as they did for their localized sense of Jewishness.

The everyday attire of scholars and elites in the shtetl, dubbed the "beautiful people" (*sheyneh yidn*), generally resembled Sabbath finery. Merchants and "common folk" (*prosteh yidn*) dressed in a type of middle-class fashion that evoked neither the "beautiful people" nor, at the bottom of the social hierarchy, the Jewish peasantry. Some tradesman and laborers unknowingly looked to the future and modified their appearance to better appeal to non-Jewish clientele. They tugged on heavy boots, shortened or removed their caftans, and trimmed their beards and earlocks. It is to that future that I now turn.

## EMANCIPATIVE HATS AND REFORM JUDAISM

In the seventeenth century, European authorities initiated the slow repeal of mandatory Jewish dress codes. Vienna annulled its regulations in 1624, followed by Mannheim (1691), Austria (1781), Rome (1798), Prussia (1812), and elsewhere. For the first time in five centuries, Jews could legally dress like everybody else.

The rationale for annulment varied across the continent, and hinged, like prior enforcement, on the economic and political strategies of local elites. In some places, civic inclusiveness promised to enlarge municipal tax receipts even as it threatened non-Jewish monopolies on power. There was much at stake in a revised dress code for Jew and non-Jew alike. Emancipation, too, arose from the broader revolutionary zeal of the new humanism that accompanied the rise of the modern era, especially after the French Revolution. Ideals such as equality and self-determination made it increasingly difficult to marginalize Jews simply on the basis of their Jewishness.

Not surprising, the process of emancipation often proved complex. Not everybody welcomed Jews as equals—and not all Jews wished to integrate. French law, for example, assigned old-fashioned yellow hats to Jews. Everybody else wore black caps. In an April 1790 festival, however, the Jews of Avignon, flush with the revolutionary promise of *Liberté, Égalité, Fraternité*, donned black hats to dance with their Gentile compatriots—themselves clad in yellow caps. Shortly thereafter, local Jews demanded permission to unlock the ghetto gates at night, to display the national cockade, and to permanently doff the yellow *chapeuax* they endured for centuries. One year later, the Jews of Avignon finally received their just prize: citizenship.[2] They could now enjoy the black hat so symbolic of French fashion and equality.

The situation proved rather more ironic at the nearby enclave of Comtat Venaissin (Szajkowski 1955). When the regional assembly in October 1790 untied Jews from yellow hats, the local populace rioted. Some Jews, fearful for their lives, requested the revival of the old dress code. In the city of Carpentras, Jews refused to swap their yellow hats lest they contravene biblical and rabbinic law by emulating Gentiles (Roth 1928: 363). The cap that for so long derided Jews now served, by their own choosing, to define them. Only a mayoral proclamation in 1791 finally convinced the Jews of Carpentras to remove their yellow caps (Bauer 1880). A year later, all French Jews were enfranchised. They could now choose their own garments. Of course, not all citizens were pleased. Some Frenchmen wished to exclude Jews from the state while some Jews longed to preserve their distinctive identity. There was little consensus in either the Jewish community or the country at large as to the precise role of the Jew in the European nation-state.

After the Napoleonic Wars, the Congress of Vienna convened in 1814 to chart the civil and political future of Europe. Delegates agreed to extend "civil rights" to Jews but not the "rights of citizenship." Jews remained primarily classified as Jews. By the end of the century, however, almost all European countries—except for Russia, Spain, Romania, and Portugal—finally recognized Jews as legal citizens. Jews could still practice Judaism, and many did, albeit largely in the privacy of the home and synagogue. But Jews were now expected to dress for the modern values of assimilation, nationalism, and the marketplace.

The emergence of Reform Judaism in the second half of the nineteenth century profoundly shaped Jewish identity and dress. This movement formally started when a group of lay Jews in Frankfort, inspired by the Jewish Enlightenment (*Haskalah*), organized the *Reformfreunde*, or Friends of

Reform, in 1842 (Meyer 1988). The reformers aimed to harmonize Judaism with the key tenets of the Enlightenment and modernity, including moral individualism, secular humanism, and progress. Reform Judaism rejected Jewish orthodoxy. The movement thus eschewed compulsory circumcision, the dietary rules, exclusively Hebrew prayer, separate male and female pews, and the belief in the invariance of the Mosaic Law. Perhaps most crucially, the reformers jettisoned from the liturgy and ethos of Judaism the traditional longing to return to Zion. For centuries, this yearning defined Judaism as a religion in exile, displaced forever until the messianic era. Jews might live in Europe, but Europe could never be home. Reform Judaism inverted this principle. As the Reformfreunde declared, "We neither expect nor desire a messiah who is to lead the Israelites back to the land of Palestine; we recognize no fatherland other than that to which we belong by birth or civil status" (Meyer 1988: 122). Jews were citizens, first and foremost, and should dress appropriately.

Of course, not all Jews wished to walk or dress in step with Gentiles and progress. By the end of the nineteenth century, then, clothing in Eastern and Central Europe increasingly divided Jew from Jew. Modernizing Jews favored new off-the-rack German styles, while traditional Jews retained a dress code that unmistakably signaled religious conservatism and opposition to any significant assimilation. Ironically, as I now show, the very same modernity shunned by traditionalists actually created their customary attire.

## MODERNIZING JEWS IN RUSSIA AND POLAND

In the late seventeenth and eighteenth centuries, Peter the Great instituted a far-reaching program of modernization that reshaped almost all aspects of everyday Russian life, from coffins and ceiling plaster to clothing (Hughes 1988: 28–88; Ruane 2002). His father, Tsar Alexis I, by contrast, sought to preserve Russia's heritage by banning German fashion in 1675. Peter did just the opposite. He compelled Russians, sometimes through forced disrobing and barbering, to adopt Western dress and etiquette, including garters, vests, Hungarian coats, and clean-shaven faces. Jews were no exception. Mannequins attired in European garb stood as mute sentries outside city gates to model the appearance of a modern citizen.

In the late eighteenth century, the imperial government under Catherine the Great, responding to concerns about the arrival of Jewish merchants in Moscow, restricted Jewish commerce and residency to the so-called Pale of Settlement. A long series of laws regulated Jewish life, at once encouraging assimilation while tolerating distinctive Jewish rites. For example, the 1804

Imperial Statute Concerning the Organization of the Jews (*Polozhenie dlia evreev*) sat Jewish children as equals in public schools and banned anti-Semitic curricula.[3] But the law also required older pupils to wear modern clothing and to speak Russian rather than Yiddish (Stanislawski 1983). The same stipulations applied to Jews serving on town councils and traveling beyond the Pale. After centuries, Russia finally welcomed Jews into society—but on condition that they shed their distinctive speech and clothing. An acceptable Jew, in other words, could hardly appear Jewish at all.

Under Tsar Nicholas I, clothing officially reflected nationalism, not religion. Jewish costumes were now confined to the home and private rituals. Authorities even levied taxes on "traditional" Jewish outfits and activities (Avrutin 2005: 151). But many Jews refused to change their clothing. Understandably, the poor viewed any wardrobe change as a financial burden. The rabbis, too, rejected modernization as a threat to their own authority and Judaism more generally. Yet Jews aspiring to integration and social mobility happily dressed in contemporary fashions such as double-breasted jackets, dark trousers, and peaked caps with visors.

In Vilna, adherents of the Jewish Enlightenment, called *maskilim*, petitioned the Ministry of Popular Enlightenment in 1843 to ban Jewish garb entirely. The "first obstacle to the enlightenment of the Jewish people," they wrote, "is their recognizable costume" (Avrutin 2005: 151). Abraham Ber Gottlober, a leader of the Russian Jewish Enlightenment, denounced men's traditional caftans for "trail[ing] behind like a woman's gown" (Mahler 1985: 38). Only by abandoning "Polish-Lithuanian Jewish garb" will the Jew appear "cultured . . . and in the course of time . . . become a useful man and citizen" (Mahler 1985: 122). Other *maskilim* appealed to more practical sentiments, noting that modern short coats and plain caps were less costly than traditional finery (Shapero 1987: 85–86). At the very least, impoverished Jews should snip their hems. Again and again, Jews debated the place of Judaism in the modern nation-state through the idiom of clothing.

By the end of the nineteenth century, imperial Russian decrees targeted all manner of stereotypical Jewish dress, including silk hoods, fur hats, short trousers, and sashes. Jewish women, declared one edict, "should wear simple garments, similar to what Russian women wear. Without question, they are forbidden to wear wigs of any sort that match their hair color" (Avrutin 2005: 152). Only the elderly received exemptions.[4] Many Jews did change "their national costume," reported one Russian official in 1845 (Avrutin 2005: 152). But others, to repeat, saw the new restrictions as an outright assault on Judaism. "Our traditional costume," reports one memoir, "was mourned like a beloved departed person" (Wengeroff 2000: 94). Some Jews refused to leave their homes. They wept, prayed, and fasted.

Similar events unfolded in the Polish territories, partly to foster Jewish assimilation, partly to revive the national textile industry (Sinkoff 2004, chapter 2). Edicts prohibited Jewish men from appearing in long beards, earlocks, silk and woolen cloaks, broad *gartel* belts, fur hats, short trousers with stockings, and old-fashioned caps lacking a modern peak. Jewish women were similarly told to dispense with their turbans, "Jewish cut" dresses, colored shoes, and characteristic ornaments. With the exception of the home and synagogue, Jews would henceforth appear like other citizens.

A modern dress code for Jews, proclaimed the Duchy of Warsaw, would assist "the progress of civilization of that people" (Mahler 1985: 199–200). As incentive, the territory granted properly attired Jews special residential and occupational privileges. But most Jews could afford to pay for neither a new outfit nor an exemption tariff, and so they were beaten, forcefully shorn, and sometimes imprisoned. Many Polish Jews, too, replaced their traditional attire not with modern European suits but with the caps, trimmed beards,[5] and long coats of Russian merchants (Mahler 1985: 201). This way, Jews swapped their old clothing for a new style that nonetheless resembled their now unlawful costume.

Ironically, edicts demanding assimilation actually fostered a self-conscious sense of Jewishness, especially among educated and urban Jews who otherwise tethered their identity to modernist aspirations (Edwards 1982). Many Jews, too, responded to these revised dress codes by investing their garments with deep emotional and religious significance. Clothing merely worn by Jews now became seen as traditional Jewish clothing, symbolizing traditional Jewish values. For example, the norm in modern male fashion is to button coats and shirts left over right. But Hasidic men, like modern women, button right over left (see Chapter 7). These conventions undoubtedly arose through happenstance. Nonetheless, Hasidic men came to see their buttons as symbolizing the triumph of divine mercy and goodness, which the medieval mystics associated with the right side of the body, over the harsh judgment and demonic powers of the left side. Jews who button in a modern fashion, declared Rabbi Menachem Mendel from Rimanov, walk in the ways of idolaters (Shapero 1987: 91–92). State-sponsored efforts to assimilate Jews, I am arguing, transformed certain garments from mere custom into a religious obligation. Modernity tailored tradition.

Neither Russian nor Polish efforts at updating Jewish garb proved wholly successful. Large numbers of Jews ignored, as in the past, dress decrees (Avrutin 2005: 154; Rubens 1967: 105). Some rabbis reacted to modernizing edicts by calling for outright martyrdom (Shapero 1987: 90–91). Yet Jewish reformers, championing the Enlightenment, dismissed these apocalyptic sentiments as anachronistic and absurd. All these contrary voices spoke to the growing significance of clothing as a key symbol for the role of the Jew in a modern society.

## DRESSING AS AMERICANS

Across the Atlantic, immigrant Jews in the United States also attributed enormous significance to clothing. A suitably tailored outfit embodied all the promises of the new consumerist society—and all the attendant anxieties. Between the 1880s and the Immigration Act of 1924, some two million European Jews steamed to America. Their arrival corresponded precisely with the rise of inexpensive, factory-made goods: electrical appliances, canned foods, gas stoves, bathtubs, soaps, mirrors, carpets, beds, cutlery, watches, and so forth, including off-the-rack clothing (see Kidwell and Christman 1974). Department stores made this merchandise accessible. Mass marketing made it desirable. Credit made it affordable. America became a land of shoppers. And Jews, as Heinze (1990) and Joselit (2001) show, took to this bounty with gusto.

Immigrants delighted in the cornucopia of cheap, mass-produced commodities. Newcomers or "greenhorns" might not learn quickly to sound or act like a proper American, but they could surely dress like one. In fact, a Jewish immigrant's rite of passage often culminated at a photographer's studio (Heinze 1990: 89–90). There, as we read in Elias Tobenkin's social fiction *God of Might*, Jews posed in "nice new clothes," then sent these portraits of affluence back to family and friends in the "old country" (1925: 33).

Indeed, novels and memoirs frequently refracted the immigrant experience through clothing. In *The Promised Land*, Mary Antin recalls journeying:

> to a wonderful country called "uptown," where, in a dazzlingly beautiful palace called a "department store," we exchanged our hateful homemade European costumes, which pointed us out as "greenhorns" to the children on the street, for real American machine-made garments, and issued forth glorified in each other's eyes. (1912: 187)

Thus phrased, as Heinze shows, a wardrobe change symbolized the casting away of the old, unrefined, despised lifestyle of European persecution and penury for American prosperity, elegance, and freedom (1990: 90–91).[6]

"The well-dressed crowds of lower Broadway," recalled Abraham Cahan in his wonderful autobiographical novel, *The Rise of David Levinsky* (1917), "impressed me as a multitude of counts, barons, and princes" (p. 91). Despite the wrenching poverty of the Lower East Side in New York City, "these people were better dressed than the inhabitants of my town" in Lithuania (p. 93). Upon his arrival in America, Cahan's alter ego, David Levinsky, rejoices in his modern "suit of clothes, a hat, some underclothes, handkerchiefs (the first white handkerchiefs I ever possessed), collars, shoes, and a neck-tie" (p. 101). The immigrant narrator in Tobenkin's *God of Might* also shed his "ghetto garb" for a "short coat" and, like David Levinsky, a shave. He now appeared "no different than any of the other Americans who stood nearby" (p. 67). And that was precisely the point.

Mass-produced commodities, especially clothing, materialized the American promise of democracy, equality, and prosperity. In "Mr. Wolfson's Stained-Glass Window," a short story originally published in *The New Yorker*, S.N. Behrman recalled his boyhood astonishment at the stately persona of the synagogue president, bedecked in "a stovepipe silk hat, a Prince Albert coat, and striped trousers" (1954: 197–98). Most wondrous, "he owned these garments outright." The president's wife was no less elegant, once returning from Boston with a "new tweed suit . . . Such a fabric as tweed had never appeared in our neighborhood before." For Behrman and most immigrants, modern clothing was something to behold, not just to wear.

In 1833, congregants in the Crosby Street Synagogue of New York City draped their prayer shawls "over modern broadcloth coats, and fashionable pantaloons with straps" (Friedman 1948–49: 178). They prayed not solely as Jews but also as stylish Americans. One can imagine these very same "fashionable" Jews purchasing their High Holiday finery, Passover shoes, and "Special Bargains for the Sabbath" at Lord & Taylor, one of several department stores that advertised in Yiddish newspapers (Heinze 1990: 67). Judaism was no longer just a religion: it was now a selling point—an opportunity to consume.

Yiddish short stories by Zalmon Libin, Jacob M. Gordin, and others, as well as Jacob Riis's jingoistic but powerful 1890 book, *How the Other Half Lives*, forcefully attest to the pervasive squalor of the tenements (see Hapgood 1965: 201–14; Schoener 1967). Still, most American Jews achieved material success in relatively short order. Compared to Europe, moreover, misery in America seemed far more tolerable given the absence of a history of anti-Semitism and the ethos and economic reality of social mobility. And there was no better way to display mastery of American materialism than competency in fashion.

Between the 1890s and the 1930s, however, fashion in America concerned not individual expression but conformity and national virtue (Joselit 2001). A well-dressed citizenry represented a healthy, progressive, democratic society. For immigrants, the seemingly simple purchase of a ready-to-wear outfit instantiated the modern ideals of affluence, opportunity, equality, and free choice (Joselit 2001: 25). No longer did Jews associate new clothing solely with a few key religious holidays (Schreier 1994: 70). For the first time in human history, the ordinary person, Jews included, could afford several outfits. Most people no longer valued clothing for sheer durability but for bourgeois notions of style and taste. Some Jews clung to an "old world" sense of decorum and layers of unadorned dresses, thick long coats, shawls, and headscarves. But most Jews happily swapped their old-fashioned garb for modern clothing.

A wonderful recollection by the daughter of an immigrant tells of a pivotal moment on her mother's steamship passage from Russia to New York City in 1902 (Schreier 1994: 4). Stashed away in her mother's trunk was a special wardrobe, carefully selected in the old country for a fresh start in the new world. But a fellow passenger, more familiar with modern styles, peeked in the chest and remarked, "These won't do in America." The trunk was tossed overboard.


## THE *SCHMATTE* BUSINESS

Jews eventually ascended to many of the more glamorous and lucrative positions in the American fashion industry, affectionately known as "the *schmatte* (rag) business." In 1847, Lob Strauss disembarked in New York City from Bavaria, changed his name to Levi, and sailed to San Francisco to open a branch of the family dry goods business. Fifteen years later, Strauss assisted a tailor from Nevada, Latvian-born Jacob Davis, originally named Jacob Youphes, in patenting a process to secure the seams and pockets of denim "waist overalls" with copper rivets. Levi Strauss paid a fee of $81.00. In 2008, Levi Strauss & Company boasted net revenues of $4.4 billion.[7]

Ida Kaganovich stands as another pivotal Jewish figure in American fashion. Emigrating from Russia in 1904, Ida changed her surname to Cohen, married William Rosenthal, and purchased a Singer sewing machine on the newly introduced installment plan. She opened shop in 1921, partnering with her husband and Enid Bisset. Allegedly, buxom Ida despised the flat-chested, boyish flapper style of the Jazz Age, which encouraged women to tightly wrap their breasts in a bandeau. Yearning instead for a garment contoured to the female body, Ida and her partners devised a brassiere in Bayonne, New Jersey. They called their invention Maidenform.[8] Company revenues now exceed over $100 million.

Ralph Lifshitz also rose to worldwide fame in fashion and, like Lob Strauss and Ida Kaganovich, changed his name to suit his style. Born in the Bronx to Russian émigrés, Ralph dropped out of City College, worked as a glove salesman, and designed neckties. With a $50,000 loan in 1968, Ralph Lauren, as he was now called, established Polo Fashions. Other celebrated Jewish participants in the American fashion industry include Calvin Klein, Kenneth Cole, Isaac Mizrahi, Lane Bryant (née Lena Himmelstein), Marc Jacobs, and Donna Karen. Jews, too, especially from Germany, established many prominent department stores, such as Gimbels, Saks Fifth Avenue, B. Altman,

Bloomingdales, Filene's, Lazarus, and even Sear's Roebuck (see Harris 1979). And let us not forget Rudi Gernreich, an Austrian-Jewish immigrant who, after arriving in the United States in 1938, designed such memorable garments as the thong swimsuit, the topless monokini, and the pubikini.[9]

The American-Jewish experience with fashion must not be restricted solely to the more swanky side of the industry. American Jews also sat at the sewing machines that tediously produced ready-to-wear. "Foreigners ourselves," uttered the narrator in Abraham Cahan's *The Rise of David Levinsky* (1917):

> and mostly unable to speak English, we had Americanized the system of providing clothes for the American woman of moderate or humble means . . . done away with prohibitive prices and greatly improved the popular taste. Indeed, the Russian Jew had made the average American girl a "tailor-made" girl.

Cahan took great pride in the Jewish role in democratizing fashion. Not all Americans were equally pleased. In 1884, *Puck* magazine charmingly judged the "vociferous Jew traders" of the Lower East Side "multitudinously objectionable."[10] The *Atlanta Constitution* in 1902 reported with similar sensitivity that "Many of New York's fashionable women brave all the vague terrors of the East Side to have their dresses fitted by an uncouth tailor who can hardly speak English."[11] But these working women not only stitched together the fashions of a nation—they did so at great occupational peril. Indeed, this very same "uncouth tailor" perhaps perished horribly in the 1911 fire that engulfed the top floors of the Asch Building in New York City, home of the Triangle Shirtwaist Factory. Most of the 146 victims were recent Jewish and Italian immigrants, all young women.

A shirtwaist, now forever connected to a needless tragedy, consisted of a somewhat frilly blouse modeled after a man's shirt (Schreier 1994: 69–70). The mass-produced shirtwaist served as the female uniform of the working class. Yet ready-to-wear also allowed the working and middle classes to emulate the wealthy. "If my lady wears a velvet gown," asked a writer for the *New York Tribune* in 1900, "put together for her in an East Side sweatshop, may not the girl whose tired fingers fashioned it rejoice her soul by astonishing Grand Street with a copy of it on the next Sunday?"[12] Or, as Marcus Eli Ravage wrote in his 1917 book, *An American in the Making: The Life Story of an Immigrant*, "one of the most curious things in America was the fact that, if you went merely by their dress, you could not tell a bank president from his office-boy" (p. 100). Notwithstanding the ideal of democracy, however, often expressed through ready-to-wear, Americans still formed exclusionary "taste communities." Jews were no exception. Thus the well-established "uptown Jews" in New York City, originally from Germany, snubbed the newer arrivals from Eastern Europe as untidy, uneducated "downtown Jews."

The wealthy looked upon the democratization of ready-to-wear as a boorish masquerade of refinement. They turned instead to custom-made haute couture (see Stubbs 1998: 162–63). The famous plot of Anzia Yezierska's 1923 novel, *Salome of the Tenements*, centers precisely on the contrast between "Cinderella clothes" and the "itching shoddiness of ready-mades." To immigrants, however, shoddy ready-to-wear seemed positively regal. Indeed, off-the-rack garments offered, especially through advertising, almost erotic pleasures and desires (Stubbs 1998: 168). Yet these fantasies, as *Salome of the Tenements* showed, no less than the garment industry in general, rested on the brutal exploitation of immigrant women (Stubbs 1998). To Jews and others, clothing represented both the promise and poverty of America.

## CORSETS, GHETTO GIRLS, AND MORAL PANIC

The manufacture of modern clothing was, and largely remains, women's work. This division of labor shaped the experiences of immigrant Jews and also, we just saw, imbued clothing with a particular, sometimes troubling symbolism. Clothing, I now show, materialized other gendered anxieties.

Mass production potentially allowed all women, not just the rich, to dress in the latest fashions. But you had to fit the style, which in the early twentieth century required a narrow waist. Unfortunately, the clichéd "Jewish figure" possessed an *un*-fashionably broad midriff. The solution? Corsets. Immigrant women quickly learned to include these constraining bodices in their urbane American wardrobes. "Putting on the corset," reminisced Ruth Gay, "was a commitment and a statement" about modern "respectability" and "containment" (1996: 192). Only a corset could reshape the "Jewish figure" into a fashionable, wasp-waisted woman. Of course, this style tragically required millions of women to loathe, and often harm, their bodies (Schreier 1994: 64; Summers 2001). Jewish women, far more than Jewish men, suffered anxiety and shame in struggling to pull on the stylish garb of assimilation.

Another gendered source of immigrant angst concerned the relationship between clothing and social context. The inaugural purchase of an American outfit often remained a lifelong memory (Schreier 1994). Women tossed aside their outdated wigs, shawls, and kerchiefs for new, fashionable hats. But not just any hat would do, as a young immigrant girl quickly learned in 1914 (Schreier 1994: 61). In America, you needed to wear the *right kind* of hat. So it was also with shoes. Immigrants learned to abandon their clunky, graceless, Old World hand-me-downs since Americans strutted in fashionable shoes with high thin heels, ornamental ribbons and buttons, and pointed toes. So astonishingly tapered were American shoes that ten-year-old Fannie Shoock, espying her first pair at Ellis Island, thought New Yorkers blighted by misshapen feet (Schreier 1994: 62). A woman's body had to fit her clothing—and her clothing had to suit the occasion. It was a lot to master.

But new fashion also meant liberation from old constraints. A columnist for *The New York Times* in 1925 applauded the popularity of "short skirts" as an "emancipation" from the long, unwieldy dresses that trailed along the sidewalk, gathering muck from horses, humans, mud, and all manner of refuse (Joselit 2001: 64–65).[13] But where the public benefits of shorter skirts seemed clear to some, others saw hidden dangers. Some consumers feared germs and contagion from garments sewn in sweatshops (Joselit 2001: 37). Others focused on the ethics of modern garb. Considerable moral panic surrounded rising hems and women's fashion in the early twentieth century. In 1919, the "women of refinement" from the Decent Dress Committee of the Women's Republican Club in New York City set off in impromptu fashion posses to censor window displays of skimpy lingerie, strapless evening dresses, and revealing bodices.[14] Jewish, Protestant, and Catholic clergy lambasted women's clothing as a threat to health, thrift, proper gender roles, and civic virtue.[15] At the fifth biennial assembly of the National Federation of Temple Sisterhoods in 1923, an eminent speaker pleaded for "a culture that teaches modesty in dress."[16] The Union of Orthodox Jewish Congregations of America denounced the "lax conduct and immoral dressing of women" in the synagogue and congratulated the Catholic Church for "barring from services immodestly appareled women."[17] Men's fashion also dramatically changed in the early twentieth century. But only women's clothing was seen as a threat to morality.

Short hems and low necklines threatened more than just Victorian virtue. In his 1893 address to the Russian-American Hebrew Society in New York City, Professor Felix Adler, president of the Ethical Culture Society, attributed anti-Semitism to "certain social defects which grate upon Americans," including the Jews' penchant for "showiness in dress."[18] Perhaps the professor had in mind the so-called Ghetto Girl.

Most immigrant Jews and their descendants yearned for acculturation—for a large degree of assimilation. They wished to dress and act like other citizens. Yet they feared rejection by the wider society on account of their Jewishness (Prell 1999, chapter 1). At the same time, Jews understood that integration would inevitably erode their heritage. If Jewishness so often precluded citizenship, then citizenship equally threatened Jewishness. The "Ghetto Girl" portrayed these twin anxieties.

Born from the collective experience of American Jews in the early twentieth century, this stereotype of a young, garish, Jewish woman received enormous condemnation in the Yiddish press. The Ghetto Girl dressed in beaded silk dresses with ornate floral décollage. She bared her shoulders, paraded pearls, sashayed in high heels, and romanticized love. In short, the Ghetto

Girl represented a *true* American—someone captivated by consumerism, enthralled with fashion, and determined to pursue individual desires rather than the demands of kin and custom. But the Ghetto Girl was an *imaginary* woman, a personification of fear. She represented, writes Prell:

> Jews who felt threatened by non-Jews, men threatened by women, the middle-class threatened by working women, native-born Protestant Americans frightened of a nation of immigrants, and participants in a changing economy frightened by their own attraction to consumption and leisure. (1999: 43)

To non-Jews, the Ghetto Girl dressed too Jewish; to Jews, she dressed too American. The Ghetto Girl represented the still emerging role of Jews in a modern consumerist society.

Off-the-rack clothing allowed men and especially women to "display and play" with novel values such as self-invention, pleasure, and romance (Peiss 1986: 63–66). Clothing also symbolized women's new freedoms to control their labor, sexuality, public presence, and economic power (see Leach 1984). Last, clothing represented the seductiveness of the "streets," as Peiss put it, and thus escape from everyday drudgery. These modern pursuits and perso-nas, while exciting, dramatically unraveled the threads of tradition, resulting in moral panic. To put a face on this alarm and uncertainty, Jew and non-Jew alike concocted the Ghetto Girl. She represented every woman, and also every man, who viewed the rise of consumerism with elation yet trepidation. The self, now liberated from conventional moorings, easily became lost amid a fast-changing world of free choice and freely available goods. Jews dressed no differently than other urban Americans. But all Americans, Jews included, dressed the Ghetto Girl in the anxieties of the era.

## "EQUAL HATS MAKE MEN EQUAL"

The Ghetto Girl garnered far more attention than her male companion, the "swell." In America, if not elsewhere, Jews and others preferred to clothe their anxieties in female attire. But public and religious authorities also scrutinized men's fashions (Joselit 2001, chapter 3). Advertisers promoted women's clothing by highlighting lavish decoration, ornamental individualism, and fan-tasies of affluence (Stubbs 1998: 162–63). By contrast, mass marketing for men's ready-to-wear stressed practical functionality and emotional restraint (see Kuchta 2002). Male fashion represented the newly masculine ideals of muted decorum and uniform propriety necessary for success in commerce and politics.

Middle-class Jews widely embraced new styles and outlooks. But devout Jews, we have seen, viewed this modernization with horror. In 1880, a young

Orthodox rabbi from Hungary, Moses Weinberger, sojourned to New York City to assess the state of traditional Judaism in America (Sarna 1981). Weinberg found an appalling neglect of almost all religious obligations. American Jews visited the synagogue for operatic entertainment, for example, not prayer; they viewed the Torah "as a glob of clay to be molded in any way they see fit." Weinberger was especially contemptuous of American democracy. "In all other lands," he wrote, "congregants are unequal and treated accordingly, each man attaining honors commensurate with his status and worth" (Sarna 1981: 43). But in America, "all are equal and treated alike." As he was often told, "Equal hats make men equal." To traditionalists like Weinberger, democracy dressed Jews in a distressing chaos that violated all the boundaries inherent in divine Law.

No longer did hats besmirch Jews or set apart the learned from the simpletons. American hats declared all Jewish men equal to all citizens (Gay 1996: 109). And proper citizenship, as Emily Post counseled in her 1922 bestseller, *Etiquette in Society, in Business, in Politics and at Home*, rested on an elaborate code:

> [A] gentleman should never take his hat off with a flourish, nor should he sweep it down to his knee; nor is it graceful to bow by pulling the hat over the face as though examining the lining. The correct bow, when wearing a high hat or derby, is to lift it by holding the brim directly in front, take it off merely high enough to escape the head easily, bring it a few inches forward, the back somewhat up, the front down, and put it on again. To a very old lady or gentleman, to show adequate respect, a sweeping bow is sometimes made by a somewhat exaggerated circular motion downward to perhaps the level of the waist, so that the hat's position is upside down.[19]

I am hard pressed to imagine Weinberger performing any such courtesies, especially to unfamiliar women. Orthodox Jews adhered to a no less stringent dress code. But they dressed for Judaism, not genteel citizenship.

Well-attired men also confronted a more prosaic peril than either the loss of tradition or the failure to dress for new manners. Modern women often shed clothing—often to scandalous glances. But protocol prevented men from doing likewise, especially in the presence of ladies. Men doffed their hats, but never their heavy coats. As a result, grumbled one writer to *The New York Times* in 1923, men dropped dead from heat exhaustion.[20]

### THE AMERICAN JEWESS

In the Weimar Republic, tells Wallach, Jewish women were keenly aware of stereotypes of Jewish affluence, and used clothing subtly and carefully "to navigate the tensions between modernity and tradition; between opulence and restraint; and between austerity and luxury" (2011). In America, the very same gendered tensions were especially in evidence a few decades earlier on the pages of the popular magazine *The American Jewess*. Despite its name, however, *The American Jewess* said little about Judaism.[21]

The magazine superbly illustrated consumerist fantasies in *fin de siècle* America. Advertisements touted a bewildering variety of products: pendent watches, glass lamps, ice cream, bicycles, encyclopedias, sewing machines, cameras, breakfast cocoa, oriental rugs, typewriters, self-heating flat irons, wallpaper, and so forth. Marketers hawked a pharmacopeia designed to make women and their families look and feel better, including mineral waters, "glove-fitting" corsets, facial bleaches, reclaimer balms, hair removers, hair regenerators, Spungia Napkins, Dr. Raub's Egg White Soap, Dr. Hobb's Sparagus Kidney Pills, and Dr. Campbell's Safe Arsenic Complexion Wafers. Readers of *The American Jewess* were courted by insurance companies, hotels, stock brokers, florists, railway lines, banks, milliners, furriers, and jewelers. The magazine even offered its own shopping bureau—"anything you desire, from a pin to a piano." The Vienna Matzos Bakery in Chicago advertised perhaps the *only* Jewish good in the entire run of the magazine! Indeed, when Best & Company Liliputian Bazaar in New York City announced the sale of 100 percent wool clothing in 1896, it was not to conform to the rules of *sha'atnez* but to boast "sure to wear and hold it's color." Advertisements in *The American Jewess* make clear the intent of the periodical and much of the age in which it was published: to integrate the Jewess into modern American society.

Toward this aim, each issue of *The American Jewess* illustrated the latest fashions. Yet many essays sternly warned against the moral perils of extravagance, especially "massive and conspicuous . . . vulgar and showy" jewelry.[22] A pervasive concern in the magazine was that the immoderation of a few might besmirch the reputation of all. The dress of women again conveyed the anxieties of everybody.

*The American Jewess* repeatedly fulminated against the transformation of the still novel confirmation ceremony, the revision by Reform Judaism of the traditional bar mitzvah rite, into an orgy of conspicuous consumption. "Before God," declared one editorial, "we are equals; that is the great lesson of confirmation; what matters the dress, the jewels, the gifts!"[23] A "Non-Jewess" offered "A Plea for Simplicity" after sitting beside a "poorly clad" child sobbing "bitterly" at one such ceremony. Why the tears? Because her family could afford neither a nice outfit nor a lavish reception.[24]

But how should the young woman have dressed? Even *The American Jewess* seemingly registered some uncertainly. In 1899, the author of "Gentle Manners" bewailed that "vulgarity of dress and manner are everywhere too prevalent."[25] Ironically, the fashion section of the previous issue of the magazine enthusiastically declared "The keynote of the present styles is— extravagance." *The American Jewess*, like the Ghetto Girl, understood well the central role of clothing in shaping a modern identity. These fantasized and fetishized women, one ideal, the other demonized, expressed through clothing anxieties over Jewish acculturation and assimilation.

## CONCLUSION

German Jews fitting into the middle class learned to shine their shoes, brush their coats and trousers, shave, walk with a proper stride, and spiff up for Sundays (Lowenstein 2005: 160). They learned, in other words, to dress like prosperous citizens, not old-fashioned Jews. Their brethren in London did likewise, infuriating Rabbi Zevi Hirschel Lewin, who raged against the Anglicized "decay of our people" (Duschinsky 1918: 177). Modern Jews, the rabbi bemoaned, acted modestly only about their faith, never their clothing. "Reverse the order! . . . We dress on non-Jewish holidays better than on our own festivals."

In America, the non-Jewish holiday that especially captivated Jews was Christmas (Duker 1949–50: 365–66; Heinze 1990: 47–79; Joselit 1992, 1994). In *The New York Times*, Mrs. Esther J. Ruskay of Temple Emanu-El lamented in 1894 that "Christmas and Easter had practically taken the place of Hebrew festivals."[26] Two years later, a writer in *The American Jewess* deplored the display of Christmas trees in Jewish homes—with nary a Chanukah menorah in sight.[27] Yet advertisers in the very same magazine promoted Christmas gifts!

Jews traditionally associated festive frivolities and gift giving with the springtime celebration of Purim. In the 1880s, however, these entertainments shifted to the minor holiday of Chanukah so nontraditional Jews could enjoy, like their Gentile neighbors, a consumerist celebration in December. Yet many Jews actually exchanged presents on Christmas. In 1900, *The New York Times* reported that "Hebrews bought toys for their children" on December 24—a full two weeks, by my calculations, after Chanukah.[28] Perhaps Ridley's department store, once the world's largest emporium of consumer goods, said it best—in Yiddish, no less (Heinze 1990: 77–78). In December 1897, Ridley's ran an advertisement in the *Yiddishes Tageblatt*, an Orthodox newspaper published in New York City, declaring that "Chanukah gifts with Christmas presents go hand in hand. There is only a difference in name." Jews partook of Christmas to celebrate not the birth of a savior but their own transformation into well-dressed American consumers.

# Fashionably Modest or Modestly Unfashionable?

[W]omen would do well to de-emphasize their bodies in order to emphasize that which is their real beauty: their inner strengths, their souls.

Dina Coopersmith, "Beneath the Surface: A Deeper Look at Modesty," www.aish.com

[I]n the Torah-oriented world great emphasis and effort is made by women to be as inconspicuous as possible in public so as not to cause males to stumble and transgress the Torah.

Rabbi Falk 1998: 341

In November 2006, thousands of ultra-Orthodox men convened in Jerusalem to address a religious crisis: spandex. "One of our generation's biggest obstacles," stated one rabbi, "is tight clothing . . . each and every one of us must stand guard and make sure his wife and daughters' clothing are modest."[1] Although the symposium focused on women's attire, only men attended.

Traditional conventions of Jewish decorum, or tzniut, apply to all devout Jews, irrespective of gender. But in regard to clothing, as we saw in Chapter 2, tzniut generally pertains to women. In this chapter, I survey the canons and implications of modesty for understanding Jewish women's attire. These matters, reminiscent of earlier concerns about the Ghetto Girl, raise questions about gender and empowerment. The rules of tzniut, too, like contemporary debates over Muslim headscarves, highlight the still uncertain relationship between citizenship and pluralism in a modern liberal democracy.

## THE MALE GAZE AND THE FEMALE BODY

Let me return to the rabbinic concept of modesty that I introduced in Chapter 2. Proper clothing, said the rabbis, like a Jew's personality, should stress restraint and humility. But the consequences of immodesty, to repeat, differ greatly with respect to gender. Men who violate tzniut insult God and erode the boundary between Jew and Gentile. By contrast, immodest women endanger men.

The rabbis, we also saw earlier, expanded the biblical concept of "naked-ness" to refer to any public baring of female skin or hair beyond a hand-breadth. Indeed, a man who glances at a woman's little finger acts "as if he gazes at her private parts" (B. Berachot 24a). As a result, ultra-Orthodox or Haredi men are prohibited from praying within sight of female "nakedness" or, by the same logic, within earshot of women's voices.[2] In the rabbinic world-view, in other words, men are possessed by innate and uncontrollable desires dangerously unleashed by the merest sight and sound of a woman. But the rabbis did not seek to constrain men by censoring the masculine gaze— a gaze that essentially transforms, as per the Talmud, the entirety of woman-hood into pudenda. Rather, the rabbis over-dressed women. A "partially re-vealed shoulder," wrote Rabbi Falk recently in his 600-page compendium on female etiquette:

> presents a stumbling block to a man who happens to see the woman or girl. It is essential that women and girls realize that it is their responsibility to ensure that men do not transgress . . . even inadvertently. (1998: 275)

Men's failings are thus made women's burden. The solution to male sexuality is for women to conceal their bodies.

To be sure, many Orthodox women applaud tzniut as a radical, liberating alternative to the sexualized and sexist objectification of female bodies that pervades contemporary culture. Religious modesty highlights inner beauty and moral substance, not superficial appearances (see Schreiber, ed. 2003). Muslim men and women often advance the same claim for veiling (e.g., Alvi, Hoodfar, and McDonough, eds. 2003). Modesty, in this view, empowers women. But this modern interpretation finds little support from traditional rab-binic sources, wherein women must cover so men can pray. From this angle, tzniut amounts to little more than male power dressed as female honor.

## MODESTY AND MORALITY

Today, a serious commitment to tzniut, pronounced *tznius* by Ashkenazi Jews, occurs only among the Orthodox. Yet devout Jews speak with no singular voice on this or any matter. Thus Modern Orthodox Jews dress in contempo-rary albeit conservative fashions. Men may pull on jeans, short sleeves, and sneakers; they often shave. More traditional women in the Modern Orthodox movement dress in long sleeves, high collars, nice shoes, and low hems. But others prefer sleeveless shirts, low necklines, denim, sneakers, and feminine-styled pants. They may also expose their hair.

By contrast, Hasidic and other Haredi Jews adhere to a far more stringent, often antimodern dress code. Men, as I discuss in the next chapter, favor black suits, black hats, and white shirts. Haredi women, writes one tradition-alist website, should:

> cover their elbows; wear skirts which reach a few inches below the knee, often mid-calf; generally avoid skirts with slits, preferring instead kick-pleats; cover their collarbones; wear stockings [thick and opaque, nothing sheer] and closed-toe shoes; avoid certain colors, especially bright red.[3]

In his study of Hasidim in New York City, Mintz writes about a husband scolded by his in-laws for lax oversight of their daughter (1992: 176–78). He failed to insist on heavy stockings. When viewed through a secular lens, tzniut may seem excessive, even medieval and misogynistic. But to strictly observant Jews, tzniut honors women as the nurturers of the community.

Each Haredi sect advocates a particular approach to modest garb. Dark or flesh-toned stockings? Wigs or scarves? Can women don the latest secular styles? Should men avoid shorts and sandals? Some groups yield to the individual's moral conscience; others defer to their rabbi. All Orthodox communities, however, permit some variation to reflect differences in devotion as well as, perhaps ironically, more secular distinctions such as taste and wealth (Figure 16). All haredim, too, agree that women's clothing requires on-going vigilance.

Take sleeves, for example. According to a contemporary Orthodox authority on Jewish law, generations of rabbis consistently censured as immodest the exposure of a woman's upper arms (Henkin 2003a). The limbs themselves are not licentious. Rather, a shirt or blouse that reveals the upper arms might also unintentionally expose a woman's breasts. For the same reason, rabbinic authorities ban loose short sleeves. Some authorities permit tight short sleeves, provided the garment covers most of the upper arm. Other rabbis permit loose sleeves that extend halfway to the elbows—but only to accommodate local custom or women with impeccable reputations. Short sleeves, in sum, warrant raised eyebrows and close scrutiny. To avert any possible impropriety, ruled Rabbi Henkin, the minimum length for a woman's sleeve is within a handbreadth of the elbows. The recommended length is for the sleeves to reach the elbows or, better yet, below them. Best of all, a woman's sleeves should extend to her wrists.

In general, writes Rabbi Falk, a properly modest woman dresses in unas-suming yet cheerful and tidy outfits that please, moreover, her husband (1998; see also Ellinson 1992). Collars should fit snugly to prevent any accidental uncovering of taboo skin. For the same reason, Rabbi Falk recommends that women sew elastic bands inside their necklines and affix clasps or snaps be-tween their blouse buttons. Garments must never cling to the body, reveal the contours of undergarments, or expose knees. A modest woman also avoids

**Figure 16**   Modest but fashionable. Photo by author.

trousers, regardless of cut or style, since these garments hint at the shape of her legs and violate the ban on cross-dressing. Many Orthodox authorities similarly assail flashy belts, close-fitting maternity wear, bold perfumes, large earrings, eyeliner, long nails, artificial tans, and garments with slogans or patterns that draw attention to the breasts or backside. "Pretty dress," summarizes Rabbi Falk, "camouflages the real body rather than shows it off" (1998: 334).

Rabbi Falk cast considerable vitriol at slitted skirts: "the Jewish population deserves to be safeguarded from this public hazard" (1998: 320–24). The former head of the Rabbinical Court of Jerusalem, Rabbi Yitzchak Yaacov Weiss, agreed. "Lately," he said, "Heaven has been shocking us with dreadful accidents and illnesses" (Falk 1998: 323). Why? Because slits in women's skirts cause "many to sin and it is they [women] who thereby invite serious retribution on the community." Women's clothing is thus made responsible not merely for male behavior but also for the ethical standing of the entire community before a wrathful God.

The rules of modesty also apply to girls' athletics, sometimes with an ironic twist. In 2007, *The New Haven Register* reported on an unusual advantage for the girls' basketball team of Beth Chana Academy, a Jewish day school in Connecticut. Team apparel includes long skirts and sleeves. The uniform of the BCA skirts inhibits certain skills. But the team believes it possesses a distinct advantage: rivals look at the skirts and underestimate the team's talent.[4] These young women manipulate traditional dress codes to challenge athletic opponents. Other Jewish women, I now show, use the very same rules to challenge the rabbis.

## COVERED HAIR: SUBVERTING OR SUSTAINING PATRIARCHY?

The prevalence of veiling in ancient Israel, we saw in Chapter 1, remains subject to ongoing debate. Some forms of veiling, both rhetorical and real, persisted into early Christianity and the second century (e.g., 1 Corinthians 11:5; Edwards 1994: 154–55). Yet canonical Jewish texts rarely mention the practice (Marmorstein 1954). The classic rabbis directed much more attention to women's hair.

Upon marriage, the rabbis reclassified a bride's hair as "nakedness" (B. Ketuboth 72a). Henceforth, any glimpse of her locks, like most of her body, remained the intimate privilege of her husband alone. Jewish religious law, in fact, requires married women, as well as divorcees and widows, to cover their hair in public. The rabbis justified this decree on the basis of the biblical *sotah* ordeal whereby an Israelite priest, recall from Chapter 1, uncovered the tresses of a suspected adulteress. Today, most devout women continue to conceal their natural hair. Even unmarried girls should, at the very least, contain their locks in braids and ponytails.

The medieval mystics saw unrestrained female hair as an invitation to demons. A woman guilty of such impropriety, declared Rabbi Chizkia in the Zohar, the central kabbalistic text, "causes poverty to descend on her home, her children not to reach the prominence they could have achieved, and an impure spirit to dwell in her home" (Falk 1998: 239). Hair itself was not the issue. Rather, I maintain, hair and clothing symbolized the rabbis' efforts to govern female agency, fertility, and sexuality.

The status of women's hair in Orthodox Judaism is far from simple. Most authorities construe a married woman's locks as intrinsically erotic and categorically immodest. They may disagree on precisely how much hair should be covered (Broyde 1991; Henkin 2003b). But they overwhelmingly agree that married women must do so. Yet some traditionalists, attributing no inherent status to female hair, permit married women to uncover their tresses in accordance with local customs (see Shapiro 1990: 150–54). In this view, Jewish law should reasonably accommodate societal standards (see Bronner 1993: 468; Weiss 2009). Of course, these Orthodox rabbis are no ethical relativists. They would never taste pork, for example, or allow men to pray "facing a woman's uncovered breasts even in islands or among tribes where women go topless" (Henkin 2003b: 134). Some rules might yield to social custom. But moral absolutes remain.

Yet even moral absolutes offer multiple interpretations. Some Modern Orthodox women now reconfigure their *hair* coverings as *head* coverings that serve, like men's yarmulkes (see Chapter 8), as a reminder of God (Berkovic 1999: 55; Landau 2008). Still, this quasi-feminist revision frames normative Judaism as masculine since women adopt a male garment, but men offer no comparable gesture. In response, many such Jewish women affirm that they actually seek to reclaim a commandment originally given to all Jews, at least in their view, but unjustly appropriated by the early rabbis exclusively for men. Head coverings thus sustain and subvert patriarchal authority. Wigs evidence a similar tension.

Jewish women in the Mishnaic and Talmudic eras, suggested Krauss, satisfied the modesty mandate in regard to hair by arranging "sumptuous" coiffures (1945–46/1970) (e.g., M. Shabbath 6:1). Only later did Jewish women put on head coverings, largely as a result of papal and royal edicts (Chapter 3) but also, possibly, to differentiate themselves from bareheaded Christian women. Women's hair thus formed, along with clothing, another plank in the protective "fence" surrounding Judaism. Wigs, however, posed a unique dilemma.

Jewish women first took up wigs in the sixteenth century (Bronner 1993). Most rabbis initially opposed this innovation for its similarity to natural hair. Perhaps, too, as Bronner suggests, the rabbis also recognized that wigs allowed women simultaneously to uphold and contest male religious authority—to breach, but not shatter, the "fence" of orthodoxy. But any transgressive intent soon faded as the rabbis, likely seeking to reestablish control over women, quickly accepted wigs. Today, many Modern Orthodox wigs appear indistinguishable from natural hair, and even emulate the latest, sometimes seductive styles. These wigs appear to mock the very modesty they are intended to uphold (Carrel 1999: 176). Thus adorned, devout women join the wider, non-Jewish world even as they announce, however slight to behold, fidelity to tradition.

We can discern a similar tension in regard to Hasidic hair. Upon marriage, Hasidic women receive a life-changing haircut, which they renew monthly.[5] Some communities trim the bride's tresses after the ceremony; others do so the following morning (Rubin 1972: 119). Each Hasidic group or "court" specifies the proper length for married women's hair. A few courts shave the head entirely. Hungarian Hasidim, such as Satmars, trim close to the scalp; Lubavitchers prefer longer hair, even a short bob (Carrel 1999: 167; Mintz 1992: 65). After shearing, women in the Reb Arelach court often save a single braid as a memento (Heilman 1992: 323). A Bobover groom's family weighs the bride's locks, and then pays her an equivalent sum (Shapero 1987: 68 n. 125). Differences aside, these matrimonial haircuts symbolize a woman's doubled rite of passage from youth to adulthood as well as from parental control to a husband's authority. The bride's snipped locks also represent the loss of her virginity since Haredi Jews typically experience their first sexual encounter on their wedding night, or shortly thereafter (Heilman 1992: 322–32). Never again, for all these reasons, will a woman display uncovered locks, now understood as her "nakedness," to any other man but her spouse. Hasidic marriage thus requires women to relinquish autonomy over their hair, clothing, and bodies, which henceforth become the property and moral concern of their husbands and community.

After marriage, Hasidic women must always cover their hair or scalp with wigs, hats, snoods, scarves, and kerchiefs (Figure 17). Beneath these coverings they may also wear a mesh or fabric headband, called a *shpitzel*, which sometimes includes artificial bangs. In preparation for marriage, Hasidic women often go wig or *sheitel* shopping. Family and friends may host a *tichel* (scarf) party, an Orthodox version of a bridal shower. Religious head coverings, it is important to note, mainly signal denominational affiliation and politico-religious sentiment rather than, as in secular culture, individualism. A "fringe dangling out of a stylish beret" signals approval of modernity and Zionism (Berkovic 1999: 47). To reject these ideologies, another woman "girds a kerchief tightly around her head." In some Hasidic groups, a woman places a small cap atop her wig "lest, God forbid, anyone should think she has not covered her hair." Ideally, a Hasidic bride adopts her mother-in-law's approach to head covering (Carrel 1999: 174). Each court prefers a particular style: uncovered wigs, black scarves over closely shorn hair, kerchiefs or hats atop their wigs, and so forth. Hair, again like clothing, signifies communal boundaries. But all Haredi wigs must look like wigs, never natural hair. Some perceptible sign—a headband, scarf, or hat, the cut or overall appearance—must clearly indicate that the wig is, in fact, a wig.[6]

Appropriate wigs, stipulates Rabbi Falk, should be short, neat, and symmetrical—no wild tresses, long locks, or irregular cuts (1998). Valid wigs and hats, too, must avoid any non-Jewish innuendo. At Wigs.com, one can purchase styles named Sorcery, Beyonce, Bad Girl, Knockout, and Beijing. These will not do. Nor would any wig in the Raquel Welch Collection. Needless to say, ultra-Orthodox hats and wigs should never appear intended to draw attention or elicit erotic admiration.

**Figure 17**    Modest attire and head coverings. Photo by author.

Since Hasidic hair, writes Carrel, represents female sexuality, a woman who exposes no hair in public laudably displays total self-control over her libidinous desires (1999). Less meritorious women show varying degrees of hair. Indeed, Carrel identified in Brooklyn a three-tiered hierarchy of Hasidic women's head coverings, from most to least observant or *frum* (1999: 171–72):

I. Scarf (*tichel*)
 entirely covers a woman's natural hair
 with headband (*shpitzel*) displaying pleated material but no simulated hair
 with headband displaying synthetic hair
II. Covered wig (*sheitel*)
 100 percent synthetic hair, and scarf
 100 percent synthetic hair, and hat
 50 percent synthetic hair, 50 percent human hair, and scarf
 50 percent synthetic hair, 50 percent human hair, and hat

    100 percent human hair, and scarf
    100 percent human hair, and hat
  III. Uncovered wig (*sheitel*)
    100 percent synthetic hair
    50 percent synthetic hair, 50 percent human hair
    100 percent human hair

We earlier saw a similar typology of sleeves, and one could doubtless try to formulate a similar schema for hems, stockings, and patterns. But Hasidim see hair as the most public and crucial sign of a woman's religious convictions. Indeed, Hasidic hair reflects themes I have stressed throughout this book, including a concern with boundaries, the assertion of masculine authority over women's bodies, the legalistic attention to everyday details, and the communal encompassment of individuality.

Despite the symbolic importance of female hair in Orthodox Judaism, some Haredi women seek to resist conventions while remaining true to tradition. For example, an online conversation about hair coverings appeared in June 2003 on "The Premier Frum Jewish Forum."[7] The dialogue touched on ever finer nuances of hair coverings, including the moral gradation between narrow and wide headbands. To this, one interlocutor posted "LOL," the texting locution for "laughing out loud." This chuckle hinted at muted criticism of the entire matter and, in consequence, at much of the authoritative rabbinic outlook.

Other critical voices are more direct. One unhappy Hasidic wife, reported Mintz, wished to eschew head coverings entirely but nonetheless consented to wigs in deference to her husband (1992: 178). Yet even this concession proved inadequate for her father, who abhorred wigs as unseemly. He preferred a kerchief over a shaved scalp. If his daughter must insist on a wig, the father continued, she should at least have the decency to cover this travesty with a hat. But the daughter, who already yielded to male authority, did neither, refusing both the scarf and the hat. For this offense, said her father, she would bear full responsibility for any tragedy that might befall her husband or children. This woman yielded to patriarchy but also resisted a puritanical conservatism, thus upholding and undermining ultra-Orthodoxy.

Many Haredi women voice deep emotional attachments to their wigs, scarves, snoods, and hats (Schreiber, ed. 2003). Wigs often become central to an Orthodox woman's sense of self, the topic of endless conversations, styled again and again for important religious holidays. Head coverings visualize personal feelings of piety, pride, and holiness—in a word, individualism. Wigs, too, say many devout women, represent a degree of control over their own bodies and identities. The wig signals not phallocentric tyranny but feminine agency and empowerment.

Yet other religious women renounce head coverings. Traditionalists lambaste these women for vanity and ignorance. But devout women who reveal their hair arrive at this anguishing decision, which may even result in rejection by family, through serious contemplation of biblical and rabbinic sources. For them, what's in your head is more important that what's atop it (Brown 2003: 194). Still, I have shown that outward appearances are often deceiving—that wigs may pose a challenge to the very male authority that head coverings otherwise sustain.

## TRADITIONAL HEAD COVERINGS AND MODERN CONSUMERISM

In the nineteenth century, Reform Judaism abandoned head coverings as part of a wider rejection of traditional authority, collective morality, and religious separatism. Understandably, Orthodox rabbis fumed (Kaplan 1991: 80). Conservative Judaism similarly rejected mandatory women's head coverings—with one exception. Most Conservative congregations now require head coverings on any congregant, male or female, who leads prayer or receives a ritual honor. In the pews, however, only men are obligated to cover their heads. In this sense, Conservative Judaism officially balances modern individualism with premodern gender.

Today, Reform and Conservative synagogues stock inexpensive ritual garments for congregants and guests, specifically yarmulkes, prayer shawls, and women's doilies or "chapel caps." In May 2008, a gross of mass-produced black and white, lace or taffeta doilies fetched about $45.00 from online vendors. Devout Jews require no such convenience. They come prepared for prayer as a matter of everyday attire. But acculturated Jews often need to fetch these items from bins and racks located just outside the sanctuary doors. No gesture or prayer attends to doilies and yarmulkes. You simply place the article atop your head and, after services, unceremoniously return it.

Inevitably, though, synagogue attendees in the United States occasionally arrive home with temple doilies or yarmulkes still perched on their heads or stuffed in their purses and pockets. Head coverings have no sacred status. They can even be tossed in the trash. But Jews generally prefer to stuff these errant items in closets, bureaus, kitchen drawers, and automobile glove compartments. This casualness introduces a brief, unintentional element of religion or ethnicity into the secular spaces of everyday life.

Many women prefer to wear personalized "chapel caps," not the cheaper coverings provided by synagogues, to match their tastes and outfits. Hello Doily sells "couture quality lace" and "special trims that are frosted with different combinations of pearls, sequins and delicate beads" (www.hellodoily.com). This retailer "provide[s] beautiful head coverings that fulfill a women's religious and traditional obligations, while satisfying her fashion needs." A century earlier, of course, readers of The American Jewess pursued the very same elusive goal of blending style with ethnicity.

Glam Doily offers "classic," "seasonal," and "junior" collections that retail for about $30.00 to $40.00 (www.glamdoily.com). These doilies incorporate European lace, designer fabrics, and "the finest Swarovski crystals." Glam Doily styles—Venice, Black Sapphire, Paris Pink, Uptown Girl, Bermuda Sky, Versailles, and so forth—evoke worldly success, fun, and upscale elegance. They "will make any woman feel proud to be wearing a head covering." Here, again, we see a fusion of religion and secular culture that allows Jewish women to express their identity as good Jews and as good consumers.

## BLEACH BRIGADES, BURNING WIGS, AND OTHER JEWISH LAW ENFORCEMENT

Women in Reform and Conservative congregations who push the limits of propriety may suffer raised eyebrows but not ostracism or worse. Orthodox and ultra-Orthodox communities resort to a far more aggressive enforcement of religious dress codes.

Not long ago, miniskirts appeared in an Orthodox high school in Boston. The troubled principal sought guidance from Rabbi Ovadiah Yossef, the Sephardic chief rabbi of Israel (Rosenthal 2001: 124–27). Clearly, the principal needed some alternative to this immodesty. But what would appeal to the young wayward women? How about trousers? True, this outfit would violate the prohibition on cross-dressing. But surely trousers would appear more modest than miniskirts.

The Torah, Rabbi Yossef responded, categorically forbids miniskirts—not directly, of course, but through divine punishment of the licentious "daughters of Zion" (Isaiah 3:16; B. Shabbat 62b). Such garb seduces God-fearing men into wrongdoing. "[T]housands of young men were killed in battle in the late Yom Kippur war," the rabbi continued. "Who knows if it was not for this grave sin?" But trousers—an immodest mimicking of Gentiles? Even worse! Still, Rabbi Yossef did permit the young women in Boston to wear pants, but only as a practical alternative to miniskirts, and then only until the day when all Jewish women finally dress in proper attire. The rabbi surrendered to secular liberalism in the hope of conserving religious tradition.

No such compromise was in evidence during the recent campaign by the Tznius Poster Committee in Crown Heights, Brooklyn. The committee, affiliated with Lubavitch Hasidim, posted signs throughout the neighborhood reminding Jewish women of their obligation to dress modestly.[8] The posters included a loose translation of Deuteronomy 23:13, "G-d walks amidst you to SAVE you and to push away your enemies, so be holy so He shall not see your PROMISCUITY and TURN AWAY from you." Heilman saw similar signs in a Haredi neighborhood in Israel declaring "Young Girl: She who wears shameless clothes, woeful are the days of her youth . . . Her sins are more numerous than the strands of her hair" (1992: 309). I caught sight of a similar poster while visiting Crown Heights in August 2009 (Figure 18). This broadside, which included the portrait of the late Lubavitcher rebbe, Menachem Mendel Schneerson, included no dire warnings, only a description of suitable styles and the simple, forceful declaration that "Modesty in all places and at all times makes Hashem [God] dwell amongst us and protect us." In this conservative worldview, a Hasidic woman wears her fate—and that of her community—on her sleeves.

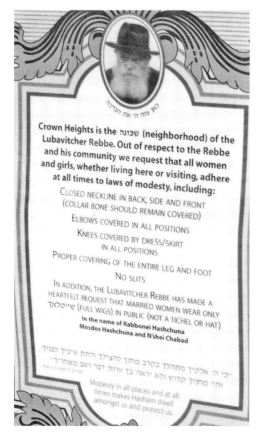

**Figure 18**  Modesty sign in Brooklyn shop window. Photo by author.

A far more violent enforcement of women's attire occurred during the 2006 spandex crisis, which I noted earlier. This outrage prompted the convening of a conference, "Strengthening and Awakening on Modesty." Attendees renewed their commitments to censor risqué sleeves, collars, hems, waistlines, colors, shoes, materials, and contours. In Israel, ultra-Orthodox men burned "clothes of impurity" in the streets, set afire fashionable boutiques, and sprayed bleach on improperly attired women.[9] A "modesty squad" horrifyingly burned a fourteen-year-old girl with acid.[10] "She cried all the way to the hospital."

In the ultra-Orthodox town of Bnei Brak, posters listed "kosher" apparel stores.[11] The Guardians of Holiness and Education issued modesty certificates to retailers who agreed to banish red garments, form-fitting clothing, and male clerks from their shops. Signs in religious enclaves throughout Israel and the United States pleaded "Please do not pass through our neighborhood in immodest clothes." A Hasidic family in the Satmar town of Kiryas Joel, New York, suffered harassing phone calls and vandalism on account of the wife's colorful skirts.[12] The Jewish blogosphere buzzed. Some fumed at the suppression of female agency and the failure of Haredi men to police their own lust. Others warned about the Talibanization of Judaism and, indeed, a fringe group of ultra-Orthodox women in Israel started veiling their faces.[13] Yet contrary voices suggested that the quickest way to quell the tempest was for secular women simply to avoid Orthodox neighborhoods.

The same debate surfaced when the two major Israeli transportation companies, Egged and Dan, ran "kosher" bus routes in the late 1990s. These particular buses, catering to ultra-Orthodox sensibilities, required modest attire and same-gender seating. Women wearing trousers or refusing to sit at the rear of the bus received verbal harassment and even beatings. In a 2007 petition to the High Court of Justice, one woman likened the experience to segregation in the American South. Others mentioned apartheid.[14] It is "inconceivable," said Justice Rubenstein, "for a driver not to allow a woman on a bus because she is wearing pants." Legally, the matter remains unresolved.[15]

Another inferno over traditional women's attire erupted in May 2004. Hasidic men from the Satmar dynasty torched hundreds of wigs on the sidewalks of Brooklyn and Israel. Until then, Orthodox women generally, albeit largely unknowingly, purchased wigs plaited from hair gathered at the Sri Venkateswara Temple in Tirupati, India. But this practice abruptly ceased when Rabbi Yosef Shalom Eliyashiv of Jerusalem ruled as *non*-kosher any locks shorn by pilgrims during Hindu purification rites. Wearing a wig now considered idolatrous was tantamount to dining on pork.

Many rabbis greeted the ban on Hindu hair with skepticism, asserting that the Gentile locks were not trimmed as an offering to a pagan god but merely as a purifying gesture prior to worship.[16] However, most Haredi men asked no such questions. Instead, they kindled pyres of taboo hair.[17] Retailers were suddenly encumbered with useless inventory—although sales in synthetic wigs boomed. "Let our shop know next year when it's the Jewish wig festival," said one such non-Jewish proprietor in Stamford Hill, London, "so we can get more in stock."[18] Other shop owners voiced less enthusiasm. "Did anyone check out this Rabbi?," asked Ace Wigs.[19] "Did he get paid off to create this new law? Is the Rabbi way out in left field?" Justifiably, the Indian community in the United States reacted with considerable dismay.[20]

Today, Hindu hair no longer enflames Haredi passions, in large part since wig stores now tend to advertise "100% European Hair" and specify rabbinic or kosher certification (Figure 19). European locks, however, cost far more than Indian and Asian hair, upward of $5,200 for a "European Kosher Human Hair" wig at A. Fox International (www.afoxintl.com). Mindful of the cost, Clary's Wigs (www.claryswigs.com) advertises a Family *Simcha* (celebration)

**Figure 19** Wig shop sign in Brooklyn, NY, advertising "100% European hair." Photo by author.

Deal: three wigs—"for *kalah* [bride], mommy, grandma, sister or any combination"—at fifteen percent off cost.

After the Hindu wig scandal, the Bostoner rebbe issued a proclamation, "Our Women of Valor be Praised," lauding Orthodox women for their steadfast devotion to the Law during the crisis. Especially admirable were those women who, refusing either to bare their heads or display non-kosher wigs, "suffered shame" by staying home, thus missing family celebrations.[21] We "should be proud of our womenfolk," the rebbe declared, and pray that God find the entire House of Israel worthy of redemption "in their merit." Here, yet again, we see masculine authority staking the fate of the entire Jewish community on the control of female attire and appearances.

## LAW AND THE LIMITS OF MODESTY

Unlawful clothing is typically a matter of too little fabric. But even modesty has its legal limits. The desire to dress in religious attire, especially for women, sometimes violates the authorized appearance of citizenship. For example, British and American passport photos may include religious headgear but never veils or any obstruction of the face. The same criteria apply to British driving licenses. In the United States, the states regulate drivers' licenses, not the federal government, and thus policies regarding hats and veils vary. Some states issue photo-free licenses in deference to religious sensibilities. (These exemptions were initially granted to Christian communities, such as the Amish and Mennonites, who object to "graven images.") Most states permit applicants to wear religious head coverings for license photos, sometimes after signing an avadavat of belief. Legislative bills in other states, however, such as Minnesota and Oklahoma, seek to ban all head coverings and veils from driver's license photos. The Florida Department of Highway Safety and Motor Vehicles, in fact, revoked the license of a Muslim woman who refused an unveiled portrait (*Freeman v State*). After litigation, the state emended the law. The issue ensnares more than Muslim sensibilities. When Missouri in 2007 started issuing photographic driver licenses, many Mennonites left the state.[22]

Legal matters occasionally entangle Jewish head coverings. In 2006, the harassment of an Orthodox woman by a license branch prompted the Illinois secretary of state to affirm the right of Jewish women to wear hats for official identification photographs.[23] A similar case occurred in 2008 when police in New York state required a Hasidic woman, arrested for welfare fraud, to remove her hat for the booking photograph. This demand, a normal protocol of law enforcement, outraged the local Hasidic community.[24]

Outside of the occasional mug shot, however, devout Jewish women today generally encounter little opposition in Western democracies when dressing Jewish. Not so for American Muslim women. They often report employment discrimination after demands by leading companies—such as McDonalds, USAir, J.C. Penny, Abercrombie & Fitch, Disney, Alamo Rent-a-Car, and Quality Inn hotels—to remove headscarves in the workplace (e.g., McCloud 1995–96; Moore 2007). In most cases, the company emends relevant policies, issues an apology, and extends a job offer. Still, the face of female citizenship in the West is far more accepting of hats and wigs than headscarves and veils.

But not all organizations refuse to accommodate Muslim sentiment. A Fitness USA health club in Lincoln Park, Michigan agreed to erect a partition between the female and mixed-gender sections of the gym. Some public pools and colleges, including Rutgers University, Massachusetts Institute of Technology, and Harvard University, now offer female-only swims, sometimes banning male lifeguards.[25] In Jerusalem, Orthodox Jews can exercise at a "kosher gym" lacking music, televisions, and co-ed workout areas (www. koshergym.com). In Montreal, a YMCA agreed to install semi-opaque windows to protect the male pupils of a nearby Hasidic school from the sight of exercising women.[26] Earlier, the school frosted its own windows—but the otherwise studious boys simply opened them or strolled outside during recess for a breath of fresh air. That the school reimbursed the YMCA did little to warm the frosty reception by some members, who saw the windows as blocking sight of Quebec's secular roots. The very same issue, rather more famously, surfaced recently in France.

Two centuries ago, as we saw in an earlier chapter, hats in France symbolized the tension between Jewishness and secular citizenship. France continues to wrestle with the legality of public displays of religious identity and clothing, only now in regard to Muslim headscarves. In 2003, President Jacques Chirac appointed a commission, chaired by long-time politician Bernard Stasi, to issue recommendations for the enforcement of *laïcité*, the official French doctrine of secularism. The concept of *laïcité* arose from a long history of strife over the role of the Catholic Church in society and governance. The doctrine permits private religious practices but mandates assimilation to ensure that "the cultural practices and ways of life of the minorities . . . converge with those of the majority" (McGoldrick 2006: 44). *Laïcité* legislates monoculture, not multiculturalism, and so allows the state to bar public expressions of ethnic and religious identity deemed antithetical to secular republicanism.

In 2004, Chirac accepted the Stasi Report and signed into law a ban on "conspicuous" religious displays in public schools. The act broadly targeted all religious symbols, including Jewish yarmulkes, large crosses worn by members of the Syro-Chaldean Church, and Sikh men's turbans. But the intent of the legislation was to curb the rise of separatist Islam by assimilating Muslims into secular society. Similar laws are under discussion throughout Europe.[27]

A full discussion of *l'affaire du foulard*, or the "headscarf affair," lies outside my scope (see, e.g., Auslander 2000; Scott 2007). But two points touch on Jewish clothing. First, public alarm about Muslims who fail to dress like proper citizens, as Sandar Gilman shows, echoes nineteenth-century arguments against the incorporation of Jews into European civil society (2006). Indeed, current efforts in the West to undress Muslim women, in a sense, recall former Russian and Polish edicts to dress Jews in the attire of citizenship.

Second, the Western vision of generic personhood actually takes root in early Christianity, specifically, the Apostle Paul's invective against distinctive Jewish practices. From this perspective, "secular" is a cipher for a particular religious identity universalized as the unmarked body of modern citizenship (see Boyarin 1994). In Quebec, for example, the Bouchard-Taylor Commission—officially, The Consultation Commission on Accommodation Practices Related to Cultural Differences—released a report in 2008 on "reasonable accommodation" to religious and ethnic minorities. Among many suggestions to enhance "interculturalism" and secularism, the report proposed relocating the crucifix prominently displayed inside the parliament building—a proposal unanimously rejected by the national assembly.

Islamic headscarves, like modest attire and wigs worn by Orthodox Jewish women, engender multiple meanings. We can view these garments as defying certain features of modernity, such as individualism, secularism, and egalitarianism. "In our country," declared French president Sarkozy in a parliamentary address, "we cannot accept that women be prisoners behind a screen, cut off from all social life, deprived of all identity."[28] But these garments may also express a thoroughly modern assertion of the individual's right in a secular nation-state to resist collective coercion (see also Bowen 2007: 142; Gilman 2006: 2). This way, women dress for religion as much as they do for free choice and citizenship.

European Jews, despite echoes of their own historical experience, largely remain silent about contemporary debates over Muslim veils (see McGoldrick 2006).[29] They do so for two reasons. First, Orthodox Jews in France generally send their children to private religious academies. The ban on conspicuous symbols pertained only to public schools. Second, Muslim anti-Zionism often results in violence against Jews in public schools—so much so that the education minister reported in 2003, "There is a trivialization of antisemitism that worries us."[30] If Muslims attack yarmulkes, so goes this logic, why should Jews defend the *burqa*? Sometimes the two religious minorities dress together against the coercive claims of the state; at other times, they dress apart.

## ONLINE MODESTY AND BOUNDARIES BLURRED AND RENEWED

The Internet, with its reputation for lurid photos, illicit trysts, and unseemly temptations, hardly seems like an appropriate venue for fostering religious decorum. Cyberspace lacks any moral center—no limits, no censoring, no constraints on individualism. Compared to tzniut, the Web is nothing if not immodest.

Ironically, though, the Internet offers new opportunities for the promotion and marketing of modest apparel. Numerous online merchants offer conservatively tailored clothing to devout Jews, Muslims, and Christians. Tznius.com, for example, strives "to keep you beautiful, modest (tznius) and looking feminine!" Other online venders of modest Jewish dress include Kosher Clothing, Frum Fashion, Kosher Casual, Below the Knee, Tznius Children, Challah and Hats, and Modest World, "the first Rabbinical approved clothing store on the web!"

The idea of modest clothing may conjure unstylish frumpiness. But many Hasidic and Orthodox women display keen awareness of contemporary fashions and thoroughly participate in consumerism (Levine 2003: 51). They dress for and against the wider society. Thus at FrumButWithIt.com, "tznius and fashion come together." Likewise, Funky Frum is "the place to shop for chic modest apparel . . . that won't compromise your femininity and contemporary sense of style" (www.funkyfrum.com). In Israel, a glossy new Haredi lifestyle and consumerism magazine, *Stylish*, showcases fashion tailored to modest sensibilities.[31]

Many Hasidic women cultivate and internalize a self-image of royalty. They see disciplined refinement as befitting a Jew's regal soul (Fader 2009: 161). A hallmark of this etiquette—polite speech, stately bearing, modest clothing— is the lack of pollution by the crassness of the wider, non-Jewish world. Yet, ironically, these Jewish "royal souls," as Hasidic women say, are drawn to expensive clothing and jewelry (Fader 2009: 164–66). Of course, a devout Jewish woman truly needs no such finery and, indeed, the very concept of tzniut stresses inner, not outer, beauty. Hasidic women's clothing thus evidences a tension between Gentile-coded ostentation and Jewish simplicity and grace—that is, writes Fader, between "the material and spiritual" (2009: 3).

A unique genre of modest apparel for Orthodox women is the Sabbath or Shabbos robe, a "long, loose, comfortable, but especially beautiful robe or dress which you can slip into quickly before candle-lighting and, wear all Shabbat night . . . the ultimate in convenience, comfort, and elegance" (http://justrobes.co.il/what-shabbos-robes.php). The Shabbos Robe exemplifies religious modesty, "with sleeves down to the wrist and hemmed at the ankles" (www.larobes.com). But it is also an eminently practical garment for devout women who rush from work on Friday afternoons to buy groceries, cook, dress the kids for synagogue, and prepare the home for the Sabbath— all before sunset. "They look like an evening gown," said one proprietor, "but fit like a jumpsuit."[32] This distinctively Jewish garment also, in this respect, represents archetypal modern values such as efficiency, pleasure, and consumerism.

Some Orthodox women shop for modest apparel at well-known retailers such as Land's End, Coldwater Creek, Talbots, and J. Jill. A now defunct website, Tznius Shopper, posted links to Wal-Mart and Sears (www.tzniusshopper. com). But they offered this caveat: "We have no control over the pictures that they use to show their clothing, and some of them show non-*tznius* necklines and sleeves or show models wearing slacks rather than skirts." Most readers will likely find the suggestion of glimpsing taboo eroticism in a Sears catalog delightfully quaint. This aside, Tznius Shopper portrayed a classic tension in Euro-American society between ethnic identity and acculturation—between a "Torah-observant lifestyle," in other words, and generic consumerism.

Another blurred vestimentary boundary in cyberspace is perhaps best illustrated by Biblical Garden Clothing Collection (www.biblicalgarden.com). This online vendor, which caters to Orthodox Jewish women, stocks the typical array of modest garb. Hence, they do not sell pants, shorts, skorts, sheer fabrics, slit-skirts, clingy knits, and solid reds. Despite this, Biblical Garden subscribes to a broad, politically conservative vision of modesty that seemingly works against Jewish religious particularism. The website posts links to Mormon Chic, Crowned With Silver ("For the Modern Christian Woman With an Old-Fashioned Heart!"), and Ladies Against Feminism. From the latter, you can click on Future Christian Homemakers, ExWitch Ministries ("God Answers Knee Mail"), TheologicallyCorrect.com ("TRUTH . . . not Tolerance"), and a t-shirt company with designs such as "Patriarch in Training" and "I ♥ Obeying My Husband." Many Christian clothiers, in fact, despite the appearance of interfaith dialogue in the guise of consumerism, endorse Jewish conversion and Messianic Jews (e.g., Jews for Jesus). The latter wear yarmulkes, tefillin, and prayer shawls but also accept the divinity of Jesus or Yeshua, thus complicating any straightforward definition of Jewish identity (Kollontai 2004). Zipporah's Thimble, for example, offers attire for "Jewish, Messianic and God fearing communities . . . in line with the final authority of the Torah" (www. zipporahsthimble.com). Modest attire encloses religious Judaism but also, in a pluralistic world, blurs this boundary.

The Web hosts a multitude of Christian clothing shops with names like She Maketh Herself Coverings, The King's Daughters, Lilies of the Field, Vessels of Mercy Dress Shoppe, Modest Prom, and Mennonite Maidens. Several online retailers specialize in the white temple attire required by the Mormon Church, such as Dressed In White, Heavenly Delight, and White Elegance. Muslims seeking modest apparel, too, can shop online (e.g., Al Hannah Islamic Clothing, Artizara, Barakallah.com, Jelbab.com, DesertStore.com, and MuslimClothing.com). Many of these stores, like comparable Jewish shops, strive to offer women modest yet trendy attire—"styled . . . for a new generation" (www.shukronline.com), or "fun and funky" (www.rebirthofchic.com).[33] IKEA, the international home furnishing company based in Sweden, now issues through the Hijab Shop in England an official headscarf for its Muslim employees (www.thehijabshop.com). In deference to veiling, some Islamic retailers use faceless mannequins or suitably crop the photos of their models. Mannequins are no less controversial to Haredi Jews. A "modesty brigade" in

**Figure 20**   Burqini. Courtesy of Aheda Zanetti and Ahida Burqini Swimwear.

Tel Aviv insisted on the placement of scarves atop the mannequins in a wig shop (Berkovic 1999: 51–52). The proprietor initially refused, then agreed to a compromise. The wigs remain uncovered. But the Styrofoam mannequins now wear unfashionable eyeglasses.

Several online Islamic retailers specialize in modest swimwear. The wonderfully named Burqini (Figure 20; www.ahiida.com) and Bodikini (www.bodykini.com) fuse performance-enhancing fabrics to Koranic morality, exposing only the face, hands, and feet. Similarly, Princess Modest Swimwear of Jerusalem sells athletic attire for "Christian, Jewish, Muslim, Druze, Atheist and all other modest dressers" (www.princessmodestswimwear.com). Aqua Modesta (Figure 21) manufactures a four-piece, quick-drying, opaque swimsuit for Orthodox women that includes a long skirt with a sewn-in brief, lined sports bra, and three-quarter-sleeve top (www.aquamodesta.net). SeaSecret (www.seasecret.biz) also offers "kosher swimwear." Here, again, we see Jewish clothing blurring boundaries between devout communities and between interfaith orthodoxy and wider secular pursuits.

**Figure 21** Modest swimwear from Aqua Modesta.
Courtesy of Regine Tessone, Aqua Modesta.

## GIRLS AND DOLLS

A few years ago, the enormously popular doll series, American Girl, introduced a Jewish character into its historical collection: Rebecca Rubin, a nine-year-old immigrant from Russia living in the Lower East Side of Manhattan in 1914 (Figure 22).[34] My daughter was thrilled.

Rebecca and the other historical dolls retail for $95.00. Add Rebecca's "Sabbath Set," school outfit, movie dress, pajamas, bed, settee, pet kittens, films, and historical novels with "Lessons of love, friendship, courage, compassion and tolerance," among other accessories, and you can spend upward of $1,000.00. American Girl also sells "Just Like You" dolls that vary in hair texture, skin tone, and eye color to match their young owners, as well as books on topics such as health, friendship, and math. American Girl, acquired by Mattel in 1998, surely contributes to the commercialization of childhood. But American Girl admirably promotes respect for ethnic diversity. Indeed, Rebecca personifies a key aspect of the Jewish encounter with

**Figure 22**   Rebecca Rubin doll. Courtesy of American Girl Brands, LLC.

modernity, namely, the synthesis of religious particularism with consumerist assimilation.

Rebecca appears as a moral, educational, modestly attired alternative to the vapid, scantily clad likes of Barbie and Bratz. In this regard, Rebecca is not alone. Gali Girls, a entirely Jewish line of dolls and books introduced in 2004 (Figure 23), also challenges the reigning ideologies of "fashion, makeup and boyfriends" that blight, in this view, the contemporary doll industry (www. galigirls.com). Gali Girls aspires "to give young Jewish girls an opportunity to incorporate positive values into their doll play"—values such as "kindness, respect, and honesty" that "kept Jewish tradition alive and growing for over 5,000 years."

Gali Girls, like American Girl, offers historical dolls: Miriam Bloom, who journeys from Russia to America in 1914; twelfth-century Reyna Li from Kaifeng, China; and Shoshana Levy, a Sephardic girl in Nieuw Amsterdam. The company also sells dolls that mirror a girl's appearance. These dolls include matching Star of David bracelets, an English and Hebrew birth certificate, and toy Sabbath candlesticks, wine goblet, and *challah* bread. Gali Girls, too,

**Figure 23**  Gali Girl doll. Courtesy of Azila Stein and Gali Girls (www.galigirls.com).

dress in modest clothing. Both Gali Girls and Rebecca seek to prevent Jewish girls from dressing like the early twentieth-century specter of the Ghetto Girl.

Neither Rebecca nor Gali Girls, despite their Jewishness and commitment to modest attire, wear distinctively Jewish outfits. By contrast, the Hasidic dolls of Mini Mishpacha or "family" (Figure 24) unmistakably dress for a "Torah-observant lifestyle" (www.minimishpacha.com). If one sees dolls as a form of *avodah zara* or idol worship, advises the website for Mini Mishpacha, "an adult can snip off a piece of the nose or a finger of each doll" to nullify any impious appearance. Two Muslim dolls, Razanne and Fulla, also dress in unmistakably religious garb, specifically, headscarves and modest "outdoor" robes that conceal more fashionable "indoor" attire (Figure 25).[35] Rebecca, Gali Girls, Razanne, and Fulla, despite doctrinal differences, all dress for common purposes: ethnic and religious pride, bodily and ethical modesty, resisting the eroticization of contemporary culture, and integration into a consumerist society.[36]

**Figure 24**    Mini Mishpacha dolls with Sabbath *challah* bread, wine, and candelabra. Photo by author.

**Figure 25** Fulla dolls—dressed for public and private. Photo by author.

## CONCLUSION

Since at least the seventeenth century, when boys dressed in new outfits for their bar mitzvah ceremonies (Pollack 1971: 61), Jews have looked to rites of passage to celebrate their worldly success. In the 1940s, American clothiers started peddling the "bar mitzvah suit" as a secular counterpart to matching sets of prayer shawls and tefillin (Joselit 1994: 93, 102). Today, reports *The Boston Globe*, the purchase of this outfit often rivals the actual ritual in significance.[37] "If there's one *bat mitzvah* fashion imperative," declared *The Jewish Week* recently, "it's The Dress."[38] The total cost of a bar/bat mitzvah party in the exclusive suburb of Scarsdale, according to *The New York Times*, can now reach upward of one million dollars.[39] The rabbis rejected impoverishment and applauded the beautification of ritual. But is this what they had in mind?

Even devout women embrace the very consumerism their codes of modesty seemingly decry. Eligible brides go *"shidduch* [matchmaking] shopping"

for glamorous clothing in anticipation of arranged dates with potential husbands (Berkovic 1999: 53). These Orthodox Jews are no less "on show,"
writes Landau, than young women in secular society (1992: 261). Indeed,
Haredi women may dress in several expensive gowns and housecoats on
the Sabbath and holidays (Heilman 1976: 54–57; Landau 1992: 274). *Frum*
hardly eclipses fashion.

Much of the contemporary rationale for tzniut concerns, to repeat, the
distinction between inner and outer beauty. Tzniut presents Jewish women
as "minds and souls" dressed for a higher calling, not as erotic objects devoted to "self-display" (Manolson 1997: 39). Modesty enables women to
reclaim their bodies and sexuality and shelters them against the inevitable
"self-loathing" that arises from comparison with the impossible, fantasized
standards of secular beauty (Safran 2007: 46). Tzniut also lends a woman
"control over when, where, and to whom she reveals her attractiveness"
(Feldman 2003: 152). Thus viewed, tzniut upholds the feminist ideal of empowerment and honesty.

Additionally, say devout Jews, tzniut protects the sanctity of femininity and
motherhood. Traditional Judaism, we have seen, sees women as the bearers
of life. Women are therefore holier than men, and so need of layers of protection, much like Torah scrolls, which Jews enwrap in fabric cloaks (Shapero
1987: 102–3). Judaism also likens women to royalty, we have seen. For this
reason, women's clothing advertisements in Yiddish newspapers often employ regal imagery—say, "Large selection of hostess dresses for the Queen
of the Seder" (Shapero 1987: 104–5). Modest garb is a gift in this view, not
a burden.

Viewed from another angle, however, tzniut appears as a form of religious
fanaticism—worse, an ideological effort to dress patriarchy in a pleasing rhetorical coat.[40] Wigs, long hems, below-the-elbow sleeves, and high collars,
like Muslim headscarves and burkinis, constitute an *anti*-fashion that rightly
belongs, if anywhere today, at the margins of normal citizenship. But tzniut,
as we have seen, works as much through fashion, advertising, the Internet, and consumerism even as it challenges these very modern pursuits.
It thus seems best to view modest apparel for Jewish women as part of a
wider, irresolvable conversation about gender, identity, and assimilation that
both resists and accommodates modernity.

# −6−

# **Black Hats and Unsuitable Suits**

> With my appearance I cannot attend a theatre or movie or any other places where a religious Jew is not supposed to go. Thus, my beard and my sidelocks and my Hasidic clothing serve as a guard and shield from sin and obscenity.
>
> Poll 1962: 65

In 2007, American Apparel posted an enormous visage of a Hasidic Jew on two billboards in Los Angeles and Manhattan. American Apparel presents itself as a hip, controversial company known for social and environmental ethics as well as sexualized advertisements that sometimes feature porn stars. The corporate ethos is decidedly erotic. Perhaps too much so. American Apparel CEO Dov Charney has received several allegations of sexual harassment.[1]

Charney sees himself as the Woody Allen of the garment industry, a well-known Jewish personality wrongly pilloried for untrue carnal improprieties.[2] It was in this spirit that American Apparel erected the billboards of a bespectacled Hasid with long sidecurls, prominent beard, and characteristic black hat and coat. Only this Hasid was none other than Woody Allen himself in a brief scene from his 1977 cinematic masterpiece, *Annie Hall*. The billboards also included the Yiddish phrase "*der heileker rebbe*," or "the holy *rebbe*," a moniker Hasidim employ only for their spiritual leaders. The gag failed, offending both Hasidic Jews and, more consequential, Mr. Allen, who sued American Apparel and eventually settled for five million dollars.[3]

Surely few viewers of the billboard or *Annie Hall* harbored any doubt as to the identity of Woody Allen's outfit. But how, and why, did this particular costume come to embody ultra-Orthodox Judaism? And what is the symbolism of this unique attire that appears, whether in Brooklyn or elsewhere, so anachronistic? I offer this chapter as an answer.

## HASIDIC HISTORIES

Hasidism arose among the eighteenth-century Jews of Podolia, Volhynia, and Galicia in modern-day Poland and the Ukraine. The movement initially centered on Israel ben Eliezer, a charismatic figure better known as the *Ba'al*

*Shem Tov*, or *Besht*, the "Master of the Good Name." This honorific referred to the *Besht*'s magical talent for manipulating divine names (Rosman 1996). But it was the *Besht*'s unconventional approach to Judaism, not his shamanism, that spread throughout Eastern Europe.

Hasidism offered a populist alternative to rabbinic Judaism and the so-called Lithuanian approach to religious knowledge. For centuries, only the privileged few could claim legitimate insight into God and Judaism—men who, after years of rigorous study, mastered the intricacies of Talmudic argumentation, Jewish law, and ritual etiquette. By contrast, Hasidism made holiness accessible to everyone. The movement eschewed rote and instead promoted dance, song, and sincerity, in short, a mystical approach to Judaism.

The rabbinic establishment, which came to be known as the Mitnagdim or "opponents," rightly saw Hasidism as an attempt to undermine the status quo. They furiously opposed the movement, and even excommunicated many early Hasids. But in the latter nineteenth century, the former bitter rivals set aside their doctrinal differences to confront the new common threats of modernity, secular culture, the Jewish Enlightenment, and assimilation.

Eventually, Hasidism branched into distinct regional groups throughout Eastern Europe, many of which endure today. Each court or dynasty revolves around the luminary teachings of a mystic, called a *rebbe*. Hasidim seek their rebbe's advice on all sorts of matters ranging from spirituality to business. They find meaning in every aspect of the rebbe's life—the cadences of his prayers, say, and the nuances of his outfits. Even in death, the rebbe may offer guidance. Lubavitch Hasidim place letters and pleas, delivered by hand or e-mail, atop the grave of their seventh rebbe, Menachem Mendel Schneerson, who died in 1994. Once a week, the entreaties are burned so the words ascend to heaven.[4]

About two dozen Hasidic courts exist today, such as Satmar, Bobov, Skyver, Belz, Viznitz, Bratslav, Ger, and Lubavitch, totaling approximately two hundred and fifty thousand adherents worldwide. Many other groups succumbed in the Shoah or Holocaust. More assimilated Jews tend to romanticize Hasidim as quaint relics of a kinder, simpler past—living embodiments of *Fiddler on the Roof*. But Hasidim often partake in thoroughly modern institutions and quarrels. For example, a feud over school districting between Satmar Hasidim and their non-Jewish neighbors in the New York town of Kiryas Joel reached the U.S. Supreme Court (*Board of Education of Kiryas Joel Village School District v. Grumet*). A squabble over dynastic leadership, allegedly erupting in fisticuffs, recently split the Satmars into two virulently opposed factions seeking control over a religious legacy and assets estimated at hundreds of millions of dollars. Similarly, rival groups of Bobover Hasidim are now litigating ownership of the very name "Bobov" after one faction submitted an application to the United States Patent and Trademark Office.[5]

And the Lubavitch dynasty offers a Send a Prayer App for the iPhone that transmits a personalized message to Jerusalem for printing and insertion into crevices in the Western Wall (http://sendaprayer.wordpress.com). Despite their premodern costumes, Hasidim sometimes participate in the most modern institutions of the secular world.

## MEN IN BLACK

In the early twentieth century, we have seen, Jews en masse dressed to assimilate into the wider fashions and morals of society. But Hasidim, especially men, resisted all calls to modernize their wardrobes. Even today, the typical Hasid dresses in black trousers, black socks, black shoes, long black coat, white shirt, and long white fringes (tzitzit) attached to a white woolen vest. Hasidim also wear black hats atop large black yarmulkes. For the Sabbath and festivals, Hasidic men generally don expensive fur hats and silk or satin caftans. Always, however, the black-and-white color scheme dominates.

In the early nineteenth century, Polish Hasidim were called "men of silk" (Dynner 2006: 2). They avoided linen as a precaution against inadvertently violating the biblical ban on wool and linen blends (see Chapter 1). Yet these silk outfits defied the Council of the Four Lands, the legislative body of Polish Jewry, which prohibited opulent attire. Through clothing, then, Hasidim signaled a strict adherence to biblical morality that also challenged both the Jewish establishment and the wider non-Jewish society. But Hasidic clothing conveys more than just the rejection of others. It also communicates the virtues of a devout Jewish lifestyle.

The early Hasidic leaders, for example, dressed in white on the Sabbath, a color evocative of purity, virtue, and mercy (Wertheim 1992: 217). They also wore satin and velvet. The Yiddish words for these two fabrics (*atlas*, *samet*) form acronyms for "this indeed is fit solely for Israel" and "avoid evil and do good." Hasidim today read similar meanings in their characteristic black garb. In Israel, secular Jews refer to Hasidim and other Haredim with the phrase "black Jews." In America, they may be derided as "penguins." But in the Hasidic worldview, black clothing represents a commitment to piety and modesty and symbolizes the mystical goal of renouncing the self in order to unite with the divine.[6] Black also stresses conformity and collectivism rather than individualism. The color, too, signifies a state of mourning for the destruction of the Jerusalem Temple and the ensuing experience of spiritual exile. More pragmatically, the antiquated otherliness of Hasidic and Haredi clothing serves as a "fence" against secular temptation and vice. "How far," asked a Haredi man rhetorically to Heilman, "can we move from our world looking like this?" (1992: 107). Not far at all, of course.

Ultra-Orthodox women, we saw in the last chapter, drape their bodies with loose-fitting layers. Haredi men do likewise. Heilman vividly conveys this style in regard to an elderly man dressing after a dip in a public ritual bath or *mikveh*:

> First came the large *gatges*—baggy, loose-hanging, yellowish-white underpants that reached down to the knees. Like the rest of his garments, these appeared to be relics of another century in Eastern Europe. His undershirt was a perfect match, loose and held together with white buttons . . . Next came the white but rather rumpled shirt, his black baggy trousers and at last a black striped *arba kanfos*, the four-cornered tunic on which the *tzitzit*, ritual fringes, are knotted. (1992: 8)

The old gentleman also donned a black caftan and, presumably, a black hat atop his yarmulke. Layer by layer, Hasidic garments contain the body and person, diminish individuality, and clothe naked human nature in the Law.

## A BLACK-AND-WHITE RAINBOW

To outsiders, all Hasidim look alike. But insiders, writes Heilman, perceive "a rainbow of differences" (1992: 289). Within the general black-and-white masculine schema, each court specifies its own unwritten dress code. Some courts favor trousers; others prefer breeches. Convention determines if a man wears the same color stockings as his rebbe, or the opposite hue. Rules, too, govern the length and shade of your coat, the number of buttons, the shape of your hat, whether you tilt it to the left or right, and so forth. Thus, at a wedding in Jerusalem, Heilman observed Ger Hasidim in knickers and tall fur hats (Figure 26), a Lithuanian yeshiva student with a doubled-breasted frock, Lubavitchers sporting their characteristic fedoras, and a Breslover with gold stripes on his coat (1992).

Hasidic clothing also communicates marital status, wealth, gender (of course), and even time (Epstein 1979: 84–95). The Sabbath and festivals warrant special finery, such as a black caftan (*bekishe*), usually woven from satin, silk, or polyester, and known for its characteristic sheen (Figure 27). Major holidays and special occasions, such as weddings, often call for entirely new outfits. Some Haredi groups, too, wear caftans in Jerusalem (Heilman 1992: 143). In all instances, Hasidic men generally avoid any garments they judge as characteristically non-Jewish, including neckties, sandals, and jewelry.

Traditionally, in fact, only brides received rings during the Jewish marriage ceremony. In the latter nineteenth century, Reform Judaism and other acculturated Jews adopted the double-ring ceremony to express their commitments to free choice and egalitarianism (Kaplan 1991: 67). Orthodox Jews maintain the single-ring ceremony. Yet some men later slip on "modern"

**Figure 26**   A gathering of Hasidic men form the Ger court, mainly wearing *spodik* hats. Courtesy of Yehuda Boltshauser / Kuvien Images.

**Figure 27**   Lubavitch Hasidic man with a patterned *bekishe* coat and a fedora. Photo by author.

wedding bands. Most Haredi men, however, shun all jewelry in deference to custom and modesty. "Are you a mother," asked a befuddled young Bobov boy to Samuel Heilman, "that you wear a ring?" (1992: 180). Most Hasidim, too, wear pocket watches attached to fobs—or strap their wristwatches to their dominant arms so as to not interfere with the mandatory placement of tefillin on the non-writing arm.

It is tempting to devise a grammar of Hasidic clothing or a catalog of dynastic insignia. But neither is possible. At best, one can offer only generalizations. The everyday outfit of Bobov men, for example, consists of black trousers, short black socks, simple black slippers (laces are deemed non-Jewish), white cotton shirt, and a knee-length silk or woolen frock called a *kapoteh* that resembles the Prince Albert coats popular during the Victorian era (Figure 28). During festivals, Bobov men dress in costlier garb: a silk coat, perhaps with black brocade, a fur hat, and knickers tucked into white stockings. During weekdays, Skyver men wear long, light-weight, dark coats called *rekel*s and wide-brimmed felt hats. On the Sabbath and holidays, they dress in long black *bekishes* ornamented with subtle patterns. Married men additionally wear fur hats and knee-high leather boots.

**Figure 28**   Bobov Hasidic man wearing knickers. Photo by author.

Most Hasidic men wear wool *rekel* coats during the workweek. Yet some Hasidim, seeking to avoid any inadvertent violation of the biblical ban on wool and linen blends, dress only in polyester or silk (e.g., Wertheim 1992: 291–95). As always, individual courts tend to favor slight stylistic variation—single- versus double-breasted cuts, concealed buttons, light striping, muted geometrical patterns, vents, and so on. Each court also specifies a preference for grooming its adherents' earlocks or *payess* in accordance with four characteristics: long or trimmed; thick or thin; straight, twisted, or coiled; and exposed or tucked under their hats or wound around the ears. A few courts restyle their *payess* for festivals.

The general Hasidic approach to clothing originally intended to differentiate the movement from other Jews, especially their rivals, the Mitnagdim. The latter tended to dress like well-to-do Europeans in starched collars, neckties, and "modish hats" (Landau 1992: 32). They also often shaved. Today, however, the Mitnagdim, more commonly called Lithuanians or Litvaks, dress and groom much like their former foes. Still, there remain subtle differences. Hasidim generally eschew hats with indented crowns (Landau 1993: 33–34). Lithuanians prefer fedoras and homburgs. Hasidim wear long shimmering coats on the Sabbath and holidays. Lithuanians favor matching suits. Hasidim pray in sashes; Lithuanians do not. Nonetheless, the overall Hasidic style dominates ultra-Orthodox Judaism. Even traditional Jews from the Middle East and North Africa have abandoned their local costumes for Hasidic fashion, writes Dan, "as if the landscape of the Moroccan Diaspora has been replaced by the landscape of the Ukraine" (1996: 419).

Hasidim do not formally join one or another dynasty. There is no paperwork, oath of allegiance, or induction ceremony. Court styles, moreover, are not centrally or officially regulated. Consequently, there is some blurring of coats and courts. Yet the threat of ostracism powerfully enforces the unwritten style of the group. In some dynasties, a ribbon affixed to the wrong side of a hat may appear as a deliberate provocation (Landau 1993: 212). A Hasidic community in Europe, needing a kosher butcher or *shochet*, passed on a scrupulously devout practitioner because he preferred short underpants (Poll 1962: 217). If he did this, the group reasoned, what more serious flaws would later appear? A single shave or outfit change, as Hella Winston powerfully shows in her book, *Unchosen: The Hidden Lives of Hasidic Rebels* (2005), can marginalize an entire family. Indeed, Winston tells of a few intrepid Hasids from Brooklyn who, longing to sample the forbidden fruits of secular society, furtively change their clothing on the subway in order to experience a few moments of cosmopolitan life in Manhattan.

Hasidic women, despite the demands of modesty, often dress in contemporary fashions and so appear modern in contrast to their archaically attired husbands. In fact, some Hasidic men vicariously partake of secular society through their wives' clothing (Heilman 1992: 56). Here, as in earlier eras, devout Jews both sustain and subvert authoritative Judaism. But we should not necessarily see Hasidic women as privileged—at least not by Hasidic standards. For while the rules of modesty, we saw in the previous chapter, clothe women as royalty, men uphold the religious integrity of the community by dressing apart from the wider society.

In the latter nineteenth century, elite European men stashed away their elaborate, colorful costumes and instead pulled on dark suits befitting the weighty political and commercial pursuits of modern manhood (Kuchta 2002). Ornate clothing now defined, and often constrained, femininity (Ruane 2002: 69). But in Hasidic society, men continue to dress in elegant, often baroque garments that bespeak an earlier style of masculine grace and power. Hasidic women tend to dress in non-Jewish fashions. Men, however, remain attired at all times for a distinct and distinctive presence in the heavenly court. Not only does this formal style exemplify the rabbinic value on dressing properly for the divine presence (see Chapter 2), but it ensures that the Hasid is always suitably dressed for prayer and the study of sacred texts. This outfit imbues every activity, no matter how trivial, with sacerdotal significance.

## SYMBOLIC ATTIRE AND HATS

The symbolism of Hasidic clothing entails far more than mere color. Many Hasidic men, especially rabbis, adorn their *bekishe* coats with velvet or felt piping that evokes tefillin straps. Some cover their *bekishe*s with a special caftan to represent, like a prayer shawl as they see it, the unique spiritual radiance of Judaism or the kabbalistic notion of the *Or Makif*, a protective aura of divine light (Wertheim 1992: 296). Hasidic men, too, generally pray in a black sash or *gartel* (Figure 29) that protects the purity of the mind from lower bodily carnality and pollution. A few courts even wear the *gartel* throughout the day.[7]

In the secular world, as I noted in Chapter 2, men button their coats left over right. But Hasidic men do just the opposite, right over left. This custom, which necessitates special tailoring and alterations, further separates Hasidim from others and also encodes an ethical outlook. Hasidim associate the "good inclination" (*Yetser ha-Tov*), or moral consciousness, with the right side, and the evil impulse (*Yetser ha-Ra*), or sinfulness, with the left. In this cosmology, men's coats represent the ascendance of goodness over sin and iniquity. Likewise, according to Mintz, long caftans symbolize the moral containment of passion and sexuality (1992: 31).

Even the Hasidic beard conveys meaning. Prominent sixteenth-century kabbalist Isaac Luria understood facial hair to channel God's spiritual abundance.

**Figure 29**  Hasidic man preparing for prayer at the Lubavitch headquarters, 770 Eastern Parkway, Brooklyn. Note the *gartel* belt and plastic Croc shoes. Photo by author.

Not only did Luria refrain from trimming his beard, but he refused even to touch his facial hair lest he inadvertently uproot a single strand. The beard, as a contemporary Hasidic website puts it, "grows down from the head to the rest of the body" and thus serves as "the bridge between mind and heart, thoughts and actions, theory and practice, good intentions and good deeds."[8] So mystically potent is the beard that some devout Jews place any hairs that fall during worship inside their prayer books.

Most people see the broad sable hat or *shtreimel* as the prototypical Hasidic garment. To some degree, they are right. This fur cap is the dearest item in a Hasidic man's wardrobe, matched only by his wife's fanciest wig. A *shtreimel* is no trivial accoutrement, costing several thousand dollars (Figure 30)—or a mere $29.99 as a masquerade costume, widely available on the Internet. A Hasid generally receives his first *shtreimel* as a wedding gift from his father-in-law. Some men own a second, less expensive *regen shtreimel* or "rain *shtreimel*" (e.g., Kranzler 1995: 48). Others purchase a long-hooded "Shabbos raincoat" (Figure 31).

Despite the centrality of the fur hat in the popular imagination, the *shtreimel* adorns only those courts originating in Romania, Galicia, the Austro-Hungarian

**Figure 30**   Enough washing, It's time for a new one, Cheap prices, as never before . . . Custom made shtreimel for a groom $1,000, for the father of the groom/bride $500. Photo by author.

Empire, and the Ukraine—groups such as Satmar, Bobov, and Belz. Moreover, the *shtreimel* is exclusively worn for special occasions such as the Sabbath, festivals, and weddings. Sometimes the rebbe alone appears in a *shtreimel*, perhaps made of white fur to match his distinct caftan. Like many items in the Hasidic wardrobe, the *shtreimel* also evokes mystical meanings. On the Sabbath or Shabbos, recall from Chapter 2, religious Jews do not lay tefillin. In Hasidic folk etymology, the Yiddish word *Shabbos* is an acronym for *Shtreimel Bimkom Tefillin*, or "*shtreimel* in place of *tefillin*." Similarly, a *shtreimel* is often made from thirteen (or twenty-six) tail pelts to evoke, like the sash knotted on some corpses, as we saw earlier, the Thirteen Attributes of Divine Mercy (Landau 1992: 34). By the same logic, the *shtreimel* refers to the unity of God since the letters in the Hebrew word for "one" total thirteen. Men in the Belz court, however, wear *shtreimel*s made from twelve tails—one for each of the biblical tribes (Heilman 1992: 87).

Legends trace Hasidic hats to Old World decrees banning distinctive Jewish dress. But since the Torah forbids the emulation of Gentiles, Hasidim could not simply reach for non-Jewish outfits. Instead, goes one version of the folktale, Hasidim literally turned these edicts and fur-lined hats inside out.

**Figure 31** Advertisement for "Shabbos raincoat" with a hood that fits over a large fur hat. Photo by author.

Legend aside, most scholars trace these hats to the national costume of Poland during the sixteenth century (e.g., Straus 1942: 70–71). The quintessential outfit of traditional Judaism was not, in this view, Jewish at all. In the seventeenth century, non-Jews upgraded their hats and wardrobes. But Jews, encumbered by pogroms, economic deprivations, and mandatory dress codes, and beholden to rabbinic rulings, remained attired in fur hats and other garb that now increasingly appeared anachronistic and distinctively Jewish.

Of course, not all Hasidic Jews are keen to derive their garments from non-Jews. After all, such genealogies violate a central precept of traditional Judaism. As a result, many Hasidim re-tailor the origins of their clothing. "Contrary to popular belief," we read on the Wikipedia entry for Hasidic Judaism, "Hasidic dress has little to do with the way Polish nobles once dressed." This "myth," the website continues, was "probably started" by assimilated Jews "in an attempt to induce younger Jews to abandon the outfit." Similarly, some rebbes and courts, especially in Jerusalem, equate their caftans with the robes worn by Abraham, the premier biblical patriarch to affirm monotheism (Ben-Zvi 1982: 58). In this scenario, the caftan later spread to the Arabs and faded entirely from Jewish wardrobes. Hasidism, however, rightfully claimed the garment back for Judaism. Hasids, then, never dressed in non-Jewish clothing. Rather, they dress like the original Jews.

The Wikipedia article also anchors several features of Hasidic clothing to the biblical purity code. Knee socks prevent the hems of trousers from dragging along the profane ground. Breeches, tied around the legs, ensure against the unintended exposure of genitals during prayer. Laceless slippers make it unlikely that a Hasid will touch his polluted shoes (see also Heilman 1992: 196–97). And so forth. But the Wikipedia contributors then correctly comment that these "connections are quite tenuous and the real reasons for the Hasidic dress code are historical and sociological and not theological." Indeed, I contend that Hasidim reacted against acculturation partly by weaving Jewish sentiments into their clothing. This way, yet again, Hasidim could singularly claim to dress as authentic Jews.

In the early eighteenth century, rabbi Yitzchak Lampronti equated the Hasidic fur cap with the biblical High Priest's mitre (Weiner 2005b). The height of these hats symbolizes a level of devotion that far exceeds the meager religious commitments of yarmulke-clad Jews. A hat, too, fully covers the head, and so better envelopes or focuses the self during prayer. A black-hatted Hasid is not merely a particular type of Jew. He is a better Jew.

Hasidic men, however, do not substitute hats for yarmulkes. They wear *both* head coverings—a hat atop a yarmulke (Figure 32). Some rabbinic authorities root this doubled head covering in an ancient prophetic vision of double-winged angels or *seraphim* hovering over the Divine Throne (Isaiah 6:2; Weiner 2005b). The final Lubavitcher rebbe, Menachem Mendel Schneerson, fit the doubled head covering into the kabbalistic notion of the soul. The uncovered body contains the lowest level of the soul (*nephesh*). Yarmulkes represent the middle layer (*hayah*), floating just above our bodies. This cap suffices for most activities. But during prayer and other sacred endeavors, a Hasid should wear a second hat to represent the highest levels of the soul (*yedidah*) that transcend material reality and touch the Godhead.

In rabbinic lore, the Hebrew letters of the word *yarmulke* can also spell "god-fearing" or *yirah Elokim*. To Hasidim, a single paltry head covering denotes the lowest degrees of this devotional "awe" (*yirah*). The additional hat signifies a more elevated or reverential level of "awe" as befitting the constant presence of the divine. In all, the black hat symbolizes a particular devotional approach to Judaism while resisting the modern values of integration, individualism, and change. The black hat, once a matter of "custom" (*minhag*), eventually gained the status of religious "law" (*halacha*). But all this, reasoned Rabbi Moshe Feinstein, is beside the point (Weiner 2005b). *Any* practice prominent in the religious community, regardless of origin and meaning, *must* be true.

**Figure 32**   Hasidic man in Boro Park, Brooklyn, wearing a *rekel* coat and a black yarmulke under his hat. Photo by author.

Despite the significance and cost of *shtreimels*, Hasidim do not always treat these items with due respect. During violent street brawls, feuding camps of Viznits Hasids in Bnai Brak, Israel, recently snatched rivals' *shtreimels* to gain the upper hand during bargaining sessions when the purloined hats are swapped.[9]

## DRESS, HIERARCHY, AND INSULT

To the casual observer, Hasidic men dress as an undifferentiated throng of religious conformity. Individualism and fashion seem evident only among women. But in many courts, Hasidic clothing varies from *zehr Hasidish*, or "extremely Hasidic," to *modernish* (Poll 1962: 65). Just as some secular garments can be tailored to suit devout sensibilities, certain Hasidic items can be modified—a higher hem, a more colorful shirt, a certain angle of the hat—to appear more worldly. Moreover, Hasidim keenly discern dress distinctions as much within as between courts. To stand apart, the rebbe in many dynasties dons a uniquely colorful and ornate *bekishe* coat—or, in some courts, an all-white frock. The rebbe of a successful dynasty, in fact, might enjoy considerable opulence (Heilman 1992: 262). Other men dress in accordance with their public renown.

The relationship between hierarchy and Hasidic clothing is perhaps most evident among the Satmar dynasty. At the apex of the court presides the rebbe. Next in status are the rebbe's coterie of advisors, men called *gabbaim* or *Shtickel Rebbes* ("piece of rebbe"). They are followed in order by ritual practitioners and religious professionals known as "beautiful Jews" (*Sheine Yiden*), learned laymen or "students of the wise" (*Talmidei Hachamim*), affluent businessmen (*Balebatishe Yiden*), and, at the bottom, undistinguished commoners (*Yiden*). For everyday activities, the latter dress in the minimal sartorial signifier of Satmar masculinity: a dark, double-breasted suit that buttons from right to left. Each ascending grade adds a few additional items to their mundane attire that serve as insignia of status. The rebbe dons the full ensemble of Satmar regalia: slipper-like shoes (*shich*), white knee socks (*zocken*), a fur *shtreimel* or beaver (*biber*) hat, and a *kapoteh* coat over a long silk *bekishe* (Poll 1962: 66–69). This baroque outfit conveys the rebbe's elite stature.

One short-lived and radically austere dynasty, Przysucha-Kock, rejected any clothing that signified hierarchy, piety, wealth, or elegance (Mahler 1985: 291–92). Its members dressed in ragged garb and aggressively tried to impose their puritanical outlook on all other Jews. Members of the court swatted fur hats from the heads of other Hasids and stripped away *kittel* gowns on Yom Kippur. No such asceticism exists today. Still, Hasidic men carefully scrutinize attire to make certain that no one dresses above his devotional station. Hasidim ridicule men whose outfits convey a sham sense of piety and harass coreligionists, especially women, who dress outside the conventions of modesty.

Most Hasidim, too, now feel entitled to dress like the *shayneh yidden* or "beautiful people" of premodern Eastern Europe—that is, like the former Jewish elite. Rubin traces this upgrading to the modernist ideal of democratization—the very value, I note, that Hasidim must also reject (1972: 248–49 n. 16). In the past, some Hasidic communities reserved the *shtreimel* for men who exhibited exceptional religious commitments (Poll 1962: 219). But now, blurted one disillusioned Hasid to Winston, "every schmuck puts one on" (2005: 120–21).

Hasidic men, much like traditional nuns in their habits, almost seem tailor-made for comedy, at least to others. Steven Brykman, managing editor of *National Lampoon*, spoofs both Hasidim and so-called American yuppies, who stereotypically dress in "preppy" clothing by J. Crew, with a mock online store named C.R. Jew (http://crjew.com/). The website purports to sell Hasidic garments. The flat brimmed hat favored by the Satmar court is dubbed "the *shvartze* [black] nipple." The slogan accompanying the long coats reads "5762 is the year for black! (but then again . . . aren't they all??)". To a large degree, the conceit of C.R. Jew rests on the widespread perception of ultra-Orthodox Jews as dull and somber. But the Haredi community hardly lacks wit. And sometimes this humor takes the form of caustic barbs directed at the dress of religious rivals.

A Torah scroll is normally tied with a sash then covered with a velvet mantle. This process is reversed to signify the non-kosher status of a marred Torah. The ultra-Orthodox Lithuanian school draws on this symbolism to deride Hasidim for tying *gartel* sashes over their coats, like blemished Torah scrolls (Aran 2006: n. 27). Hasidim, too, jeer Lithuanians, allow their rotund bellies to sag ridiculously over their belts, thus trapping their Hasidic souls in corpulent excess. In reply, Hasidim laugh at the "modern" neckties and other accoutrements of the so-called Enlightenment favored by Lithuanians (Aran 2006). Hasidim also chortle at Lithuanian belts, perched so absurdly high that they highlight the lower body, the corporeal site of sin and filth. Lithuanians thus appear ruled by their genitals, not their hearts and heads.

Despite these internecine insults, both Hasidim and Lithuanians scorn Arab attire. They call the black band (*akal*) on the Arabic head covering or *kaffiye* a "Mohammedian *gartel*" (Aran 2006). This slur transforms the entire body of the male Muslim into base flesh. Underneath the outer façade of piety that clothes ultra-Orthodox Jews, we might say, lurks a bawdy undercurrent of comedic, vestimentary nastiness.

## HASIDIC CONSUMERISM

Men in the Lubavitch court, more so than their counterparts in any other dynasty, dress in hybrid garb that weaves tradition with modernity. They wear dark business suits during the week and caftans on the Sabbath and festivals. Most distinctively, Lubavitcher men put on black felt fedoras or homburgs (Figure 33), not fur hats, which they first acquire prior to their bar mitzvah ceremonies. This stylistic blend befits the Lubavitcher program of outreach to non-Orthodox Jews worldwide through the Chabad movement. (*Chabad* is a Hebrew acronym for *chochmah*, wisdom, *binah*, comprehension, and *da'at*, knowledge.) While other dynasties aim for a cloistered Jewish existence and dress the part, Lubavitch Hasidim move with relative ease in the modern world and thus favor slightly more contemporary clothing. Indeed, many Lubavitcher men aspire to wear not just any fedora but the rakish Italian Borsalino.

Yet all Hasidim bargain an uneasy relationship with consumerism. Hasidic Jews, as we might expect, largely spurn secular leisure. Instead, Hasidim

**Figure 33**   Young Lubavitch Hasidic man asleep at his studies in his characteristic fedora. Photo by author.

may splurge on their homes and clothing (Kranzler 1995: 38). Yet many Hasidim also snub coreligionists who lavish too much attention on attire and style. Satmar in one district of Brooklyn look askance at Hasidim in another neighborhood for evaluating a person's merit on the basis of fine clothing, wigs, and jewelry (Kranzler 1995: 81, 101, 173). Nevertheless, Satmar acknowledge that lavish displays of finery and dress improve the matrimonial prospects of their daughters, and so parents shop accordingly (Kranzler 1995: 184). Likewise, Satmar husbands purchase elegant outfits for their wives as "small tokens of our appreciation of their constant hard work of keeping the house clean and in proper shape; of bearing and raising our children" (Kranzler 1995: 175). Clearly, many Hasidim find it necessary to dress in support of the very conspicuous consumption they also dress against.

Polish Hasidim do not generally wear a *shtreimel* on the Sabbath and festivals. Instead, they prefer another fur hat, the tall black *spodik* (see Figure 26) or brown *kolpic* (Mintz 1992: 29). These hats are no less expensive than the *shtreimel*, and are similarly made from sable, mink, and fox. So concerned was the Gerrer rebbe with the exorbitant cost of these hats that he now allegedly allows his court only to purchase faux fur hats—or threatened to adopt fedoras if manufacturers raise the prices. At the other end of the spectrum of Hasidic consumerism is a Lubavitcher designer, Mendy Sacho, who recently opened a haberdashery in Toronto called Sartoria Sacho. He offers, among other services, to sew a touch of "funky" haute couture to the traditional *kapoteh* coat (http://kapotas.com). That the name and logo for Sartoria Sacho is written in Italian rather than Yiddish suggests that some Hasidim are not as immune to modern secular pretensions as their distinctively antiquated attire might otherwise suggest.

Hasidic Jews, as I mentioned earlier, often shop for new outfits in preparation for major Jewish holidays. Here, again, Hasidim partake of the very consumerism they reject. "In honor of the Holy Days," declared one Yiddish advertisement in Brooklyn, "With the help of God, May He be blessed, I announce to all my customers that I have received a great lot of beautiful doubled-breasted suits" (Poll 1962: 212–20). "In honor of Passover," advertised another shop, "the most beautiful double-breasted children's suits . . . Also, right-to-left underwear, also long underpants, women's gowns with long sleeves . . . With blessing for a kosher and happy holiday." Hasidim, much like their secular coreligionists, also seek to pray as fashionable Jews.

## THE TABOO TEXTILE

The biblical books of Leviticus and Deuteronomy, as we saw in an earlier chapter, ban wool and linen fabrics or *sha'atnez*. The classic rabbis elaborated greatly on these forbidden fibers. They also classified the law of *sha'atnez* as a *chok*, that is, a divine decree based on otherworldly logic that defies human understanding. But *sha'atnez* nonetheless commands considerable attention by Hasidim and other Haredi Jews.

Scholars trace the word *sha'atnez* to an ancient non-Semitic language. But the rabbis of the Talmud (B. Niddah 61b) and Mishnah (M. Kilaim 9:8) creatively derived the term from three methods of combining fibers: combing or hackling (*shu'a*), spinning (*tavui*), and weaving (*nuz*). Today, legal decisors or *poskim* understand the law to forbid any potentially permanent blend of wool and linen. The rule prohibits knotting and gluing, for example, but not buttons, snaps, Velcro, and, according to some authorities, zippers. Moreover, the rabbis restricted "wool" to the fleece of sheep, not camels, hares, goats, alpacas, angora, and other animals.

The rule of *sha'atnez*, also spelled *shatnez*, applies both to garments and any textile in direct contact with the body that confers some benefit, such as warmth. This includes handkerchiefs and towels but not, say, umbrellas. Strictly speaking, the law does not extend to furniture, rugs, tablecloths, and drapery. But the rabbis feared that a part of these textiles might inadvertently cover a portion of the body. A carpet tuft may cling to a pant leg. Thus the rabbis largely forbade Jews from utilizing any such items that include *sha'atnez*, especially if bare skin might brush against the fabric (e.g., B. Yoma 69a).[10]

The "benefit" clause of the *sha'atnez* rule allows merchants to sling taboo textiles over their shoulders and heads, but only for the sole purpose of carrying, never for shelter from rain or sun (B. Pesachim 26b). To avoid even the appearance of unlawfully using forbidden garments, a truly pious Jew would carry the items at the end of a pole. The rabbis also forbid Jews from selling garments containing minute quantities of *sha'atnez* to Gentiles (B. Pesachim 40b). Otherwise, another Jew might unknowingly purchase the item. But illicit blends can be made into burial shrouds since death, as I noted in an earlier chapter, releases Jews from all commandments (B. Shabbath 30a).

Violators of the *sha'atnez* rule, declares the Talmud (B. Makkoth 21a–b), are liable for a flogging. I know of no evidence that any Jews actually suffered this punishment. Indeed, I surmise that the rule of *sha'atnez* was confined for most of Jewish history only to rarified rabbinical conversations. After all, Jews in earlier eras often dressed in clothing made by non-Jews. Given the state of interfaith relations in premodern Europe (see Chapter 3), it seems rather unlikely that Jews expected, never mind demanded, compliance. Moreover, Jewish communal legislation about clothing, which I discussed in Chapter 4, consistently fails to mention the forbidden mixture (Daxelmüller 1995: 42). I doubt this silence arose from widespread observance. Rather, the rule largely faded from everyday practice except for the truly devout.

Today, the website for STAM, or Shatnez Testers of America, lists over sixty-five "laboratories" worldwide (http://www.shatnez.n3.n3t/).[11] Since each species of fiber has distinct properties, *sha'atnez* investigators snip small pieces of cloth from non-visible parts of garments, then run a battery of identifying tests. They peer through microscopes, observe the breaking points of threads, drizzle olive oil to separate the microfibers, and dye and dissolve the colors.[12] Then the tester may approve the garment, suggest necessary alterations, or ban it altogether. *Sha'atnez* testing is a part-time occupation, fueled by religious commitment rather than any promise of worldly wealth. Testers charge minimal fees for inspection and alterations, after which they may affix a *sha'atnez*-free label (Figure 34). The amount of business received by *sha'atnez* labs, remarked one rabbi, and the expense of the garments tested, serve as impromptu economic indicators of the Orthodox community.[13]

*Sha'atnez* generally, to repeat, refers to potentially permanent blends. Can a devout Jew therefore pull woolen garments over linen clothes, and vice versa? Not necessarily. Ashkenazi authorities permit this layering only if the inner garment can be extracted without also removing the outer item. According to this criterion, any mixing of shirts, blazers, and neckties poses little peril. One may also perch a linen-lined hat atop a wool yarmulke. But wool trousers, for example, could never be worn over linen undergarments.

Many shoes, according to Shatnez Testers of America, contain linen threads and so may violate the *sha'atnez* rule when slipped over woolen stocks. Yet some rabbis permit this combination, especially when the stitching occurs on the outside of the shoe. If the stitches are located on the interior, then it is best to cover them with tape. Rabbi Yitzchok Zev Soloveitchik,

Boston Shatnez
Laboratory

Brighton, MA   617-782-2624

All textile materials found
Non-Shatnez

Zvi Solomon
Member of
I.A.P.S.L

**Figure 34**   Non-shatnez certification label used by the Boston Shatnez Laboratory to confirm that garment had been found to be free of shatnez. Courtesy Rabi Zvi Solomon/Boston Shatnez Laboratory.

known as the Brisker Rav, took a more stringent approach. He only wore linen-stitched footwear over woolen hosiery after first cutting holes in the shoes so he could pull off his socks without also removing the shoes.

Garment labels are unreliable indicators of *sha'atnez*. In the United States, the Federal Trade Commission does not require manufacturers to list any fibers comprising less than two percent of a garment. An item described as "100 percent wool" might therefore contain a small amount of linen. Moreover, garment labels are not legally required to list the content of linings, trims, button threads, linen stiffeners sewn into collars and shoulders, and appliqués. For these reasons, devout Jews vigilantly examine their clothing and consult with testers. STAM advises careful checking of myriad items and features, including coats, patches, collars, cuffs, fleece-lined boots, wool sofas, fur coats, potholders, sleeping bags, baseball gloves, business suits, sport jackets, sweaters or jumpers, linen tablecloths, polyester neckties, and anything made with "reprocessed," "mixed," or "other fibers." STAM also warns devout Jews against wearing certain clothing lines known to contain *sha'atnez*, including styles from Ann Taylor, Armani, Banana Republic, Barney's, Brooks Brothers, Burberry, Eileen Fisher, Gucci, Polo, Prada, and Saks Fifth Avenue. Many *sha'atnez* laboratories periodically issue consumer alerts.

Sometimes *sha'atnez* causes a minor uproar. The flagship store of Zara, a Spanish clothing company popular in Israel, publically apologized in 2007 for selling suits that blended wool and linen.[14] The company offered to reimburse customers for the cost of removing the taboo blend. Even religious articles sometimes demand vigilance. In 2009, *sha'atnez* appeared in a particular style of prayer shawl, the so-called Turkish Tallis (although really made in Tunisia), favored by Hasidic men in the Skvere and Belz dynasties.[15] Ironically, Hasidim and other devout Jews look to modern chemistry and optics to make possible the fulfillment of a premodern dress code.

## CONCLUSION

During the first Intifada in 1988, a small group of women, appalled by allegations of human rights violations by the Israeli military, held vigil at a busy intersection in Jerusalem on a Friday afternoon, just prior to the Sabbath. Dressed in black, holding aloft a sign declaring "Stop the Occupation," this group, later called Women in Black, protested killings on both sides of the conflict. The movement quickly spread (www.womeninblack.org). Local groups of Women in Black have stood against neo-Nazism in Germany, racism toward guest workers across Europe, nuclear weapons in India, and ethnic conflict in Croatia and Bosnia. In December 2001, upward of five thousand Israeli and Palestinian women, all attired in black, marched in Jerusalem beneath banners stating "The Occupation is Killing Us All!" and "We Refuse To Be Enemies."

When Women in Black first gathered in Israel, passing motorists hurled insults and obscenities. They saw Women in Black as traitors to the Jewish people. Indeed, a rival and militant group, Women in Green, offers the far different mission of "safeguarding our G-d given Biblical Homeland" (www.womeningreen.org). Their hats signal a fierce opposition to any suggestion that Israel revert to the so-called Green Line, or the borders that preceded the 1967 Six Day War. This conflict allowed Israel to occupy—or rightfully regain, depending on your sentiments—the West Bank or, as the settler movement calls it, Judea and Samaria.

The strong response to Women in Black, I suggest, pertains to more than just the color of grief. In Israel, black clothing evokes the religious and political convictions of Hasidim and other Haredi Jews. In this worldview, black symbolizes the perseverance of Torah-true Judaism amid an immoral secular society. Black, too, conjures the destruction of the Temple and ensuing spiritual exile that will only cease with the advent of the messianic era.

Secular Jews in Israel see black rather differently. For them, the color evokes the unwarranted and appalling prominence of religious fanaticism in a modern society established on the secular ideals of the Enlightenment. From any perspective, a gathering of black-clad women on the streets of Jerusalem, on the eve of the Sabbath, is sure to raise hackles. Both groups, Haredim and Women in Black, dress in dark tones to mourn—but to very different purposes amid a never-ending conversation, often phrased in clothing, about the moral center of Judaism.

# Straps, Fringes, Snails, and Shawls

Women are moved by the physicality of a *tallit*'s embrace, as well as its talismanic power to protect.

Schnur and Schnur-Fishman 2006: 26

[S]he should strengthen her ties to Judaism through other means.

Henkin 2003c: 33

The Hebrew Bible mandates the attachment of fringes or tzitzit on Israelite clothing. Consequently, devout men dress all day, every day, in a tasseled undershirt (Figure 35). But most Jews wear fringes only in the synagogue, when they slip on a prayer shawl. Formerly, these ritual garments generally clothed men in dark-striped and white uniformity. Today, fringed wraps and scarves often transform the pews into a colorful patchwork that sews tradition to modern notions of taste, individualism, and egalitarianism.

Fringed garments also represent acculturation—to devout and acculturated Jews alike. Orthodox boys start wearing the tasseled undergarment or *tallit katan* on their third birthdays, during a rite called *upsherin*. This ceremony marks the transition from maternal care to male teachers (Bilu 2000). Boys also receive their first haircut during the rite, thus swapping feminine locks for masculine fringes. Despite this traditional symbolism, a young boy's *tallit katan* is now as likely to display Barney, Power Rangers, and Scooby-Doo as the Hebrew alphabet and Torah scrolls. This playful iconography harnesses pop culture to the reproduction of a traditional religious system that rejects those very same secular values. Indeed, these fringed undershirts represent Judaism as an irresolvable dialogue between tradition and modernity.

## EXACTING ESOTERIC STRAPS

Before I detail the symbolism of the fringes, I want first to decode the ritual boxes and straps equally crucial to a devout wardrobe. Prior to weekday morning prayers, we saw in earlier chapters, religious Jews, starting at age thirteen, lash a black box containing biblical verses around the forehead, and

**Figure 35**    Hasidic man in Brooklyn with a *tallit katan*. Photo by author.

another down the arm (see Chapter 2, Figure 4). The apparatus is called tefillin.

A religious scribe (*sofer*) inks the scriptural verses on parchment. The texts are folded, wrapped in cloth, tied with calves' hair, inserted into the leather cases, then stitched shut with sinews. Everything derives from kosher animals. Precise rules, as we saw in Chapter 2, govern the shape, color, and dimensions of the boxes as well as the manner of folding the parchment, the method of stitching, the knotting and width of the straps, and other details. As sacerdotal objects, tefillin demand careful etiquette. The penalty for accidentally dropping tefillin is a charitable donation or a period of fasting.

The myriad rules governing tefillin exemplify the legalistic outlook of rabbinic Judaism. Only Jews possessing clean bodies, as I detail shortly, lacking even perspiration, may "wrap" or "lay" tefillin. One dresses in tefillin before reciting morning devotions but after donning a prayer shawl. Ashkenazi Jews generally lay tefillin while standing; other Jews often sit. Wrapping must occur without interruption—not even, say some rabbis, a wink. Right-handed Jews position the box or "house" of the arm piece (*shel yad*) on the center of the left biceps, tilting slightly inward toward the heart; left-handers do the opposite. Some rabbis precisely arrange the lowest point of the box at the beginning of the muscle swell (never below it), so the uppermost edge of the case rests between the midpoint of the upper arm and the upper end of the swell[1]. After properly positioning the "house," one coils the black strap down the arm—seven times toward the body if Ashkenazi, eight times in the other direction if Sephardi or Hasidic. Next, the case of the headpiece (*shel rosh*) is arranged in the middle of the forehead, at the hairline. The straps encircle the head and drape down, from a knot at the back, over the chest. Last, the arm piece strap is wound around the hand.

Intriguingly, a recent article in the *Journal of Chinese Medicine* correlates the bodily location of tefillin with acupuncture points (Schram 2002). But Jews generally discern a different symbolism. Over the years, authorities devised at least four different hand-winding patterns: Ashkenazi, Hasidic, Chabad (Lubavitch Hasidim), and Sephardi. While each style engenders its own meanings, all four methods wrap the strap around the middle finger to symbolize the wedding of Israel to God (see Hosea 2:21–22). Often, this winding resembles the Hebrew letter *dalet* (ד). The coiling around the top of the hand forms a *shin* (ש), while the knot at the palm suggests a *yod* (י). Together, these letters spell the divine name *Shaddai* (שדי). The *yod* additionally alludes to the Tetragrammaton, or *YHWH* (יהוה), often pronounced *Yahweh*. Moreover, the knotted head straps resemble the letter *dalet*, the headpiece itself exhibits a *shin*, and the knot at the arm piece recalls a *yod*. These letters also spell *Shaddai*. Before prayer, then, a devout Jew doubly tethers himself to God.

The headpiece case actually displays two *shin* letters. One *shin* exhibits the normal three prongs. But the other *shin* shows four prongs. Nowhere else in Judaism do we find a four-pronged *shin*. The origin of this alphabetic curiosity remains unknown. But interpretations abound. For example, the two variants represent the two ways of ancient writing. The three-headed *shin* resembles raised ink on parchment, while the four-headed *shin* conjures, like figure to ground, a regular *shin* chiseled in stone. Alternatively, one *shin* represents the three Forefathers (Abraham, Isaac, and Jacob), while the other refers to the four Foremothers (Sarah, Rebekah, Rachel, and Leah). Rabbinic numerology, or *gematria*, reveals further symbolism. Each of the two *shin* letters designates the numeral 300. As a word, *shin shin* spells *shesh*, or "six." There are seven prongs total. Taken together, we arrive at the sum of 613, the exact number of commandments in the Torah. This way, devout Jews each morning enwrap themselves in the totality of the Law.

Twelve stitches, three on each side, attach each case to the base. These stitches symbolize the dozen angels surrounding the heavenly throne, the twelve Israelite tribes, and the number of months in the year. The seven arm windings signify the days of creation. The black color of the cases, which conceal white parchment, represent the yearning to glimpse, through prayer, some clarity into the mystery of God. Since no color mixes with black, tefillin also signify God's uniqueness. Jews wind tefillin on the left arm, which represents evil and temptation, to restrain our animalistic urges and human failings.

The headpiece straps drape downward to unite the upper spiritual and lower physical sides of existence. In the religious imagination, I am suggesting, tefillin bind Jews to the central precepts of their cosmos.

The two major styles of tefillin, named after the great medieval sage, Rashi, and his grandson, Jacob ben Meir, better known as Rebbeinu Tam, arrange the four biblical passages differently. Rashi tefillin, favored by Ashkenazi Jews, lists the verses as they appear in the Torah; Exodus 13:9–10, Exodus 13:11–16, Deuteronomy 6:4–9, and Deuteronomy 11:13–21. Rebbeinu Tam tefillin, however, worn by Hasidic and other Haredi Jews, reverses the order of the Deuteronomy passages. The reason for this medieval dispute is unclear. In one modern view, the final passage of the Rebbeinu sequence, the famous *she'ma* prayer that declares the unequaled oneness of God, reflects the messianic yearning for ultimate judgment (Emanuel 1985: 404–5). The Rashi version, by contrast, concludes with a poetic reference to divine loving-kindness (see also Kaplan 1975). A few devout Jews don both types of tefillin, sometimes at the same time—hedging their theological bets.


## CLEAN BODIES

Traditional Judaism holds tefillin as the privilege and obligation of men alone. The rabbis restricted tefillin to "clean" bodies unsullied by illness, impure thoughts, or flatulence (e.g., B. Shabbath 49a). Originally, this stipulation made no reference to gender. Later, however, some rabbis drew upon the cleanliness principle to bar women from laying tefillin since menstruation, in their view, evidenced an inability to maintain adequate bodily purity (Berger 1998). Many rabbis, too, judged women's use of tefillin as a forbidden act of cross-dressing that disrupts the "natural" balance of the sexes.

I propose a cross-cultural or anthropological explanation for traditional rabbinic unease with women enwrapped in tefillin. This explanation draws on my ethnographic experiences among the Iatmul people of Papua New Guinea (Silverman 2001). In many tribal and kinship-based societies, men dominate the political and religious systems yet ritually emulate female fertility. Of course, any direct expression of this envy would undermine the cultural prominence of manhood by acknowledging the general primacy of motherhood and uterine fecundity. Consequently, the official ideology of many cultures, including ancient Israel, defines menstruation as polluting. By barring women from full participation in key religious rites, men appear as the reproducers of society and the cosmos (see Margalit 2004; Silverman 2006). Judaism today is not tribal in any serious sense of the term. But ancient Israel was surely a tribal polity. And thus Judaism, like the Iatmul, endures not by actively recruiting new members or engaging in proselytizing, but through procreation.

Most Jews are born Jews. Until recently, moreover, Jewish identity was exclusively conferred through matriliny. Ritual privileges such as tefillin therefore sustain male privilege while both acknowledging and denying the reproductive prominence of women.

In fact, the prominent twentieth-century Orthodox theologian and philosopher Rabbi Aryeh Kaplan viewed the boxes and straps of tefillin as symbolizing the womb and umbilical cord (Kaplan 1975). Similarly, writes Rabbi Falk, men cover their arms and heads with tefillin while women do likewise with long sleeves and hair coverings (1998: 195–96). Moreover, the tefillin case is called a "house" (*bayit*) to parallel the home overseen by women. According to this logic, women have no need for tefillin. On them, the sacred objects would appear redundant. Worse, at least from a traditionalist perspective, women enwrapped in tefillin compromise the religious ideology of manhood.

Tefillin, too, must be worn in the morning. The early rabbis, however, exempted women from rituals timed to specific hours (e.g., M. Berakoth 3:3; M. Kiddushin 1:7). Some rabbis based this ruling on female inferiority. But others understood women to possess a superior sense of innate spirituality. Women, in this view, require fewer ritual prompts than men to shun temptation (see Berger 1988; Rapoport 2000). Why burden women, moreover, who are already so busy with their domestic chores, with additional tasks? And what could be more important than tending to home and hearth? Last, many rabbis censure women attired in ritual garments for impious and immodest flamboyance. At most, rules Rabbi Henkin, women may wear prayer shawls in private (2003c). In public, they must restrict themselves to the fringed undergarment (*tallit katan*)—so long as they conceal the tassels beneath their clothing. But no traditionalist today yields to any such compromise in regard to tefillin.

Some rabbinic texts do mention, without reproach, women laying tefillin (B. Eiruvin 96a–b; Cohn 2008: 113–18; Golinkin 1997). Likewise, some classic rabbis included women in the obligation to wear tzitzit fringes (e.g., B. Menachoth 43a; B. Eiruvin 96b; Cayam 1998). Yet the majority of authoritative rabbis, to repeat, barred or dissuaded women from both practices.

Early Jewish writings, argues Cohn, suggest that women once wore a unique amulet, comparable to men's tefillin, called, after the biblical talisman, "women's *totafot*" (2008: 117) (e.g., M. Shabbat 6:1–5; B. Shabbath 57b). These charms were akin to the magical cords mentioned in the Testament of Job, composed around the year 200. But all further references to women's *totafot* ceased by the Talmudic era. Early rabbinic texts also mention children wearing tefillin (e.g., B. Sukkah 42a). But this practice, too, long ago faded, partly out of concern for the sanctity of these objects (see Cohn 2008). Indeed, tefillin are never tossed in the trash. Damaged tefillin, like any tattered or discarded Hebrew text that contains the divine name, must be buried in a Jewish cemetery.

## TEFILLIN DATES

Rabbinic laws governing tefillin permit little variation other than size and quality. Tefillin range in price from $150.00 for the "bar mitzvah" grade to upward of $1,000.00 for large, hand-made, carefully inked, and proof-checked tefillin cut, moreover, from a single piece of flawless leather. But all tefillin cases are more or less plain, black, and square. The black straps exhibit no greater variation. Tefillin appear utterly resistant to change, and so aptly symbolize orthodox Judaism. The storage pouches, however, which lack any hallowed significance, could not be more different.

Most traditional tefillin bags are made from dark plush velvet, lined with white cotton, and sealed with a zipper. They typically display some minimalistic, Jewish-themed decoration, such as a Star of David or the Jerusalem skyline. But many tefillin bags now express individualism. Internet vendors sell all manner of tefillin bags: needlepoint, embroidery, hand-dyed silk, fabric appliqués, and so forth. Coby Classics of Cleveland, Ohio, offers chenille, tweed, and blue jean pouches, in a variety of colors and patterns such as paisley, houndstooth, royal crushed velvet, and leopard spots (www.cobycomclassics.com). Leather Exclusive stocks over 100 styles (www.leatherexclusive.com). Another online shop sells All Star Sports, Art Deco, Bat Mitzvah Rose, Fruit of the Vine, and Modern Star, among many other patterns (http://www.gonestitching.net). One retailer suggests selecting a style that matches your personality—say, ocean waves for nautical enthusiasts (www.tallitmaaven.com). They also sell "Eco-Friendly Textile options." Danke Judaica offers tefillin bags styled after the Pop Art movement of the 1960s (www.dankejudaic.com). A red and white case, evocative of Andy Warhol, incorporates the Hebrew word *tefillin* (תפילין) into a popular soft drink logo. "For the fun-loving Bar-Mitzva boy or Coca Cola fiend, this novelty Tefillin bag is sure to bring a smile to everyone's face." This pouch fuses Jewishness with entertainment and consumerism.

Many tefillin satchels now feature plastic materials, shoulder straps, various compartments, and a handle. Hard waterproof cases with camouflage patterns and built-in compasses, used to ensure proper orientation toward Jerusalem during prayer, seem far more suitable for wilderness expeditions than for the pews.[2] (The iPhone store offers several tefillin apps to assist with the proper placement of the headpiece.) In Brooklyn, I noticed tefillin bags adorned with stickers proclaiming the deceased rebbe of the Lubavitch Hasidic dynasty, Rabbi Menachem Schneerson, the messiah or *moshiach*.

Tefillin bags allow contemporary Jews to clothe their devotional commitments in individualism—that is, to make a statement.

Perhaps the best synthesis of modernity and tradition in this regard is the "tefillin date"—when a Modern Orthodox man totes his tefillin to an evening rendezvous in case he spends the night with his paramour (Berkovic 1999: 185; Winston 2005: 57). This way, he can fulfill both traditional and transgressive desires. And what should one bring as a gift to a potential lover? Why, chocolate tefillin, of course! While these *parve* (neither dairy nor meat) treats are generally marketed for bar mitzvah celebrations, and widely available on the Internet, I see no reason why they could not tempt other, rather less sanctified, events. And should you misplace your tefillin during your date, I add, you can post an announcement on TefillinFinders.com. There is much about this traditional ritual item that speaks to thoroughly modern tastes and practices.


## SYMBOLIC KNOTS

Modern fringes, even more so than personalized tefillin bags, speak to the hybrid nature of contemporary Jewish identity. I earlier intimated as much in regard to the appearance of cartoon characters on children's fringed undershirts. Religious Jews dress in these garments upon arising in the morning, after a ritual hand washing that starts the Orthodox day. In theory, one also recites a benediction which, in practice, most Orthodox Jews omit. Later, as they prepare for morning devotions, they utter a blessing over the large prayer shawl that also retroactively applies to the fringed undergarment.

Since the Torah, as I discussed in an earlier chapter, explicitly calls on the Israelites to *see* the fringes, many devout Jews understand the commandment as binding only, or minimally, during daylight. To ensure visibility, too, many arrange their fringes on top of their shirts and trousers. Other Jews disagree with this stance. They judge the point of the commandment simply to wear fringes, not necessarily to behold them. They may tuck their tzitzit inside their trousers—but over their underwear, of course, to protect the sacred from lower bodily defilement. Some Jews, too, look at the overt display of fringes as a sign of religious vanity. All Jews, however, must hide their tzitzit before the dead, including in cemeteries, to avoid slighting the deceased, who can no longer perform religious obligations.

A few Jews wear two sets of fringes, one concealed, the other exposed. Some strive for middle ground by winding their tassels around their belts or tucking them into their pockets. These accommodations might also serve a practical purpose since dangling tzitzit are allegedly prone to such modern hazards as getting caught in car doors, sprayed at the urinal, zipped in the fly of one's trousers, and snarled on bicycle spokes.[3]

Most rabbis define the minimum size of a valid *tallit katan* as one biblical *amah* in width by one and three-quarters *amot* in length. (An *amah* equals about forty-eight cm.) The *tallit katan* of a Haredi Jew often displays a black stripe as a symbol of mourning for the ancient Temple (Heilman 1992: 262). But while these garments symbolically point to the traditional past, they also exhibit modern ingenuity. NeaTzit, for example, a preshrunk cotton t-shirt with fringes, features patented stainless-steel snaps and "form-fitting design . . . You'll look fresh and composed all day!" Each NeaTzit contains special pockets to protect the fringes from unraveling during laundering. The garment also boasts "kosher certification from Torah giants." A rival shirt, Perftzit, lacks the sewn-in pockets—but one can always stuff the garment into a mesh Wash-Tzit Bag to protect the fringes from the washing machine. These items are all widely available on the Internet.

The larger prayer shawl, or *tallit gadol*, generally conforms to two styles, as noted earlier, the narrow scarf and the broad wrap. The scarf is easier to wear, less expensive, and lightweight. It often appears as a religious accessory to secular attire. Many rabbis and cantors wear this style to better suit the long vertical folds on their clerical robes. By contrast, the larger tallit enwraps the entire upper body, thus enclosing a Jew in the Law and heightening devotional focus. This garment evokes a greater sense of religious dedication than the scarf while nonetheless, we will see shortly, illustrating the modern value of expressive individualism.

A valid *tallit gadol* should drape fully over the shoulders, with the four corners—two in the front, two in the back—dangling below the waist. The tallit is not simply tossed willy-nilly over the shoulders. There is a precise procedure—which you can readily glimpse from numerous instructional videos on YouTube. Sephardi Jews first examine the fringes for any frays or mars that might invalidate the garment (Yitzhak 2006: 20–23). Then they kiss and gaze at the fringes, imagining, for reasons I will explain shortly, that the tassels are blue rather than white. Sephardi next unfurl the tallit and, holding the garment aloft in both hands, uninterruptedly recite the blessing. Silently, the tallit is placed on the head, and the two right corners swept over left shoulder; after a brief pause, the same is done to the left corners. Then Sephardi Jews unfurl the garment and pray.

Ashkenazi Jews tend to follow a different procedure. They also examine the fringes, sometimes with the tallit draped over the right shoulder. The garment is then unfurled and held aloft. Many *tallitot* display an ornamental band or "crown" (*atarah*) that contains an embroidery rendition of the appropriate blessing. You kiss the upper edge of the prayer, from the end to the beginning, and recite the benediction while swinging the tallit over your shoulders.

Some Ashkenazi Jews enfold the shawl over their head for a moment of private reflection. They may also sweep the corners over their left shoulder and clutch the fringes atop their heart. If you temporarily remove a tallit—say, before visiting the restroom, which is especially important if the garment bears the divine name—you need not repeat the benediction. But if the tallit falls to the ground, you must do so.

Interestingly rabbinic law is of two minds in regard to folding a tallit after Sabbath morning prayers. For some, folding along preexisting creases violates the Sabbath ban on "work." Instead, you randomly fold the tallit, or wait until after the Sabbath. For others, a Jew should always properly fold a tallit, even on the Sabbath, since it is a religious responsibility to beautify ritual duties.

For most Jews, any fabric suffices for a prayer shawl except the taboo wool and linen or *sha'atnez* blend. Yet some religious circles exempt the tallit from this prohibition (see Chapter 2). Some devout Jews also shun synthetics. The archetypal tallit consists of white woolen fringes attached to a white woolen wrap ornamented with black or blue stripes. These ritual garments may cost upward of several hundred dollars. Reform and Conservative synagogues tend to purchase low-priced, bulk *tallitot*, often made from rayon, acrylic, or polyester. These prayer shawls are typically slung on racks for use by congregants and visitors (Figure 36). Jews who regularly attend services, however, generally possess their own *tallitot*.

A legitimate tallit must satisfy several requirements. The fringes must be attached to four squared corners, two in the front, two in the back. No slits are permitted; you cannot, for example, attach fringes to a tuxedo coat.

**Figure 36**  Tallit rack in a synagogue. Photo by author.

The tallit must be made from a proper garment and not, say, a blanket. Only Jewish adults—males over the age of thirteen, women over twelve—can spin the fringes, provided they are not deaf, mute, or cognitively challenged. The fringes must be set into a garment large enough to encircle a toddler. And only Jewish men can traditionally attach the fringes although a "praiseworthy" wife, writes Rabbi Yitzhak, will inspect her husband's tassels (2006: 197). Last, a ritual fringe, as noted in Chapter 2, consists of eight strands tied into five double knots separating a precise number of loops. Ashkenazi fringes contain a pattern of seven, eight, eleven, and thirteen windings. Sephardi fringes display ten, five, six, and five. Lubavitch Hasidim and various other communities follow slightly different patterns (Figure 37).[4]

Tzitzit fulfill a divine decree but nonetheless embody no intrinsic holiness. One can toss ragged fringes in the rubbish bin. Still, devout Jews prefer to use old fringes as bookmarks in prayer volumes or as bindings for discarded holy texts awaiting burial. The fringes evoke, through the logic of rabbinic numerology, a rich symbolic algebra. The twenty-six loops on a Sephardi fringe equal the sum of the letters in the divine name *Yahweh*, or the Tetragrammaton (יהוה). The first two sets of windings on an Ashkenazi fringe, seven and eight, also convey an ancient significance. In biblical culture, as I show elsewhere, the number seven, drawing on the average length of menstruation, represented worldly creation, fertility, and renewal (Silverman 2006: 75–76). Eight signified the masculine, often ritual, transcendence of everyday reality—to wit, the consecration of male procreative potency during the circumcision rite staged on the eighth day after birth.

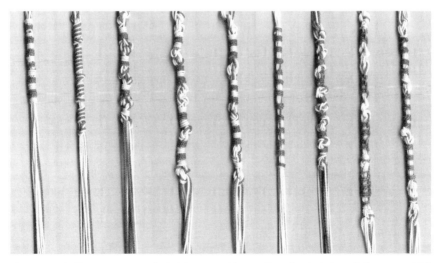

**Figure 37**   Different patterns of tzitzit loops and knots. Note the dark thread. Courtesy of Ptil Tekhelet and Baruch Stermn.

The fringes thus represent feminine, earthly fecundity as well as the superior realm of a male divinity.

The five knots on each fringe variously represent the Five Books of Moses, the dedication of all five senses to God, and the first five words of the famous *she'ma* prayer that declares the unparalleled uniqueness of God (Deuteronomy 6:4). The first two sets of Ashkenazi loops (seven plus eight) equals the numerical equivalent of the first pair of Hebrew letters in God's name *Yahweh*, while the third set (eleven) represents the last two letters. The final windings (thirteen) recall God's singularity by totaling the letters in the word "one" (אחד)—a term symbolically spelled from one (א) tallit and its eight (ח) strings and four (ד) corners. The thirty-two tzitzit strands on each prayer shawl equal the sum of the letters in the Hebrew word "heart." The thirty-nine loops do likewise for the phrase "The Lord is One." The eight strings, together with the five knots, total the Thirteen Attributes of Divine Mercy (Exodus 34:6–7). As I mentioned in Chapter 2, moreover, the tassels visualize the 613 commandments in the Torah. The fringes, in other words, again like tefillin, enclose Jews in God's moral order.[5]

Traditionally, men surround themselves with a "fence" of ritual accoutrements that include tefillin and tzitzit (e.g., B. Shabbat 118b). In a famous tale, a devout Jew tests his piety by visiting a prostitute (B. Menachoth 44a; Harvey 1986). Alas, he was not as pious as he hoped. But just when he is about to yield, his fringes slap him across the face! So impressed was the wayward woman that she converted to Judaism.

## KIND OF BLUE

Most fringes today are white. Nonetheless, the Torah calls for a thread of "blue" (*tekhelet*)—really, a deep indigo (Numbers 15:37–41). The ancients paid dearly for their blue. A gram of *tekhelet* in 200 b.c.e. cost the equivalent of $164.00 or an astounding $74,389.00 per pound.[6] Accordingly, only the wealthy and powerful dressed in blue and purple. Yet the Torah implies that all Israelites could afford a few blue threads. The indigo strand thus conveyed a powerful message in the ancient world about the divine election of Israel (Milgrom 1983)—or at least Israelite men.

In the postbiblical era, the rabbis added mystical symbolism to the blue thread. In the Talmud, Rabbi Meir famously interpreted the color through a series of associations that shift from earthly to heavenly: the blue resembled the sea, which recalled the sky, which evoked sapphire, which conjured the divine Throne of Glory (B. Menachoth 43b; the throne is mentioned in Exodus 24:10 and Ezekiel 1:26). The blue thread thus surrounded Jews with divine protection. Other rabbis devised a more ominous interpretation by tying the biblical word for blue, *tekhelet*, to the Hebrew verb "to destroy" (*kalo*). The color reminded Rashi of a darkened, punitive sky and the tenth Egyptian plague through linguistic similarity with the Aramaic term for "bereavement" (*tikhla*). For him, the blue thread invoked divine judgment, itself likened to the searing, inner part of a flame (Bokser 1963: 18–20). Despite this rich symbolism, few Jews today have worn, or even seen, a ritual thread of blue. The tassels long ago faded into nostalgia and yearning. As a memorial to the lost commandment, in fact, Jews added black, purple, or navy stripes on the tallit. What happened to the blue?

Ancient writers describe the blue dye as deriving from a marine animal called a *chilazon* in the Talmud (e.g., B. Menachoth 42b, 44a; B. Shabbat 75a). Unfortunately, nobody knows what it is. The Talmud offers only a few enigmatic clues: the *chilazon* lives in the territory of Zebulum, resembles the color of the sea and the shape of a fish, possesses a shell, and appears every seventy years. We also learn that the expensive blue dye was rare, made from the blood of the *chilazon*, manufactured at a Hittite town, and easily counterfeited (B. Sanhedrin 12a; B. Baba Metzia 61b; B. Menachot 42b–43a). Alas, these remarks allow for no definitive identification.

Rome restricted production of the dye to the ruling classes and generally reserved the color for the emperor and royalty (Bridgeman 1987: 160). Between the seventh and thirteenth centuries, the Levantine Coast experienced a series of traumatic upheavals—the Islamic conquest, Christian massacres of Jews, the rise and fall of Byzantium, the Crusades, and the ascent of the Ottoman Empire—all of which slowly reduced, then halted, the large-scale processing of marine creatures into blue dye. Thereafter, European Jews lacked the knowledge and the means to revive their blue fringes. The vanished color was best left, like the lost land of Israel, to the imagination.

In the latter nineteenth century, Jews renewed interest in both the land and the blue. Religious fantasies of rebuilding the Temple, and thus fulfilling the entire Law, fueled the search for the *chilazon* in the coastal waters of the eastern Mediterranean (e.g., Cohen ed. 1996; Spanier ed. 1987). In Poland, Rabbi G. H. Leiner, also known as the Radzyner Rebbe, identified the *chilazon* as the common squid-like cuttlefish (*sepia officinalis*). He enlisted an Italian chemist to produce a blue dye. Rabbi Leiner wrote voluminously on the topic, and attracted a sizable following. But not all religious Jews were convinced. The cuttlefish failed to satisfy several Talmudic criteria. The creature lacks a shell, for example, and its abundance hardly speaks to an ancient luxury. Most Jewish fringes remained white.

In the early twentieth century, Isaac Herzog, the chief rabbi of Ireland, wrote a doctoral dissertation at London University on *tekhelet* (reprinted in Spanier, ed. 1987). He discovered that Rabbi Leiner's chemist unwittingly introduced

Prussian Blue, a modern synthetic dye, into the process. Moreover, Leiner's blue seemed rather too purple to qualify as the sky blue known from Jewish traditions. But Rabbi Herzog could do no better with his own candidate for the *chilazon*, the *Murex trunculus* sea snail. The biblical blue remained a mystery.

Today, most scholars vindicate Rabbi Herzog and attribute the ancient blue dye to the colorless mucus secreted from the hypobranchial gland of the banded-dye murex snail, or *Murex trunculus* (Milgrom 1983; Ziderman 2008). Archaeologists, in fact, unearth vast middens of these snails at Bronze Age commercial sites throughout the eastern Mediterranean. Ancient manufacturers obtained biblical blue (*tekhelet*) and indigo (*argaman*) by steeping the mollusks in hot seawater baths, adding an alkaline reducing agent such as wood ash or fermented urine, and cracking the shells to extract the biochromes. The animals are plentiful but yield an infinitesimal fleck of color. In one experiment, twelve thousand snails oozed less than two grams of dye.

For decades, no technique could synthesize a sky blue hue from the murex snail. Darker violets were the best anybody could do. In the early 1980s, however, Otto Elsner of Shenkar College of Engineering and Design in Israel discovered the missing ingredient: sunshine. Wool dyed with the snails on cloudy days appeared purple. On sunny days, the dye turned blue (Sterman 1999). The key component is ultraviolet radiation. Professor Elsner rediscovered *tekhelet*.

In 1993, Rabbi Eliyahu Tavger of Jerusalem and several other devout Jews established the Ptil Tekhelet Foundation to produce trunculus-derived blue tzitzit strings (see Figure 37). Jews so inclined can now, after centuries of enduring white tassels, pray in blue. They can do so, moreover, with the aid of science, the hallmark of modernity so often seen as opposed to traditional Judaism. Indeed, notes Sterman, the blue molecule in murex dye absorbs light at 613 nanometers—the exact number of commandments in the Torah (1999).

Numerous papers in the online library of the Ptil Tekhelet Foundation vigorously defend the trunculus snail as the source of authentic *tekhelet* (www.tekhelet.com). But other Jews with a vested interest in fringes promote the cuttlefish and so-called Radzyner blue. After all, they note, the murex snail, like the cuttlefish, only partly conforms to the Talmudic description of the *chilazon*. The snail, for example, hardly resembles a fish. This debate, as in all matters pertaining to Jewish law, hinges on finely tuned conventions of rabbinic argumentation and linguistic nuance. (see, for example, McGovern and Michel 1987; Sterman 2002). When the rabbis likened the *chilazon* to a "fish," for example, did they narrowly refer to scaly oceanic vertebrates or broadly imply sea creatures in general? Acculturated Jews will hardly find such matters compelling. To pious Jews, however, this dispute is fraught with theological implications (Navon 2003–4). What if further research falsifies a particular blue dye? Would well-intentioned Jews who dressed in false fringes suffer divine retribution or forfeit some heavenly reward?

Proponents of murex-dyed blue tend to affiliate with Modern Orthodoxy, especially the pro-Zionist settler movement.[7] By contrast, Hasidim from the Radzin and Breslov dynasties favor Radzyner blue. (Most other Hasidim shun blue fringes until the messianic era.[8]) Despite these generalizations, no official dogma attaches to either fringe. Radzyner blue retails at online Judaica shops for as low as $16.95 (e.g., www.judaica.com). Many Christian retailers, such as Holy Land Gifts (www.shofartallit.com) and Messianic Marketplace (www.messianicmarketplace.com), also sell these fringes. Beged Ivri, the ultra-Orthodox organization devoted to rebuilding the "Holy Third Temple," which I mentioned in Chapter 1, also sells Radzyner blue, and thus ties these fringes to Jewish fundamentalism.[9]

Murex-dyed fringes are more expensive than Radzyner tzitzit. The Ptil Tekhelet Foundation sells three styles, ranging in price from $70.00 to $140.00. This group also sponsors snorkeling excursions to collect the snail, billed as "the ultimate family experience—combining Torah and fun." Some Judaica shops stock both types of blue fringes. But white fringes alone adorn the vast majority of Jews and prayer shawls. Blue remains a rarity—as if convention, even to the Orthodox, supersedes the Law, thus allowing most Jews to dress against divine decree.

## FEMININE TEFILLIN

Earlier, I discussed several traditional justifications for excluding women from certain ritual obligations. Today, many devout Jews reject these stipulations as *ex post facto* rationalizations seeking to maintain male dominance in religious Judaism (e.g., Berger 1998; Cayam 1998; Ross 2004). Women in many Conservative and especially Reform congregations now regularly pray in tallit and tefillin. Often, they seek neither to emulate men, and so violate the Torah, nor to challenge overtly male privilege. Rather, writes Wiesberg movingly, women dress in these ritual garments only to obey the commandments given to *all* Jews, in their view, but illicitly seized by male authorities (1992) (see also Berkovic 1999: 26–27). The high visibility of these items on women ironically belies the simple desire to pray, in Wiesberg's words, as an "unremarkable member of the congregation." Modern feminism, in other words, allows religious women to dress as traditional Jews.

In the late nineteenth century, Reform Judaism jettisoned tefillin as a religious obligation. Nonetheless, the movement promotes "religious equality" and therefore offers "no real objection" to women who wish to pray in tefillin or *tallitot*.[10] Any Reform synagogue that requires congregants to dress in ritual garments, moreover, must impose this rule equally on all adults. By contrast, Conservative Judaism formally classifies tefillin, head coverings, and prayer shawls as *obligatory* for men but *optional* for women (Berger 1998). A recent study, in fact, showed that most young women at a Conservative Jewish high school pass on wearing tefillin and *tallitot* (Kellner 2004). Any girl who wraps herself in these articles breaches both institutional and peer norms. She dresses entirely on her own. Yet two playful renditions of women enwrapped in tefillin seek to challenge this taboo.

Jen Taylor Friedman, a devout *sofer* or religious scribe and the first modern woman to ink a Torah scroll, wonderfully weaves together Jewish tradition, modern feminism, and American consumerism in her religious makeover of a Halloween Hip Barbie doll. Friedman dresses her Tefillin Barbie as a Modern Orthodox woman in a modest denim skirt, hat, prayer shawl with blue fringes, and tefillin (Figure 38).[11] Tefillin Barbie also carries a prayer book

**Figure 38**   Tefillin Barbie. Courtesy of Jen Taylor Friedman.

**Figure 39**    Rosie the Tefillin Wearer. Courtesy of Miriam Attia.

and a volume of Talmud. Similarly, Miriam Attia-Holt, author of the blog *Rose-Colored Glosses*, featured tefillin on the classic American icon from World War II, Rosie the Riveter (Figure 39).[12] Both religious portrayals of Rosie and Barbie seek to wrap women in ritual equality. Not all Jews, however, favor this refashioning. "Seriously disturbing," remarked one viewer on the Tefillin Barbie website, "like watching a car accident . . . disgusting."

Barbie and Rosie both pray in traditional tefillin. Other women, however, shun the canonical straps and boxes. Ayana Friedman designs oval-shaped, feminine tefillin ornamented with beads and gold threads and "made of synthetic fabric, not dead animal's skin" (Figure 40).[13] She also includes a new prayer for women. No Orthodox rabbi would certify Friedman's tefillin as valid. But that is precisely her point: to wrest away religious authenticity from traditional, masculine authority.

Some readers may scoff at Friedman's remark about "dead animal's skin." But the fulfillment of this leather-bound commandment poses an ethical quandary to devout vegetarian and vegan Jews. Rabbi Jordan D. Cohen,

**Figure 40**   Women's tefillin by Ayana Friedman. Courtesy of the artist.

the "Reb on the Web" (www.kolel.org), proposes several alternatives, including finely crafted wooden boxes and natural fiber straps. A Hasidic-trained scribe in Israel sells a different type of "vegetarian tefillin" (www.soferoftzfat. com). At first, he tried making tefillin from naturally deceased cows. But the leather often proved unsuitable. So he devised the macabre technique of using the hides of unborn calves that die by miscarriage or in utero when the mother also expires from natural causes. Either way, stresses the rabbi, no intentional killing occurs.

Traditionalists will surely sneer at vegetarian tefillin, Tefillin Barbie, and Tefillin Rosie. But these ritual innovations seek to dress age-old Jewish ritual in modern sensibilities. The same process of gendered renewal, I now show, vividly occurs on feminine prayer shawls.

## MATRIARCHS IN PASTEL

Today, many Jewish women pray in the very ritual fringes once deemed the prerogative of men (Emmett 2007; Herz 2003; Schnur and Schnur-Fishman 2006). Judaica shops now stock countless styles of prayer shawls woven expressly for women. What was once the unnamed white and dark-striped woolen norm, worn by most men for lack of any alternative, is now known as the "traditional" or "classic" tallit. This prototype now competes with hundreds of other colors, styles, and ornamental motifs—in wool, silk, acrylic, rayon, and other fabrics, in fact, in *any* fabric (www.greenfieldjudaica.com). You can purchase a complete tallit, often with matching bag and yarmulke, or order separate components—shawl, fringes, crown, satchel, and decorative clip to prevent the garment from sliding off your shoulders.

The tallit no longer dresses Jews solely for prayer. The garment now reflects personal taste and fashion, that is, quintessential facets of modern identity. Contemporary tallit styles, all readily available on the Internet, include Jerusalem in Blue, Twelve Tribes, Tree of Life, King David, Carmel, Seven Spices, Festivals, Jerusalem Wall, and Joseph's Coat. The governing organization of Conservative Judaism in North America, the United Synagogue of Conservative Judaism, devised its own prayer shawl—gold and burgundy stripes on white wool—with the official logo. One can even purchase a tallit displaying the Official Jewish Tartan (www.jewishtartan.com), registered with the Scottish Tartans Authority.

Women's prayer shawls are typically woven from silk, hand-painted with pastel colors, and decorated with delicate, curving figures and motifs (Figures 41–44). Common styles, all readily located on the Internet, include Miriam's Tambourine, Queen Bathsheva, Galilee Silk Pink Flowers, Four Mothers, Dancing Girls, Peace Shalom, Pomegranates, Sheaves of Wheat, Blossoming Tree of Life, Birds in Gold, and so forth. Judaica Mall sells Matriarchs in Color, Jerusalem in Silk, and Vista in Blue (www.judaica-mall. com).The Tallis Lady offers Renee, Eden, Alissa, and Sheera (www. thetallislady.com). Pray in Style sells Pink Roses, Silk Fruit, Earthtones,

**Figure 41**   Iris tallit. Copyrighted design by Nicole Curl and Jan Lanier of Silk Bijoux.

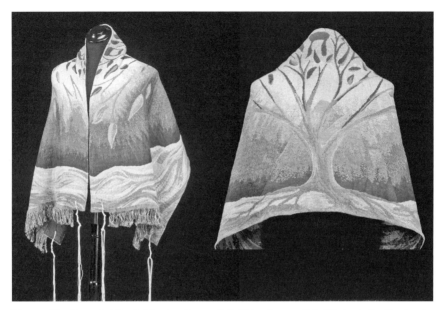

**Figure 42**   Tree of Life tallit. Courtesy of Debbie Secan, FabriChai; Seth Tice-Lewis, photographer.

and Celebration (www.tallit.org). All these *tallitot* aim for a distinctly feminine aesthetic that contrasts with the heavy wool and thick, dark stripes of the masculine tradition.

Women's prayers shawls, too, often convey an ethos of feminist empowerment. Edna Sandler Judaica has this to say about its Moon Tallit: "By adopting the moon as a symbol of womanhood, we reclaim the positive aspects of our female cycles . . . sanctify our bodies and celebrate the physicality of our lives" (www.tallit.net). During silent morning devotions called the *amidah*, men traditionally praise God, "who has not created me a woman." To this, the decorative crown of the Moon Tallit offers a rejoinder, "For I was born a woman." Tallit for Women echoes similar sentiments in describing their floral-patterned Teal Tallit: "The feminine vine of life that connects heaven and earth is within you, creating a delicate sense of balance that is both inspiring and everlasting" (www.talit-for-woman.com). These *tallitot* consecrate the very female fertility that traditionally excluded women from praying in ritual garments.

Many Jews voice deep emotional attachments to their prayer shawls (Smith, ed. 2005). "I have nice tactile memories," one congregant e-mailed me, "of the blue velvet embroidered bag my father carried to our synagogue." Despite these emotions, many men reach for *tallitot* out of rote or convention. By contrast, women find the act of enwrapping profoundly meaningful, and report feeling "swathed in God's love, wrapped in a huge hug, embraced in

**Figure 43**    Rainbow tallit. Courtesy of Debbie Secan, FabriChai.

warm and comforting folds . . . cradled, cushioned, loved, sheltered, swaddled, embosomed," and other expressions of nestled shelter (Schnur and Schnur-Fishman 2000: 26). These sentiments, of course, all evoke nurturing motherhood. Women, too, often see their *tallitot* as a form of artistic self-expression. "Your worship and beliefs are very personal," states Joan Richman at handpaintedtallit.com. "Your *tallit* should be also."

A quick survey at my own Reform synagogue, Congregation Beth El in Sudbury, Massachusetts, confirmed that many women knit personal meanings into their *tallitot*. A "lovely gift from my in-laws," said Marla Platt. A "prize possession," reported Lisa Breit, "hand-painted by an artist in Northampton." Several mothers told of attending tallit-making workshops with their daughters in preparation for a bat mitzvah. Cantor Lorel Zar-Kessler's elegant prayer shawl, uniquely tailored for women, resembles a vest that can fold and enlarge outwards, thus fitting the moment. Prayer becomes flexible, not staid. Pam Shira Fleetman tied ritual fringes to a crewel-work shawl she purchased long-ago while traveling in India. Helen Morrison Probst created an off-white tallit with contrasting tartan stripes to "honor" her paternal family's Scottish roots. All these ritual garments personalize the sacred while enveloping the congregation in colors, patterns, and sentiments unseen, and unfelt, in earlier eras. They also allow women to join men in prayer as equals—not merely to emulate men—and thus to resist the conventional masculine norms of

**Figure 44**   Raw silk tallit made in Israel by tallit-for-women.com. Courtesy of Tzila Amihud and www.tallit-for-women.com.

ritual decorum. Today, women's prayer shawls recolor the experience of prayer and thus the relationship between humanity and God herself.

## POLITICAL FRINGES

In the 1890s, the early Zionists transformed the tallit into a political banner by affixing a stylized Star of David onto on a white background with blue bands (Berkowitz 1993: 23–25). This emblem would later, after slight modification, fly as the official flag of modern Israel. The iconic hexagram on this tallit is often, yet fancifully, traced to King David's battle shield. The earliest appearance of the star in connection with Judaism dates to the biblical era. But the star did not begin to signify Jewishness until the medieval and renaissance eras (Oegema 1996: 129; Putik 1993). Still, universal association of the symbol with Judaism only emerged, argues Gershom Sholem (1949), in the nineteenth century when emancipated Jews, seeking a secular insignia for Jewish nationalism, rejected religious icons such as the menorah and took up instead the star (see also Oegema 1996: 115–20). The Israeli flag thus embodies, like many forms of Jewish clothing, the irresolvable tension between modernity and tradition.

That only men traditionally wore the prayer shawl clothes Zionism and Israeli nationalism in a masculine ethos. Ironically, women attired in the very same ritual garment now challenge that masculinity. In December 1988, a group of women assembled at the gender-segregated Western Wall in Jerusalem to chant aloud from the Torah, a sacred task reserved exclusively for men in Orthodox Judaism. They sang and prayed, some wearing *tallitot*, and opened a Torah scroll (Chesler and Haut, eds. 2002). This act of communal piety violated not only Jewish custom but also Israeli law. State security guards dragged the women from the Wall. *Haredi* Jews yanked away their prayer books. They were cursed, shoved, and spat upon—even called Nazis and blamed for the Holocaust. Men hurled chairs. A young girl was struck and hospitalized.

In Israel, the Chief Rabbinate governs Jewish religious sites. This ultra-Orthodox institution feverishly opposed the religious aspirations of the group now known as Women of the Wall or WOW. Women may pray quietly at the Wall, but not aloud lest they disrupt men on the other side of the partition. Nor may women appear at the Wall dressed in *tallitot* and tefillin, or chant from a Torah scroll. Women who do so are liable for fine or imprisonment.

WOW took to the courts in pursuit of the legal right to wear prayer shawls and chat from the Torah at the Western Wall (http://womenofthewall.org.il).[14] The state submitted statements from leading religious authorities. "This is definitely the work of Satan" declared Rabbi Avraham Shapira, the Ashekenazi Chief Rabbi. "They neglect their husbands and their children," said another. When the Israeli Supreme Court in 1994 issued a split decision, the Knesset or Israeli parliament formed a commission consisting entirely of men. They recommended that WOW pray outside the Old City altogether. Undeterred, WOW set up a "tallit table" in Zion Square inviting women to pull on prayer shawls and to utter the appropriate blessing. A *Haredi* man smashed the table. Even today, women are still unable to pray and dress as Orthodox Jews at the Wall.

Women attired in prayer shawls anywhere in Jerusalem, but especially at the Western Wall, infuriate the ultra-Orthodox establishment. To avoid verbal and physical assaults, some members of WOW disguise their *tallitot* as secular clothing. For several years, WOW sold the fringed undergarment or *tallit katan* (see Ochs 2002). The group now sells prayer shawls on its website. One style, called Four Mothers, depicts "Sarah, Rebekah, Leah, and Rachel" to provide a "uniquely feminine prayer garment that recalls these women and their spiritual significance."

In November 2009, police arrested a woman at the Western Wall for wearing a prayer shawl.[15] In May 2010, a man beat a young woman at an

Israeli bus stop.[16] He noticed marks on her arm and asked if they were made by *tefillin* straps. She said "yes."

## SACRED AND PROFANE

A tallit is holy. Its satchel is not. The liminal space in between is often filled with a unique, sometimes unexpected confluence of sacred and profane. A decade ago, Schnur and Schnur-Fishman explored the contents of women's tallit bags (2006). They discovered pacifiers, Tums, band-aids, recipes, lipstick, photographs, hair gel, Kleenex, personal keepsakes, candies, tea bags, even tampons and a bra. Women, in other words, filled their tallit bags with tokens of their children, bodies, and emotions. And inside men's tallit bags? Only prayer shawls.

In November 2009, I conducted an impromptu e-mail survey of my fellow congregants at Beth El in Sudbury, Massachusetts. What did they stuff into their tallit bags? Women reported:

- Bodily items such as hairbrushes, handkerchiefs, cough drops, decongestants, Tylenol, Lactaid, Sudafed, ChapStick, lip glosses, tampons, hair ties, eating utensils, and mints.
- Ritual items, including maracas for musical moments during services, extra yarmulkes (often for husbands), old High Holiday tickets and memory (*yizkor*) books, notes from Sabbath morning study classes, copies of previously chanted Torah portions, personal prayers, prayer books, and, for synagogue officiants, the names of congregants receiving healing prayers (*misheberach*).
- Children's amusements and necessities: disposable diapers, pens, pencils, notepaper, chewing gum, hard candies, granola bars, packaged cheese snacks, and small bags of Cheerios and crackers.
- Personal mementoes: a paper fan made by a little girl, photographs, dinner invitations, a father's old handkerchief, a mother-in-law's necklace, yarmulkes from a child's bar or bat mitzvah, a personal prayer uttered for a son while he attended college, a blessing recited at a daughter's bat mitzvah, "it will stay there, forever."
- And, last, an iPod.

I also received this playful response: "I'm not interested in having the contents of my tallit bag made public."

I received far fewer responses from men—perhaps, as a number of women grumbled, because men's garments often have the benefit of pockets. At any rate, men's tallit bags mainly contained religious and institutional items, such as a book about Jewish prayer, yarmulkes, hair clips, a small Hebrew-English copy of the Five Books of Moses with abundant marginalia, an old Israel Bonds brochure, and synagogue bulletins. Men also reported ibuprofen, Zantac, an envelop of photographs, and a handkerchief—but only in case someone else is moved to tears. I should also add another comment I received to my query: "I definitely heard of more than one nice Jewish boy who hid his dope stash in his tallit bag back in the 1960s and 1970s."

From iPods to tender keepsakes, the tallit bag today conceals and contains many layers of Jewish identity. Contemporary prayer shawls, too, I argued, weave together traditional meanings with thoroughly modern commitments to self-expression, consumerism, the search for personal meaning, and devotional egalitarianism.

## CONCLUSION

In 2009–10, the Jewish Museum featured an exhibition, *Reinventing Ritual: Contemporary Art and Design for Jewish Life* (see Belasco 2009). Several items addressed gender and ritual: Liora Taragan's "Wedding Dress," which includes a *tallit katan* to blend male and female; Jen Taylor Freidman's re-fashioned tank top as a *tallit katan* (perhaps also worn, in a smaller size, by her Tefillin Barbie); and Rachel Kanter's "Fringed Garment," a 1950s-style

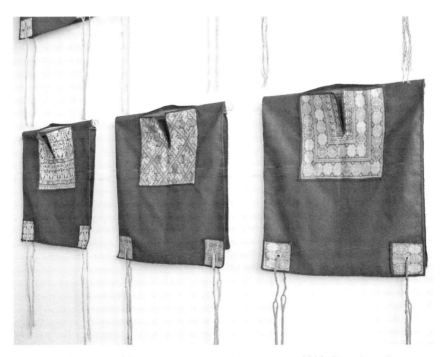

**Figure 45**    Garments of Reconciliation, made by Andi Arnovitz, 2009. Photo by author.

kitchen apron with tzitzit tassels (http://rachelkanter.com/tallit.html ). One item, a prayer shawl, commented on the wider Middle East conflict: Azra Aksamija's "Frontier Vest," a blue and white, bullet-proof, Kevlar flak jacket that doubles as a tallit or a Muslim prayer mat (http://www.azraaksamija. net/frontier-vest/). Similarly, at the Women's Studies Research Center at Brandeis University in 2010, Andi Arnovitz's vibrant installation Tear/Repair (*kriah/ichooi*) included "Garments of Reconciliation," a series of black vests ornamented with colorful tzitzit fringes and Palestinian embroidery (Figure 45). Arnovitz elegantly used traditional garments to powerfully redress the Middle East conflict.

Other recent attempts to clothe this conflict in new political garb involve the iconic black-and-white, fringed and checkered Palestinian headscarf called the *keffiyeh*. To some, this scarf represents a legitimate struggle for nationhood. To others, it signifies murderous terrorism. Yet the *keffiyeh* is often worn as an item of fashion and, indeed, street vendors in New York City hawk the garment in a bright rainbow of colors. Jews wishing to wear this wrap, but not wanting to conjure the Palestinians, can now purchase the *kaffiyeh yisraelit*, a fringed scarf ornamented with blue Stars of David (www.themagic wand.co.uk). A similar garment, the Israeli Keffiyeh, appeared to widespread

**Figure 46**    Israeli Keffiyeh. Photo by author.

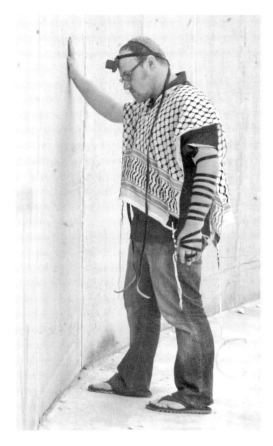

**Figure 47**   Tallit Katan Shel Shab-batai Tzvi created by Daniel Sierad-ski. Courtesy of the creator; Kitra Cahana, photographer.

press in 2010 (Figure 46). This scarf, too, displays fringes and Stars of David but also the Hebrew phrase *Am Israel Chai*, "The Jewish People Live" (www.shemspeed.com/thekef). The designers intended both scarves to compete with the Palestinian garment for prominence and authenticity. They seek to validate Jewish claims to the Holy Land through the idiom of ancient clothing, thus dressing Jews as indigenous Middle Easterners, not recent settlers. Of course, many Palestinians view the Jewish *keffiyeh*s as yet another example of the Zionist appropriation of their culture and land.[17]

Far different is the message offered by Daniel Sieradski, a young and brilliant Jewish-American online writer and activist who established several influential weblogs, including Jewschool, Radical Torah, and Orthodox Anarchist. Sieradski fashioned a prayer shawl from a *keffiyeh*, which he calls a *Talit HaKatan Shel Shabbatai Tzvi* (Figure 47).[18] This tallit aims at rapprochement, not appropriation or colonization. Indeed, Sieradski expressly intended his garment to dress Jews, especially Zionists who invalidate the Palestinian struggle, in the ideal of a common humanity. Why wear the ritual fringes, asks Sieradski rhetorically? "So that you should remember," he answers, evoking the rabbis, "that all of humanity are the children of Adam, that we are all created in the image of G-d, and that you should love your brother as yourself." His tallit enwraps Jew and Palestinian alike in a plea for universal human rights and dignity, and implores "mainstream Jewry" to abolish all walls, especially the controversial partition that now separates Israel from Palestinian territory.

In ways the classic rabbis could never have imaged, the tallit today represents consummately modern, and thoroughly contested, identities. The same is true, I now show, for perhaps the most obviously Jewish garment: the yarmulke.

# I ♥ Yarmulke Day

*Yarmulkas* must be black or dark blue, and at least size 5 or larger. *Yarmulkas* with names or logos are NOT allowed.

Dress Code, Yeshiva Chanoch Lenaar, Brooklyn, NY, www.yeshiva.org

This week's sign that the apocalypse is upon us: For $75 a sports memorabilia company in New Jersey has sold what it bills as yarmulkes signed by Sandy Koufax.

*Sports Illustrated*, May 15, 1995

What could be more Jewish than a yarmulke? Indeed, perhaps no other article of clothing so publicly and unmistakably signals Jewishness. Yet contemporary yarmulkes often display images and phrases far removed from traditional Jewish identity and rabbinic exhortations to piety. Yarmulkes now express personal preferences for sports teams, cartoon characters, rock-and-roll bands, hobbies, consumer goods—really anything. The yarmulke, in other words, wonderfully illustrates the ongoing tension between defining Judaism as a distinct religion, set apart from the wider society, and as just another ethnic group, defined by the very same generic citizenship and individualism embraced by everybody else, and so hardly distinct at all.

## DOES SIZE MATTER?

Devout Jewish men—today, some women—wear yarmulkes throughout the day, removing them, if at all, only for sleeping, bathing, and swimming. (Should a yarmulke fall to the ground, one simply picks it up and, perhaps with a slight kiss, unceremoniously replaces it.) So objectionably do some traditional Jews view bareheadedness that, as we saw in an earlier chapter, they don *two* head coverings. That said, Rabbi Moshe Feinstein, a leading authority on Jewish law, issued a twentieth-century ruling allowing Orthodox Jews to remove their yarmulkes in the workplace. Like all ritual garments in Judaism, the yarmulke conveys multiple meanings and expresses contrary devotional commitments.

No rules govern yarmulke fabrics except, of course, the biblical ban on wool and linen blends. But many Orthodox institutions, especially religious day schools, impose their own regulations in order to promote reverential decorum. Most religious Jews, too, I add, reject toupees as valid head coverings, and permit the use of hands and arms only for mundane tasks in unusual circumstances. Does Jewish law prescribe a minimum size for a yarmulke? This question receives considerable deliberation (e.g., Morris 2006). In one view, a legitimate yarmulke minimally covers the majority of the pate.[1] Yet another authority offers a more subjective ruling: any yarmulke is valid so long as one can rightly say that it "covers" the head. For profane tasks, pronounces a third rabbi, the yarmulke must be visible from all sides. Prayer, however, necessitates a larger cap. Rabbi Hillel Posek offers perhaps the most precise response (Zimmer 1992: 350). A proper yarmulke must cover the equivalent area of the head that would be left *un*covered after laying two headpieces of tefillin.

Recently, several rabbis in Israel railed against the increasing popularity of small yarmulkes among the ultra-Orthodox (Zimmer 1992: 350). One rabbi even attributed the high rate of Israeli automobile fatalities to this impious attire. Yet Rabbi Ovadia Yosef ruled as sufficient any size yarmulke, at least for everyday activities in Israel. In the diaspora, however, small yarmulkes sinfully "emulate the ways of the Gentiles" (see Chapter 2). Similarly, many Orthodox rabbis forbid men from wearing yarmulkes that match the color of their hair lest they give the impression of striving to pass as a non-Jew or a secular Jew.

In practice, all these regulations pertain solely to strictly observant or *frum* communities, where male head coverings form an essential part of the daily wardrobe. By contrast, Conservative Judaism requires men to wear yarmulkes only for prayer, synagogue activities, and the study of religious texts. Conservative women may also wear yarmulkes, but merely as a personal preference and not, recalling the ruling on prayer shawls and tefillin, as a compulsory obligation. For years, Reform Judaism rejected ritual head coverings. Today, however, many Reform congregations require yarmulkes on anybody, male or female, who chants from the Torah or guides religious services. For all other purposes, including prayer in general, head coverings are optional in Reform synagogues. In short, yarmulkes do more than simply communicate generic Jewishness. They express a Jew's personal preference for Judaism, thus balancing communal needs with individualism.

## FROM CUSTOM TO LAW

The Torah never orders the Israelites to dress in headgear with the sole exception of priests. But the elaborate mitres of the priesthood conveyed no religious meaning. These hats simply signified, as throughout the ancient world, ceremonial rank. Clearly, Jewish men took up caps after the biblical era.

But when? The postbiblical literature detailing the Maccabean revolt in the second century B.C.E., celebrated by the festival of Chanukah, briefly mentions caps. Traditional Jewish leaders, we read, furiously objected to a campaign of Hellenization that included efforts to induce "the noblest of the young [Jewish] men to wear the Greek hat" (2 Maccabees 4:12). But the tale never indicates that these caps replaced Jewish headgear. A few hundred years later, the New Testament similarly provides no evidence for Jewish hats. In fact, first-century Jews prayed bareheaded (2 Corinthians 3:15–16). Indeed, while the Apostle Paul relentlessly berated Jews for their distinctive bodily practices—specifically, circumcision, the dietary laws, and the Sabbath rest—he never mentioned hats.

The Mishnah is equally silent on the matter. Only in the Talmud do we first find sustained comments about Jews and head coverings. But the Talmud speaks to the issue infrequently and inconsistently. The tractate Kiddushin, for example, places head coverings on certain rabbis as well as on married men judged "great." We occasionally read about "covered" prayer (B. Berachoth 60b; B. Shabbath 10a). Most famously, Rabbi Huna declared, "May I be rewarded for never walking four cubits [about two meters] bareheaded" (B. Shabbat 118b). Why? Because the Shekhina, Rabbi Huna declared, or the feminine manifestation of God, "is above my head" (B. Kiddushin 31a). Despite these offhand remarks, the Talmud nowhere mandates head coverings as a condition of divine Law. Indeed, "Men sometimes cover their heads and sometimes not" (B. Nedarim 30b). The only reasonable conclusion for the Talmudic era is that head coverings were optional expressions of private belief and etiquette, unrelated to any communal norms for ritual or prayer. Moreover, all relevant Talmudic comments refer solely to Roman garments, never to any hats that seem characteristically Jewish.

Male head coverings originally seemed restricted to the Babylonian diaspora (Zimmer 1992: 327). But slowly, the practice spread to Palestine and beyond (Lauterbach 1928/1970: 231; Zimmer 1992: 329). Or, as Krauss sees it, head coverings arose haphazardly throughout the Jewish world during the medieval era (1945–46/1970). Regardless, Jewish men did not widely adopt hats until the fifteenth century, when Rabbi Israel Bruna issued a responsum, or legal pronouncement, declaring male bareheadedness a violation of religious law (Zimmer 1992: 333–35). But why then?

Perhaps Rabbi Bruna could no longer suffer the degrading edicts that for centuries aimed to besmirch Jews with derisive dress (Zimmer 1992: 334–35). Simply put, he had had enough. But the largely powerless rabbis had few options to voice their discontent with the dominant society lest they invite further persecution. Within these constraints, the rabbis perhaps resisted domination by transforming their experience of vestimentary apartheid into a condition of Jewish law. No longer would Europe push Jews to the margins of society and fashion. Now Jews would dress themselves to reject the wider, non-Jewish world. "We dwell," wrote Rabbi Israel in fifteenth-century Moravia, "among the nations that go bareheaded" (Woolf 2000–1: 55). To stand apart, Jews would henceforth wear hats and anchor this practice to the Torah, not the church. From the threads of custom, to invoke Lauterbach, the rabbis spun hats into defiance, and then into Law (1928).

The rabbis did not, however, yet spin yarmulkes. Illuminated Hebrew manuscripts from the latter Middle Ages show Jews in a wide variety of headgear (Metzger and Metzger 1982). Yet many Jews, especially in France and Germany, still went bareheaded, even during prayer. In the fourteenth century, Rabbi David ben Judah the Pious sternly rebuked any Jew who prayed with an uncovered head, declaring "woe to his soul . . . This is a practice of the cursed [Christian] nations among whom they assimilated . . . they conduct themselves in a degrading manner due to haughtiness and pride by standing bareheaded before the Almighty God" (Zimmer 1992: 333). But despite the severity of this denunciation, Jews did not uniformly view head coverings as an absolute masculine obligation until the mid-sixteenth century publication of Rabbi Joseph ben Ephraim Caro's codification of Jewish law, the *Shulchan Aruch*.

Nonetheless, many Ashkenazi men continued to pray bareheaded. Even Rabbi Caro's contemporary, Rabbi Solomon Luria, admitted "I do not know of any prohibition against praying with uncovered head" (Lauterbach 1928: 236). As late as the eighteenth century, Rabbi Elijah ben Shlomo Zalman, the famous sage or *Gaon* of Vilna, could only justify devotional hats on the basis of "good manners" (Zimmer 1992: 335). How, then, and when, did the yarmulke gain its iconic status as the central garment of Jewish masculinity? It is to that puzzle that I now turn.

## THE APOTHEOSIS OF THE YARMULKE

Scholars disagree on the origins of the word *yarmulke*. Older, now discredited etymologies traced the term to the Ottoman Empire and a Turkish "rain-cover" (*yagmurluk*) or to the old Germanic country fair (*Jahrmarkte*) allegedly popular with Jews (Plaut 1955). In reality, the word derives from an ecclesiastical hood worn by the medieval church, a garment called an *almucia* in Latin or, in its diminutive form, *almucella* or *armucella*. The latter was often pronounced *armukella* (Gold 1987; Plaut 1955). Over time, the term came to connote a generic hat. In the eighteenth century, Yiddish-speaking Jews in Eastern Europe borrowed some variant of the word, which now became known as a *yarmulke*. From this point onward, the cap and term conveyed an unmistakable Jewish affiliation.

Jews in Poland and Central Europe, however, continued to refer to the small cap by another Yiddish term, *kapl*, which survives today only in southern Britain (Gold 1987: 183). Today, British Jews sometimes speak of a *"cupple,"* a term unknown to most Americans. Most Jews now refer to the small ritual cap as a yarmulke or, using modern Hebrew, a *kippah* or *kipa*.

Of course, as we saw in the previous chapter, devout Jews generally prefer Jewish origins for their garments. Hence, they often derive the term *yarmulke* from the Aramaic phrase "god-fearing" or *yare melakhim*. But in truth, the yarmulke largely owes its existence to non-Jews. Let me elaborate.

In the latter nineteenth century, Reform Jews officially doffed hats in the synagogue as part of a wider effort to modernize Judaism—to dress, in short, like other citizens. In response, Jews who rejected acculturation retained their caps as a sign of fidelity to tradition. They also wore conspicuously large yarmulkes. When Reform Jews tossed aside religious headgear as an antiquated custom, in other words, Orthodox Jews responded by looking upon bareheadedness as a repudiation of divine Law. The presence or absence of a hat now served as a self-conscious sign of a male Jew's relationship to traditional Judaism. Indeed, Rabbi Shlomo Kluger ruled ingeniously in the Ukraine that all earlier edicts seemingly assenting to bareheaded prayer actually intended *only* to permit Jews to forgo hats, never their yarmulkes. Bareheadedness was a figure of speech (Grossman 2010: 131). The head must *always* be covered—minimally with a yarmulke. In fact, some devout Jews actually *forged* head coverings in republished portraits of originally hatless Orthodox clergy (Rabinowitz 2007). Thus the original engraving of Rabbi Moshe Hefez Gentili that appeared on the frontispiece of his 1710 commentary on the Torah, *Melekhet Mahashevet*, depicts no head covering, as befitting the era. But in the second and posthumous edition of the book, published in 1860, Rabbi Gentili miraculously appears in a large yarmulke.

Initially, debates over head coverings pertained only to prayer and the synagogue since social convention required all men, Jewish and otherwise, to appear becapped in public. Hats could not distinctively characterize religious Jews until other men removed their caps as a matter of everyday protocol. (*The New York Times* first mentioned Jewish "skull-caps" in 1874, "it being one of the points of Hebrew etiquette to have the head covered on ceremonious occasions, dinner-parties included"—that is, indoors.[2]) And this innovation did not occur until the early to mid-twentieth century. In this respect, the religious symbolism of Jewish hats and yarmulkes arose from the most irreligious force of modernity: secular fashion.

Pictorial evidence suggests that yarmulkes were in little use prior to the modern era. Rabbinic portraits from the seventeenth century display a wide variety of headgear, including fur caps, turbans, and berets (see Cohen 1998, chapter 3). Jewish portraits from the American colonies show no yarmulkes

(Brilliant, ed. 1997). At the turn of the twentieth century, Orthodox and Con-servative Jews dressed in all manner of hats, including bowlers, top hats, fedoras, pillbox hats, and peaked caps, but rarely yarmulkes. We see few yarmulkes depicted on early twentieth-century American Jewish New Year cards (Smith 2001), or in nineteenth-century Passover religious guides called *Haggadot* (Yerushalmi 2005), or in photographs from Eastern Europe before the Holocaust or Shoah (e.g., Avrutin, et al. 2009; Levine, ed., 2002). Like-wise, two early twentieth-century surveys of religious practices among Reform Jews in America never mentioned yarmulkes.[3] In the main, Jews wore local hats. The yarmulke existed, to be sure, but only as an occasional garment worn by some Jews and not as a universal icon of Jewish manhood.

In the 1880s, as I discussed in Chapter 5, a young Hungarian rabbi, Moses Weinberger, penned a scorching indictment of American Jewry. But Weinberger wrote nothing about exposed pates. Were American Jews scrupu-lously observant about religious head coverings? Of course not. Rather, most Jews in America adopted secular fashion which, at that time, included hats. For this reason, turn-of-the-century literary descriptions of immigrant Jews, which often remarked on tefillin and prayer shawls, scarcely mention yar-mulkes. Likewise, the Anglo-Jewish Historical Exhibition of 1887, which por-trayed the history of English Jewry through the display of twenty-six hundred objects, included betrothal rings, amulets, tefillin, and prayer shawls but no yarmulkes. Most Jews in England dressed to resemble, as in America, their non-Jewish neighbors.[4] They wore hats as citizens, not as Jews.

The first European synagogue to declare men's head coverings an op-tional ritual accessory was probably the Berlin Genossenschaft für Reform im Judentum in 1845. In Hungry, Rabbi Aron Chorin scorned headgear as an "Oriental" custom ill-suited for enlightened Europeans (Zimmer 1992: 341). In New York City, Temple Emanuel formally institutionalized uncovered male prayer in 1874. Other Reform temples in the United States soon did likewise. Several decades later, Rabbi Lauterbach issued a famous Reform responsum validating bareheaded prayer (1928). The appearance of men's heads, like the state of their genitals amid heated debates over the relevance of ritual circumcision (Silverman 2006: 17–87), suddenly split Jewry into two bitterly feuding camps.

The rabbis of old, we saw in earlier chapters, repudiated asceticism and ad-monished Jews to honor God by dressing in pleasant outfits. In the Victorian era, many Jews dressed formally for religious events. The October 1895 issue of *The American Jewess* featured an engraving of Orthodox men parad-ing with Torah scrolls during Yom Kippur services.[5] They dressed in prayer shawls as well as in fashionable knee-high boots, Prince Albert frocks, and top hats. (Today, the Jewish Center, an Orthodox synagogue in Manhattan, still requires officers to dress in formal wear for Sabbath services.[6]) In this elegant yet sanctified setting, a yarmulke would surely have appeared woefully diminished in moral and civic stature.

To summarize, I pin the birth and apotheosis of the yarmulke as the signal garment of Jewish masculinity on the rise of Reform Judaism and especially on two shifts in early twentieth-century fashion, namely, the general decline of formal attire in the synagogue and the banishment of hats from men's everyday attire—that is, sometime around the 1930s.[7] Folklore traces the demise of men's hats in the United States to John F. Kennedy's 1961 presidential inauguration. Yet Kennedy did, in fact, wear a top hat for most of the event. He doffed his hat only prior to the inaugural address, while sitting beside and chatting with outgoing President Eisenhower—who did likewise. After speaking to the nation, Kennedy replaced the hat for the inaugural parade and, later, the inaugural ball. The decline of hats long preceded President Kennedy.

The earliest appearance of the word *yarmulke* in any major American newspaper was in 1946, when *The New York Times* described the attire of Mayor O'Dwyer, who attended the groundbreaking ceremony for the Rego Park Jewish Center in Queens, New York.[8] For it was only in the 1940s, I suggest, that Jews and non-Jews could first truly notice this garment *in public* as a distinguishing sign of traditional Judaism. Any years earlier and Mayor O'Dwyer would likely have donned a formal hat. But in 1946, long before Kennedy's inauguration, he wore a yarmulke.

As early as 1925, Jewish caterers included yarmulkes in their wedding packages (Joselit 1994: 28). But yarmulkes did not become a major retail item until mid-century when, now enshrined as the *de rigueur* sign of respect for Jewish tradition, the *"yarmulke* cult," as Abraham Duker called it, firmly took hold (1949–50: 375). No other hat would suffice. But as I have shown, this textile token of tradition arose from thoroughly modern trends in Judaism and secular fashion.

## YOU ARE WHAT YOU WEAR

Several types of yarmulkes emerged during the second half of the twentieth century, each generally representing a particular religious and often political affiliation. Consider, for a noteworthy example, the small crocheted or knitted yarmulke called the *kippah serugah*, which gained popularity in Israel in the 1950s (Figure 48). These yarmulkes first appeared among members of Bnei Akiva, a fervently nationalistic and Orthodox youth organization (www.bneiakiva.org). These yarmulkes represent religious Zionism.

The *kippah serugah* is known for its colorful designs, which often include the owner's Hebrew name (Baizerman 1992). Sometimes the patterns visually express personality types—say, subdued motifs for businessmen or

**Figure 48** Stack of yarmulkes in the *kippa seruga* style. Photo by author.

bright hues for extroverts. Men may even request a new such yarmulke to match a recently purchased pullover or shirt. Most *kippot serugot* are crocheted by women for kin, friends, and especially romantic interests. In fact, the gift of a *kippah serugah* often conveys the desire for courtship, even marriage. Young women, writes Berkovic, "spend hours poring over and discussing the intricacies of the patterns the same way a man dissects a page of *Talmud* . . . it amounts almost to sexual foreplay as they think about the man they are crocheting a *kippah* for" (1999: 164).

Men who wear the *kippah serugah* display a fierce devotion to the Israeli Defense Forces and disproportionately enlist in the infantry. Yet the military voices concern that these soldiers might refuse orders to dismantle illegal settlements defended by men wearing the very same yarmulkes (Cohen 2007). Not surprising, secular Jews in Israel see the *kippah serugah* as a symbol of dangerous fundamentalism and religious fanaticism. But Hasidic and Haredi Jews, who view secular Israelis and religious Zionists with equal distain, dismiss the *kippah serugah* as a frivolous masquerade of piety.

To many American Jews in the Conservative and Reform movements, the *kippah serugah* often and ironically evokes a countercultural ethos.

Liberal Jews, too, may wear the *Bukharan* yarmulke, often called a *Bokhara kippah*, that originated in Central Asia. These large needlepoint caps resemble pillbox hats. They display vivid colors and baroque patterns, sometimes enhanced by tiny sewn-in mirrors, and communicate a hip and artsy demeanor. They also celebrate ethnic pluralism by loosely conjuring romanticized notions of non-European or indigenous Jews. When worn by women, these yarmulkes may additionally signal a liberal feminist outlook.

Modern Orthodox Jews tend to wear small, often knitted and colorful yarmulkes. These *kippot* represent, I propose, an acceptable compromise between ultra-Orthodox hats and bareheaded Reform Jews. The Modern Orthodox also prefer what Israelis sometimes call "American *kippot*," that is, plain suede or leather yarmulkes. To Traditional Orthodox and Hasidic Jews, however, any small yarmulke betokens a diminished sense of religious commitment and an illegitimate liberalism. Instead, Haredi men prefer large, black, velvet or satin yarmulkes covered, we have seen, by a black hat. (Other Jews unflatteringly call Haredim "black hat Jews" or "black yarmulke Jews.") These hats, writes Heilman, signify the weighty responsibility of marriage that rests upon the "head" of the household (1976: 54–57). Over time, the hat rubs a dull sheen into the yarmulke that connotes the strict, scrupulous observance of Jewish law.

The placement of a yarmulke and hat, and not just the style, may also convey denominational and political significance. Traditionalists tend to push the yarmulke toward the front of the head; liberals toward the back. Among yeshiva students, who typically dress in dark jackets and trousers, leather shoes, and white shirts, the slight tilt of a black hat conveys an attitude of youthful *insouciance* (Helmreich 1982: 148). The yarmulkes of religious Jews never show creases, the telltale hints of lax Jews who rarely wear their yarmulkes and instead stuff them, folded and forgotten, in their pockets and bureaus.

A fringe, splinter sect of Breslover Hasidim devised their own pseudo-yarmulke style. These large, crocheted, typically white and tasseled hats display the Hebrew mantra, *Na Nach Nachma Nachman Me'uman*. This incantation derives from the name and birthplace of Rabbi Nachman of Breslav (1772–1810), the eponymous founder of the Breslover court. Followers of the group, called Na Nachs, sing the magical mantra while ecstatically dancing to blaring "techno-Hasidic" music in order joyfully to hasten the messianic redemption.[9]

Reform Jews, recall, removed their hats in the nineteenth century and even banned caps in some synagogues. In 1955, the Ritual Committee of the Reform movement in the United States unequivocally declared yarmulkes to be antithetical to modern etiquette: "in our time, and in this land, it is the very best of manners to express respect by uncovering the head, [so] we should think it an act of willful and useless self-isolation when an American Jew chooses to make of the skull-cap an important symbol of Jewish piety." Yet Reform Jews today, men and women alike, increasingly take up this symbol during prayer. In an earlier era, Jews feeling too Jewish joined the Reform movement. Today, many Reform Jews evidently feel not Jewish enough, and so ironically, even controversially, seek to revive the Jewishness they once abandoned.[10]

The few women who wear yarmulkes outside the synagogue report considerable anguish and struggle (e.g., Ner-David 2002; Wages 2001). Of course, most Orthodox congregations reject female yarmulkes as an unseemly feminist intrusion. "According to Kabbalah," states a Hasidic website, "the feminine soul" is uniquely attuned to spiritual matters and thus women require nothing "so superficial" as a yarmulke (or tefillin as we saw earlier) to remind them of their "innate connection with G-d."[11] A woman's modest hair and attire, in this view, as well as her natural gift for domesticity and child raising, amply attest to her dedication to the Law. Thus phrased, yarmulkes are not a right denied to women. Rather, yarmulkes evidence men's inherent wrongs.


## PERSONALIZING THE SACRED

In Conservative and Reform synagogues, as I noted in Chapter 5, Jews and others can readily borrow yarmulkes from public bins or baskets. These yarmulkes—unadorned white or black, made of taffeta or rayon, and unlined—retail online for about $30.00 to $40.00 a gross. Many synagogues and catering halls in the mid-twentieth century provided stacks of cheap, white, crêpe paper yarmulkes for major ritual events. Worn once, they were tossed in the trash.[12] (Such items still exist at shrines in Israel, such as the Western Wall, one of which I recently saw auctioned on eBay.) In the synagogue today, paper caps would seem downright uncouth—unless the yarmulke was manufactured, as I discuss shortly, from recycled cardboard.

In the 1940s, the hosts of large Jewish occasions in the United States, such as weddings and bar mitzvahs, started purchasing glossy satin or plush velvet yarmulkes, often lined with cotton and frequently bordered by faux silver or gold filigree. These yarmulkes likely originated with caterers as part of the overall wedding and bar mitzvah package (Duker 1949–50: 379). This style would eventually dominate American synagogue celebrations. Guests wear these yarmulkes during the religious service, then take them home as souvenirs. The distinguishing feature of these keepsakes, which has changed little over the past sixty years, is an imprint on the lining that records the names of the honorees, the date and type of event, and the location (Figure 49).

Personalized yarmulkes, no less than the ritual occasions they commemorate, symbolize the retention of Jewish tradition—even if that tradition was only recently invented, as in the case of the bat mitzvah as well as the yarmulke itself. But the formulaic autograph transforms tradition and community into a celebration of unique lives and fortunes. Personalized yarmulkes, too, signaled

**Figure 49**   A personalized yarmulke. Photo by author.

the material successes of American Jews as they ascended into the middle class during the postwar era. By the 1970s, personalized yarmulkes seemed almost obligatory for any large celebration among acculturated American Jews.

Today, synagogue bins brim with imprinted yarmulkes, as do the hall clos- ets, living room hutches, kitchen drawers, and automobile glove compart- ments of many Jewish families (Figure 50).[13] These yarmulkes often form a stratigraphy of memory. Many Jews periodically tote excess yarmulkes back to their local synagogue, dumping them into the public baskets. (In picking through many such bins, I have found yarmulkes dating back over twenty years.) During my own family gatherings, such as Passover, the names in- scribed on these yarmulkes often prompt lively recollections.

The personalized yarmulke weaves together consumerism, Jewish identity, and individualism. Indeed, Jews today can select from a wide range of yarmulke fabrics, including silk, denim, terylene, and chino. To accessorize, one can order various trims, buttons, metallic embossing, and all manner of colors, patterns, images, logos, and phrases, even photos of the honorees. The website for A1 Skullcap, for example, lists a dozen styles, including moiré, brocade, velour, knit, and suede (www.skullcap.com). A click on satin brings up twenty-six pos- sible colors, from aqua, dusty rose, and hot pink to lime green, peach, and teal. Each yarmulke can also receive one of eleven different trims. Weinfeld Skullcap Manufacturing offers a similar assortment of styles, including Patriotic, Silver & Gold, and Camouflage (http://yarmulkes.com). The plush monochrome yar- mulke, unadorned save for a modest imprint, now seems almost "retro."

Until fairly recently, four Brooklyn-based manufacturers, all managed by Orthodox Jews, dominated the yarmulke market in the United States:

**Figure 50**  Yarmulkes
stuffed in a kitchen drawer,
beside the coffee filters.
Photo by author.

A1 Skullcap and Weinfeld Skullcap Manufacturing, which I just mentioned,
as well as Mazel Skullcap (www.kippah.com) and Brucha Yarmulke (now Yofah
Religious Articles, www.yarmulka.com). In January 2006, I contacted these
shops to arrange a visit. Not all four firms responded to my requests—largely,
I was told by one proprietor, because Orthodox Jews, abiding by the traditional
ethos of modesty or tzniut (see Chapter 5), often shun the spotlight. Yet two
businesses kindly agreed to a visit.

Both shops hire seamstresses, printers, and cutters—upward of thirty,
I was told, depending on the pace of business. I actually saw employees in
only one location—an older Eastern European man in a plain black yarmulke
at a cutting machine, and a half dozen Latina women, earning minimum wage,
with needle and thread (Figure 51). The décor of neither shop offers much
glitz or elegance. One showroom is tucked away, upstairs, in a nondescript
warehouse; the other lies in a graffiti-besmirched brick building, its name
barely discernable on the plain steel door.

Neither shop was particularly forthcoming about sales figures and revenues. Both shops, however, consent to almost all requests so long as the
event or design does not clash with Orthodox sensibilities. (An order for

**Figure 51**   Sewing trim. Photo by author.

yarmulkes with images of unclad women was decisively refused.) When in doubt, one proprietor consults his rabbi. Both shops, too, begrudgingly supply yarmulkes for gay and lesbian weddings and interdenominational church seders at Passover. And like any venerable New York City business, both shops claim to be the original source of the imprinted yarmulke.

For Conservative and Reform Jews, yarmulkes blend a dedication to religious tradition with the thoroughly modern values of self-gratification, stylishness, and sometimes mere amusement—the precise qualities associated with secular fashion. As A1 Skullcap advises, "choose a color to suit your taste, or your décor." (For my own wedding in 1996, a seamstress made yarmulkes from fabric we purchased in Hawaii that displayed a Polynesian *tapa* cloth pattern; see Figure 52.) Contemporary yarmulkes thus represent the contrary relationship between Judaism and modernity. This suggestion is nowhere more in evidence than in what I call the pop culture yarmulke. These yarmulkes communicate the inescapable conclusion that most American Jews are as thoroughly American as they are Jewish.

## POPULARIZING THE SACRED

Many yarmulkes today appear cute, playful, and witty. They display almost every icon, insignia, slogan, and pop culture character imaginable. No longer is the market dominated by a few unassuming retailers in Brooklyn.

**Figure 52** Yarmulke from the author's wedding, made from a Polynesian *tapa* cloth pattern. Photo by author.

Jews today can point their web browsers to Kippah King, Kool Kipah, Design Kippot, Best Kippah, Kippa Connection, Kippah Corner, Kippot World, Mazel Tops, Kids Kippot, Ego Kippot, and Lids for Yids, among others. Myriad brick-and-mortar Judaica shops also stock yarmulkes, from J. Levine Books & Judaica in Manhattan (www.levinejudaica.com) and Judaica Place in Flatbush, Brooklyn (www.judaicaplace.com), to Shuki's Judaica (www.shukisjudaica.com) in Framingham, Massachusetts, and Golds World of Judaica in Sydney and Melbourne (http://www.golds.com.au).

"The *yarmulke*," declared *The New York Times* in 1990, "is now a fashion item."[14] And so it is. Contemporary designs include:

Sports team logos and mascots: mainly American baseball, basketball, football (gridiron), and ice hockey but also British football (soccer) teams such as Manchester United, Arsenal, Liverpool, and Tottenham.

Comic book and television superheroes such as Batman, Superman, and Green Lantern.

Movie characters, including Yoda and Obi-Wan Kenobi (*Star Wars*), Buzz Lightyear and Woody (*Toy Story*), *Little Mermaid*, *Beauty and the Beast*, *Cinderella*, and *James Bond*.

Endless creatures and figures from Disney, Looney Tunes, and other children's television programs: Mickey Mouse, Big Bird, Cookie Monster,

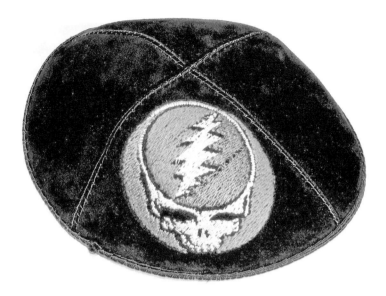

**Figure 53**  Yarmulke decorated with the Steal Your Face design affiliated with the Grateful Dead. Courtesy of Rhino Entertainment Company

Elmo, Bart Simpson, Blues Clues, Pikachu, The Wiggles, Snoopy, Charlie Brown, Spongebob Squarepants, Avatar, Tinkerbell, Dragon Tales, Bob the Builder, Telletubbies, and others.

Rock-and-roll iconography: The Beatles crossing Abbey Road, Phish's logo, the symbols from Led Zeppelin IV, the Rolling Stones tongue, the iconic image from Pink Floyd's album *Dark Side of the Moon*, AC/DC, The Who, Metallica, Black Sabbath, and the Steal Your Face design of the Grateful Dead (Figure 53).

Consumer preferences, including Apple computers, Hershey's Kisses, Fender electric guitars, and Harley Davidson motorcycles.

And hobbies: poker hands, bagpipes, drum sets, bowling pins, golf clubs, chess pieces, sailboats, fishing rods, NASCAR, karate kicks, and so forth.

Yarmulkes display the national emblems of military branches, Harry Potter on his broomstick, the Cat in the Hat, Winnie the Pooh, Hello Kitty, Teenage Mutant Ninja Turtles, Shrek, Clifford the Big Red Dog, Garfield, Thomas the Tank Engine, Bart Simpson, the numerical constant pi written in binary code, Super Mario, dog paw prints, flags, dolphins, Godzilla, smiley faces, yin and yang, hearts, construction machines, shamrocks, flowers, fish, and even— and here I am being only slightly facetious—the occasional Jewish motif such as Stars of David, menorahs, and *matzah* patterns (Figures 54–57). Seemingly no aspect of secular culture is barred at the sanctuary doors.

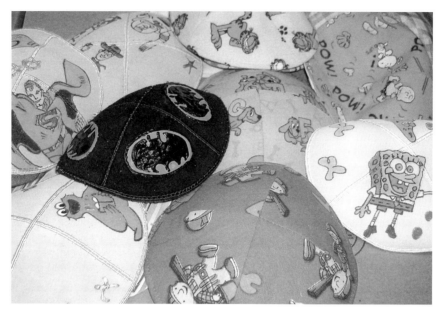

**Figure 54** Pop culture yarmulkes. Photo by author.

**Figure 55** Yarmulkes with smiley faces. Courtesy of Ugo Luzzati (www.egokippot.com).

On September 19, 2011, a search for "yarmulke" on eBay yielded thirteen hundred and thirty-nine hits. These yarmulkes displayed Star Wars Clone Troopers, University of Florida Gaters, Scottish plaid, Green Bay Packers, University of Alabama, Spiderman, Scooby Doo, penguins, geckos, South Park, bagels, dollar signs, Darth Vader, Curious George, Kermit the Frog, Luke Skywalker, sharks, New England Patriots, baseballs, peace symbols, Red Sox, Caillou,

**Figure 56**  Yarmulke with the *she'ma* prayer (Deuteronomy 6:4–6) written in binary code. Courtesy of Ugo Luzzati (www.egokippot.com).

**Figure 57**  Basketball, karate, and poker yarmulkes. Courtesy of Mazel Tops (www.mazeltops.com).

Ben 10, Tweety and Sylvester, the Beatles, the solar system, Donkey Kong, Yoshi, Smurfs, a surfing dog, and the logos for Rush, Yes, and Kiss. Surely few readers will recognize, never mind identify with, all these cultural references. Yarmulkes today celebrate an astounding pluralism within Judaism as much as they index any global Jewish identity.

The L.E.D. Kippah flashes a personalized message on a programmable display (http://ledkippah.com). Krazy Keepas makes yarmulkes from corduroy, men's suit fabrics, fleece, argyle, flannel, seer sucker, and sports mesh (www.krazykeepas.com). They also offer plastic "krok kippas" to match popular Croc footwear. The Yamulkap combines a yarmulke with a visor (www.yamulkap.com). The website for KlippedKippas.com shows colorful designs for over sixty North American Jewish day schools. The names are unmistakably Orthodox—Hebrew Academy of Tucson, for example, and Yeshiva of Central Queens—but the totemic eagles, ravens, leopards, lions, bulldogs, and wolves dwell in the non-kosher world of secular sports. Contemporary yarmulkes all but dissolve the fence between sacred and profane.

Many yarmulkes appeal to multiculturalism. At UncommonYarmulke.com you can download the book *Yarmulke-gami: E-Z Paper Fold Jewish Art Hats*. Design Kippah in Australia (www.designkippah.com) offers yarmulkes with Aboriginal patterns and even the Aboriginal flag (Figure 58). African Home

**Figure 58** Yarmulkes from Australia, sold by Design Kippah, including Aboriginal designs and, at bottom, an Aboriginal flag. Photo by author.

(www.africanhome.co.za) sells tin yarmulkes made in the townships from discarded soft drink cans (Figure 59). The London 2012 Olympic Games provided an official *kippah* to Jewish volunteers to match their uniforms.

Today, one can purchase "kosher *kippot*" certified sweatshop-free by the Progressive Jewish Alliance (www.pjalliance.com). Sources of "kosher *kippot*" include Global Goods Partners (www.globalgoodspartners.org) and Maya Works (www.mayaworks.com), two organizations fostering the economic development of women and girls in Guatemala and elsewhere. In the United Kingdom, the Jewish Social Action Forum offers "fair trade *kippot*" woven at a women's cooperative in India (www.faritradekippot.org; see also www.amsteinart.com and www.mayanhands.org). Kippot for Hope sells yarmulkes crocheted by the indigenous Jews of Uganda (www.kippotforhope.org). Proceeds support the local community.

Kosher *kippot* are part of a wider Jewish movement today, driven mainly by Reform Jews, advocating for ethically manufactured clothing. The moral outlook of "kosher clothing" arises partly from Jewish experiences with ancient enslavement and the modern garment trade.[15] In an earlier era, the so-called Milliner's Bill, introduced into the New York State Assembly in 1911, sought to prevent the extinction of certain birds by prohibiting the sale of wild plumages used to decorate women's hats. When leading Jewish millinery

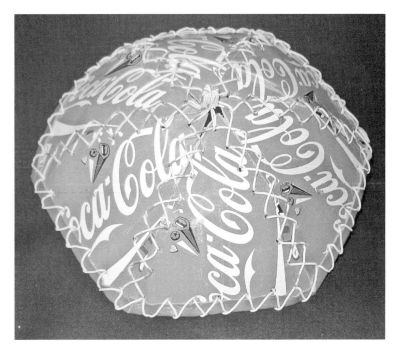

**Figure 59**  Yarmulke made from discarded FIFA World Cup Soccer Coca-Cola cans from South Africa. Courtesy of Claudette Davis, African Home (www.africanhome.co.za).

**Figure 60**   Eco-Suede Kippah label. Photo by author.

firms opposed the legislation, the Yiddish newspaper *Die Wahrheit* reminded its readers that Jews "were the first in the world to preach about mercy to animals."[16] A similar environmentalist ethic prompted the production of yarmulkes from recycled cardboard, dubbed "eco-suede," which Zara Mart (www.a-zara.com) describes as "The eco-friendly vegan alternative to suede-leather *kippot*" (Figure 60).

Kosher *kippot* are not the only political style of Jewish religious head-gear. During the 2008 presidential election, Jewish voters could pray in the "Obamulke" (Figure 61) or "McCippah."[17] Obamulkes.com released a 2012 reelection yarmulke just in time for the 2011 High Holy Days. The following summer, Judaism.com sought to appeal to all voters, selling both "Romney 2012" and "Obama '12" yarmulkes. One can readily find other candidate kip-pas on eBay, including the "yarMITTkah" and, some months earlier, "Don't Mess with Sarah" and "Palin Power." Here we see a seemingly traditional Jewish garment lending voice to one of the most cherished, private acts in a modern liberal democracy: casting a ballot.

## LITIGIOUS YARMULKES

To the extent that yarmulkes express key values of modernity, it should come as little surprise that these ritual garments periodically appear in the court-room. In 1981, for the most noteworthy example, Captain Simcha Goldman, an ordained Orthodox rabbi and a clinical psychologist in the United States

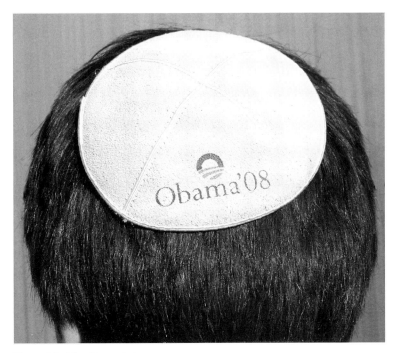

**Figure 61**    The Obama-kah.

Air Force, was ordered by a superior officer to remove his yarmulke in accordance with regulations barring indoor headgear. Goldman refused and sued the military (*Goldman v. Weinberger*) for violating his constitutional right to the "free exercise" of religion.[18]

A district court ruled for Captain Goldman. But the Court of Appeals reversed the decision. The captain then appealed to the United States Supreme Court in 1986, which issued a 5–4 decision affirming the right of the military to regulate dress to promote order and solidarity. In response, several members of the U.S. House of Representatives and the Senate authored legislative "*yarmulke* amendments" allowing Jewish and Sikh servicemen to wear "neat and conservative" religious headgear. After several iterations, President Ronald Reagan signed the "Religious Apparel Amendment" (10 U.S.C. § 774) into law as part of the 1988 Defense Authorization Bill.

In dissenting from the majority opinion on the Goldman case, Justice William J. Brennan recognized that the apparent stance of religious neutrality endorsed by the U.S. military actually permitted "only individuals whose outer garments and grooming are indistinguishable from those of mainstream Christians to fulfill their religious duties."[19] Justice Brennan also wrote that "a *yarmulke* worn with a United States military uniform is an eloquent reminder that the shared and proud identity of United States servicemen embraces and unites religious and ethnic pluralism." But the Court opted instead to legitimize the ideal of the unmarked body of citizenship—an ideal originally enshrined in the first-century Letters of Paul.

The courts, however do not always endorse this ideal. In 2003, the Ben Franklin Science Academy in Oklahoma City banned hats, including yarmulkes and Muslim headscarves, to curtail gang activity. The Justice Department intervened, and the school district agreed to pay restitution to a suspended eleven-year-old Muslim girl and to amend its dress code.[20]

Some Jews refuse to see the yarmulke as an essential, unmovable sign of Jewish identity. In an essay in *Antioch Review*, Harry Steinhauer bemoaned the "war over a minor grievance" during the Captain Goldman affair and the "undeserved importance" many Jews attribute to this vestimentary "fetish" (1990). Steinhauer was particularly dismissive of fund-raising letters, accompanied by yarmulkes, mailed to Jewish voters by Senator Daniel Inouye of Hawaii on behalf of New Jersey Senator Frank J. Lautenberg's reelection campaign. (Not incidentally, Lautenberg co-sponsored the "*yarmulke* amendment.") "All *yarmulkes* are sacred," wrote Inouye, "That's why I hope you'll keep the one I'm sending you today . . . as a reminder that we can never take our freedom for granted." Of course, the senator slightly erred. The sacredness of the yarmulke arises from the United States Constitution, not Jewish law—from secular society, in other words, not religious tradition.

Ongoing litigation over the yarmulke, however, suggests that few American Jews seem willing to divest this garment of its symbolic power and sacredness. Likewise, not all non-Jews agree with Senator Inouye. Thus in 1996, for example, a judge in Texas asked an Orthodox Jewish law professor to remove his yarmulke before testifying as an expert witness in her courtroom (see Renteln 2004). The judge was concerned that the yarmulke might imbue the professor's testimony with religious authority and so undermine jury impartiality. Conversely, an appellate court in 1978 reversed an earlier decision by a trial court ordering a Jewish defendant to choose between retaining his yarmulke or attending his own trial (*Close-It Enterprises, Inc. v. Weinberger*). In 2005, the international movie rental chain Blockbuster settled with the U.S. Equal Employment Opportunity Commission after a store manager in Arizona asked a salesman to remove his yarmulke or face dismissal for violating the company dress code. In 2007, an Orthodox Jewish police captain brought suit against the Las Vegas Metropolitan Police Department for refusing to accommodate his beard and yarmulke. (The court ruled in favor of the beard; the department settled over the yarmulke.) In 1997, Jewish parents sued the Pike County School Board in Alabama for allowing students to wear crosses but neither Star of David pins, which apparently resembled gang symbols, nor yarmulkes. The case was settled.[21] I could cite additional litigation. But the point should be clear: the role of the yarmulke in outfitting a citizen remains, despite Senator Inouye's pronouncement, an ongoing controversy.

Jews share legal entanglements over dress with other ethnic and religious minorities, especially Sikhs and, as we saw in Chapter 5, Muslim women. The Sikh Code of Conduct, or *Reht Maryada*, requires all baptized adherents to carry a small ceremonial sword (*kirpan*). Sikh men must also wrap a turban over their untrimmed hair. Predictably, this outfit raises alarm in public schools, airports, and government buildings, especially after 9/11.[22] Many countries now wrestle with the *kirpan*. The sword is illegal in Denmark, for example, but permissible in the United Kingdom, Belgium, and the United States—but not necessarily when boarding an airplane.

Even the basketball court is not immune from litigation over yarmulkes. Many Jews secure their yarmulkes with bobby pins or "*kippah* clips"—really, ordinary hairclips with small ornaments. Some referees see *kippah* clips as potential hazards, and thus require Orthodox sports teams to remove their yarmulkes or forfeit the game. In 1982, Jewish basketball players sued a school district that banned yarmulkes (*Menora v. Illinois High School Association*). But the court argued that athletes "have no constitutional right to wear *yarmulkes* insecurely fastened by bobby pins." The court similarly upheld a no-yarmulke policy for pugilists (*Harris v. New York State Athletic Commission*). Yet schools permit the use of eyeglasses during basketball games, observes Renteln (2004), and thus these legal fisticuffs may involve more than just safety. Yarmulkes, even when decorated with the most secular patterns and slogans, still largely attire Jews outside the norms of proper citizenship.

Athletes can now purchase a few entrepreneurial alternatives to the metal fasteners. Kippon, a Velcro-like strip that adheres both to hair and yarmulkes, but easily pulls away, advertises as "No more bobby pins, No more clips! Say goodbye to anxiety trips!"[23] Likewise, a coach at Weinbaum Yeshiva High School in Boca Raton, Florida, developed a yarmulke with a hidden clip (http://klippedkippahs.com/). It is "roller coaster strong."

Finally, one other genre of illegal yarmulkes bears noting: unauthorized reproductions of copyrighted logos and characters. Nike and Sesame Street both asked Judaica shops to remove yarmulkes featuring pirated renditions of the famous swoosh and Big Bird.[24] I heard similar reports about *Peanuts* and *Where's Waldo*. The yarmulke may be sacred to Senator Inouye—but not to American copyright law.

## CONCLUSION

Not long ago, Jews transformed the yarmulke from a minor article in the liturgical wardrobe to a potent sign of religious identity. So powerful is this symbol that rebellious Haredi men in Brooklyn remove their yarmulkes before secretly setting off to go clubbing (Levine 2003: 162)—while secular criminals in Israel don yarmulkes in the hopes of receiving lighter prison sentences.[25] The Ethicist, a column in *The New York Times Magazine*, weighed in on a similar issue in 2006. Is it moral for an devout Jew who ordinarily goes hatless, asked the writer, to wear a yarmulke in the hopes of receiving a discount at an Orthodox-staffed camera shop? No.

In 2006, a yarmulke signed by Sandy Koufax, the legendary left-handed Jewish pitcher who threw for the Brooklyn and Los Angeles Dodgers in the 1950s and 1960s, fetched $3,838.00 at AmericanMemorabilia.com. A year later, a plain black yarmulke, allegedly swiped by the owner's uncle after Koufax wore it at a wedding in 1971, was auctioned on eBay. The winning bid was $91.00, and the money donated to a synagogue.[26] A purple yarmulke with a Grateful Dead logo, similar to Figure 53 and once worn by Jerry Garcia, the virtuoso guitarist, singer, and composer for the band who died in 1995, received a winning bid of $639.60 at an online auction in March 2011 hosted by Gotta Have It! Collectables, Inc.[27] The sacredness of these yarmulkes expands well beyond any rabbinic fence.

In December 2003, a high school student named Dan Torres in upstate New York asked his friends to wear yarmulkes in school as a humorous response to the Santa Claus hats allowed by teachers despite a general ban on caps. A few years later, this "joke" expanded into an annual "Yarmulke Day" that celebrates the values of difference and tolerance.[28] Yarmulke Day even has its own line of t-shirts and messenger bags that celebrate Judaism through a version of that most ubiquitous of contemporary American slogans, "I ♥ Yarmulke Day" (http://yarmulkeday.spreadshirt.com/). This, as much as anything, attests to the full incorporation of Jews and yarmulkes into modern society even as this small cap still dresses religious Jews at the margins. To some, the yarmulke signals resistance to the domineering institutions and mores of modern society (Boyarin and Boyarin 1995). But as I argued, the yarmulke today also accedes to the very consumerism and individualism it seemingly rejects.

At the beginning of this book project, I purchased for my daughter a yarmulke displaying Dora the Explorer, the popular Latina girl, and her decidedly non-kosher pet monkey, Boots. For my son, I selected a yarmulke with an anime character—a boy named Goku, my son informed me, from the series Dragon Ball Z. These yarmulkes comment wonderfully on the prominence of globalization, ethnic fluidity, and multiculturalism in contemporary Jewish culture. They also, at least in regard to my daughter, evidence the impact of feminism on the religious practices of many, if not most, American Jews.

Surely the most ribald use of the *kippah* today is the "yarmulkebra"—yes, a bra made from a pair of yarmulkes (www.yarmulkebra.com). The yarmulkebra comes in several sizes, including *Bat-mitzvah* and *Boobooshka*. It is rivaled only by the *bramulke*, a yarmulke fashioned from a bra.[29] Even Orthodox Jews may invest their yarmulkes with erotic intent. Devout couples shun sexuality, and all physical contact, during menstruation and for seven days thereafter. To learn if this taboo period has passed, a husband may toss his yarmulke onto his spouse's bed, hoping she tosses it back (Gold 1987: 193). Far less prurient is the Mazel Tov Curly Teddy, a stuffed toy bear complete with yarmulke and tallit, available from the popular Build-A-Bear chain of shops (www.buildabear.com). More objectionable, at least to devout Jews, is the placement of yarmulkes upon dogs during the unorthodox canine ceremony practiced by some American Jews, the "bark mitzvah."

I can scarcely imagine what the rabbis of the Talmudic era would have made of the yarmulkebra, Dora the Explorer, Yarmulke Day, bark mitzvahs, and the iKippa app for your iPhone (for when you need a yarmulke and don't have one; alas, no longer available). Surely they would be appalled. Or maybe not. Yarmulkes now display the quintessential signs of modern identity. They also allow Jews to resist, even as they embrace, acculturation—a process far more traditional to Jewish life than the yarmulke itself. Indeed, the yarmulke is simply a recent version of a time-honored predicament I have traced throughout this book and which continues to vex many Jews: How to dress for Judaism as much as for integration into the wider society.

# –9–

# Jewtilicious

Oy vey! Tempest in a T-Shirt.

*Brandweek*, April 19, 2004

For centuries, clothing mapped the everyday and ritual coordinates of Jewish identity. But rarely did Jews agree on proper attire, especially after the rise of modernity and the enshrinement of individualism and citizenship. Indeed, perhaps it makes more sense to think about Jewish clothing not as a set of symbols or boundaries but, rather, as an unresolved conversation about the very meaning of Jewishness. I now turn to the latest controversial garment in a long and tempestuous history of Jewish attire: t-shirts.

Around the turn of the most recent, albeit non-Jewish, millennium, groups of young American Jews—decidedly urban, progressive, intellectual, and rebellious—established several webzines, blogs, magazines, and communities both real and virtual aimed at reinventing Jewish identity. They go by many names, at least in the popular press, including Hipster Jews, Generation-J, Heebsters, Cool Jewz, and New Jews. But they all seek to challenge mainstream Jewry. New Jews see established modes of Jewish identity as anachronistic and alienating, inert and dull, rooted in stale theology, and anchored to historical events no longer resonant. New Jews also find conventional Jewishness either too parochial or too invisible—that is, too Jewish or not Jewish enough. In consequence, New Jews yearn to push Jewishness to the cutting edge of contemporary culture by lending powerful Jewish voices to debates over multiculturalism and the politics of identity. They want, in short, to make Jewishness relevant—to themselves, of course, but also to everybody else. And they wear their Jewishness on their sleeves.

## OPEN SOURCE JEWISHNESS

Before we turn to the apparel of the New Jew Cool we need first to explore this novel rendition of Jewish identity. More and more, young Jews today, especially in America, view their Jewishness as "cultural" or "ethnic" rather than "religious." The rabbis of old pinned the survival of Judaism on an impermeable "fence," which included clothing, that would cloister the community.

By contrast, New Jews hinge Jewish survival on the dismantling of any such fence in order to promote a forceful, self-identified Jewish presence in the wider, non-Jewish society.

Traditionalists premise Judaism on a "primordial non-contingent commitment" to the Torah. Ethnic Jews eschew formal institutions and fixed, communal codes of religious conduct (Klaff 2006; Zenner 1985). New Jews confer no authority to time-honored gatekeepers. They experience Judaism as a negotiation for personal meaning, a broad cultural affiliation, and an ethical and aesthetic sensibility. It is enough today simply to *feel* Jewish.

Ethnic Jews do not wholly spurn traditional ritual performances. They may light the Chanukah menorah and attend synagogue on the High Holidays. But ethnic Jews tend to identify as postdenominational and therefore mainly "do" Judaism through the consumption of Jewish-themed films, books, magazines, music, television shows, and food (Horowitz 2003). They are drawn to "entertaining, playful, ironic . . . [and] generationally distinctive" expressions of Jewishness (Cohen and Kelman 2005: 5). Above all else, ethnic Jews seek to reinvent Jewishness to fit, like a garment, their contemporary lifestyles and worldviews.

Although New Jews might seem committed to assimilation, they actually aspire to *un*-assimilate (Rakoff 2003). But they anchor their particularism not to religious practices, as noted, but to a Jewish style of blurring ethnic boundaries. New Jews emphasize what the theorist James Clifford calls "cultural hybridity" and "inventive impurity" (1997: 176). But although New Jews reject ethnic invisibility, they ironically dress their Jewishness in the same racy, swaggering tones that characterize contemporary pop culture. Think Jewish hip-hop.

From an Orthodox perspective, these novel expressions of identity amount to Jewish-lite. But New Jews value personal ownership over Judaism, not fidelity to the past. They reject essentialism, that is, the tenet that authentic Jewishness entails some absolute core set of beliefs, practices, and rites. They generally believe that "the only things that Jews share in common is the fact that they self-identify" (Aviv and Shneer 2005: 175). Kirshenblatt Gimblett wonderfully calls this unstable, iconoclastic, and multicultural *un*-movement "open source Jewishness" (2005). But despite the wider currents of multiculturalism coursing through contemporary society, argues Gilman, Jews remain largely outsiders—too much the victim, too much the success (2006). Young Jews respond to this doubled predicament, I now show, by dressing to resist and play with both stereotypes.

## T-SHIRTS YOUR MOTHER WARNED YOU ABOUT

I began this book with a photograph of my grandmother, a young girl somberly posing amid her family for a portrait of nascent worldly success in the early twentieth century (Figure 1). How, I wonder, would my grandmother greet a t-shirt that shows a gun-toting Hasid who taunts, after a famous wisecrack uttered by Clint Eastwood's character Dirty Harry in the 1983 film *Sudden Impact*, "Go Ahead, Make My Shabbos"?[1] Would she dare to venture the streets in a shirt emblazoned with Jewcy, Jewlicious, or Jewtastic? I suspect not.

Indeed, I propose that few Jews who migrated to the United States during the classic era of American immigration would don a shirt that exclaims "Jews Kick Ass" (Figure 62). The six personalities depicted on this shirt, never mind the expletive, hardly embody an earlier generation's view of authentic Jewishness. This garment seeks to put a heterodox face onto normative Judaism: Henry Winkler, better known as The Fonz on the television sitcom *Happy Days*; Albert Einstein; Sammy Davis, Jr., the African American convert legendary for boozily crooning with Frank Sinatra and Dean Martin in the Rat Pack; William Shatner, famous as Captain Kirk on *Star Trek*; Bob Dylan; and Jesus Christ. This shirt vividly illustrates the irreverent, sardonic refashioning of Jewish identity by The New Jew Cool, as Fishkoff (2004) calls them, and the subversion of mainstream Jewry.

Not all contemporary Jewish t-shirts, however, break with the past. AccentriciTees.com, the "home of Talmudic Tee-chings," offers "cool t-shirts with positive, uplifting messages gleaned from the Talmud" (www.accentricitees. com). These garments affirm traditional yet somewhat liberal religious

**Figure 62**    Jews Kick Ass. Courtesy of JEWS KICK ASS—2003. © Bruce Jefferies Reinfeld (www.highfidelitydisco.com).

sentiments such as "613 Mitzvot" (the number of commandments or *mitzvot*, recall, in the Torah), "If I am only for myself, who am I?" and "We do not see things as they are . . . we see things as we are."[2] But most Jewish t-shirts that catch notice today do not, as I stated earlier, represent Judaism through traditional theology and decorous sensibilities. Indeed, these garments intend to make the Jewish establishment wince.[3]

The flagship institution of the New Jew Cool is often identified as the magazine *Heeb*. The title attempts to flip a term of derision into an icon of ethnic pride. In name, *Heeb* has much in common with the provocative use of the term "nigga" by African Americans and the hip-hop community (see Kennedy 2002). *Heeb* received startup funds from the Joshua Venture Fellowship, itself partly supported by Steven Spielberg's Righteous Persons Foundation and the Andrea and Charles Bronfman Philanthropies. Despite these utterly mainstream roots, *Heeb* delights in assaulting the etiquette and sensibilities of the American Jewish establishment. For example, most Jews greeted Mel Gibson's controversial 2004 film *The Passion of the Christ* with alarm. But *Heeb* went one step further with its winter 2004 parody, "The Crimes of Passion." The Anti-Defamation League, a fierce critic of the film, also berated *Heeb* for the "shocking" photos of "Jesus as a sex object with his genitalia wrapped in a Jewish prayer shawl."[4]

Much in the same spirit, *Heeb* sells a t-shirt announcing "Moses Is My Homeboy." This phrase, like many slogans of the New Jew Cool, defines Judaism through a hip-hop idiom that simultaneously challenges Christian cultural hegemony. This garment, we might say, offers a much-belated response to the vestimentary edict of Pope Innocent III and the Fourth Lateran Council in the thirteenth century (see Chapter 4). *Heeb* also offers a shirt stating "Jesus Saves, Moses Invests" (Figure 63). This phrase transforms the old canard of Jewish wealth, dating to the New Testament, into a comical expression of ethnic bluster. Indeed, many garments in the New Jew Cool proudly make public the very stereotypes that earlier generations of Jews found degrading and unsettling.

Many other contemporary Jewish t-shirts respond brusquely to Christianity. YidGear, "the shirts your rabbi warned you about," printed "I didn't kill your God; get off my back" (http://yidgear.com). In the 1990s, American evangelicals often wore jewelry, clothing, and accessories festooned with "WWJD," an acronym for "What Would Jesus Do?" To this, Rotem Gear responded with a shirt steeped in Jewish history and theology, asking "What Would Maimonides Do?" (Figure 64; www.rotemgear.com). *Heeb* magazine offers a similar, albeit less intellectual, retort that features the likeness of Barbra Streisand and asks WWBD or "What Would Barbra Do?" Both garments proclaim Jewish identity through a witty rejoinder to Christianity, thereby defining Judaism in terms of, yet against, the dominant culture. Symbolically, these

**Figure 63**    Jesus Saves, Moses Invests. Courtesy of Heeb Media, LLC.

shirts dress Jews far beyond any boundaries endorsed, or even imagined, by the classic rabbis.

Many shirts merge Jewishness with a generic American identity. PopJudaica.com, also called ChosenCouture.com, sells a "Yo Semite" garment that amusingly calls attention to Jewishness while referring to Yosemite National Park. The "Green Jew" shirt by YidGear shows a recycling logo made from Stars of David. Both designs add new voices to the long-standing dialogue between Jewish distinctiveness and generic citizenship. At the same time, the comedy of "Yo Semite" seemingly casts Jewishness as mere humor or, worse, frivolous. Another Pop Judaica garment proclaims "No Limit Texas Dreidel." LuckyJew.com offers a comparable comedic repertoire, such as "I Prefer Kosher," "Jews for bacon," "Jews for cheeses" (a play on messianic "Jews for Jesus"), and "Shalom Out," a twist on a youthful parting gesture whereby you thump your chest and flash a peace sign while uttering "peace out." The "chosen shirts" at Everything's Jewish include "Kosher hottie," "Got Guilt?," and "You had me at shalom" (www.cafepress.com/oygevalt). The latter is a variant of a famous line, "You had me at hello," uttered by Renee Zellweger to Tom Cruise in the 1996 film *Jerry Maguire*. Everything's Jewish also promotes a "Schmutz Happens" shirt that puns with the crude witticism, "shit happens." Judaism thus appears as a variant of the wider cultural cadence, not a language all its own.

**Figure 64**    WWMD: What Would Maimonides Do? Courtesy of R. Jean Roth; Rotem Gear.

Often, garments marketed to the New Jew Cool affirm Jewish ethnicity by transgressing, as I suggested earlier, the decorum and taste of the Jewish establishment. Thus YidGear sells a shirt with a marijuana leaf and the phrase, "Light One Up This Hanukkah." KosherShirts.com, a defunct company, offered "On Hannukah we smoke Marijuanica," alluding to the lyrics from the first of Adam Sandler's many Chanukkah Songs. These ditties seek to soothe Jewish angst during the Christmas season by naming and honoring famous American Jews.[5] Sandler's song, like the "Jews Kick Ass" design, engages in "Jewhooing," that is, the "outing" of unidentified Jews (Glenn 2002). But Jewhooing undermines the very aims of the New Jew Cool by construing Jewishness as innate rather than self-selected.

While some modern t-shirts define Jewishness as intrinsic or embodied, other designers, such as Cool Jewish T Shirts, present Jewishness as all surface or façade, with little substance. They sell a "Just Jew It" slogan with a ram's horn (*shofar*) that resembles the Nike swoosh logo (www.cooljewishtshirts.com). This shirt ironically un-assimilates by dressing Jews in the very same footwear, as it were, worn by the rest of society. Designs by the oxymoronic clothing company KosherHam (www.kosherham.com) include "Winnie the Jooh" (with a yarmulke atop the famous bear, of course), and a Dr. Seuss-like rhyme, "One fish, two fish, red fish, Jew fish" (beside a jar of gefilte fish). Jtshirt.com offers a "Shofar Hero" motif that visually recalls the Nintendo Wii game *Guitar Hero*. Shalom Shirts similarly represents Jewish-ness through a droll phraseology drawn from pop culture (www.shalomshirts.com). Their garments include "Do the Jew," which resembles the logo for the soft drink Mountain Dew, and a dancing Hasid listening to an mp3 player accompanied by the phrase "חי Pod." The latter, pronounced *chai* pod, refers to the talismanic Hebrew word for "life." Shalom Shirts also parody rock-and-roll bands. Instead of Guns N' Roses, they offer "Guns N' Moses," complete with a skull sporting a beard, *payess*, and a black hat. On another shirt, a silhouette of two Hasids appears next to the name of an AC/DC song, "Back in Black." The historical tension between Jewish distinctiveness and acculturation, so often sewn into clothing, remains no more resolved today than in the late nineteenth century or the Middle Ages. The vocabulary of this far-reaching dialogue has surely changed. The conversation, however, endures.

Several online venders, such as JewTee.com, Matzoh Ball Mamaleh (www.zazzle.com/jacki1959), and Hebrew American (www.cafepress.com/hebrewamerican), sell Holocaust remembrance shirts that boast of Jewish survival. These designs typically depict a yellow star, often with the German word "Jude." The shirt may also declare "Never Again," "*Am Yisrael Chai*" ("the people of Israel live"), or similar sentiments. These garments, like the *Heeb* shirt, turn icons of anti-Semitism into signs of ethnic pride. But they also dare to represent Jewishness through a taboo symbolism that many Jews would likely find beyond the realm of any moral, or consumerist, possibility.

Most *bon mots* and motifs that adorn garments of the New Jew Cool do not seek to delineate Jewishness as a serious alternative to generic American conventions. Instead, these garments define Jewishness through consumerism and popular culture, thus positioning Jews as both outsiders and insiders. In fact, shopping for an ethnic identity and publicly celebrating one's heritage are now commonplace American pastimes (Halter 2000). No longer is ethnicity begrudgingly toted as a liability that impedes social and economic integration. Rather, ethnic identity today accrues considerable cultural cachet. Many Americans seek their "roots" to serve as existential anchors amid the anonymity of generic citizenship, the vapidity of runaway consumerism, and the superficial, sound-bite flotsam and jetsam of postmodern society. Ironically, though, we often express our ethnicity through the very same consumerism we hope to escape.

A century ago, most Jews spurned characteristic ethnic garb and dressed for acculturation and even, in some cases, outright assimilation. Today, many Jews use shirts, no less than the yarmulkes I discussed in the previous chapter, to celebrate Jewish identity—in fact, to make Jewishness fun. But these garments, I argued, express a tone, outlook, and style that simultaneously dissolves any deeply rooted Jewish particularism. Do the shirts represent new, exciting, and empowering Jewish voices? Or do they reduce Jewishness to the very caricatures that for so long barred Jews from full citizenship? Regardless, the shirts are hardly the apparel that my grandmother would have worn. And that, to say the least, is the point.

## MERRY JEWISH CHRISTMAS

Many vestimentary proclamations of new Jewish identity, as I intimated earlier, playfully blur ethnic boundaries. These garments celebrate Judaism as ethnically distinct as well as multicultural, diffuse, and cosmopolitan. Judaism thus again appears as a variant of American culture, not as a distinctive tradition defined on its own terms.

Many t-shirt designs, for example, allude to hip-hop and African Americans. Of course, dialogue between blacks and Jews is a long-standing, integral facet of modern American history. For centuries, as we have seen, Europe categorized Jews as demonic Others who could only join proper society after a dip in the cleansing waters of baptism, thereafter dressing in Christianity. Upon immigration to the United States, however, Jews encountered a hierarchy of color, not religion. The path to legitimacy in the New World was to become white. Jews achieved this status and hue partly by darkening their faces with burnt cork in the popular amusement of blackface.

As a form of "racial cross-dressing," argues Rogin (1998), minstrelsy allowed Jews and, before them, the Irish, to mock the only group that dwelled beneath themselves in the urban social hierarchy. By turning black in theater and film, Jews turned white in everyday life and thus, despite their Jewishness, "passed" in a highly racialized society. The shift from white to black, and then again to white, thus reflected the transformation of Jews into Americans (Rogin 1998: 49). But while blackface admitted Jews into American society, minstrelsy still barred the door to the very people whose creativity blackface usurped.

The nativist movement was hardly fooled by burnt cork. Jews had no place in their vision of a white America. As a result, Jews came to think of themselves as both white *and* different, and so often allied with other minorities. To be sure, blackfaced Jews helped perpetuate a racist America, especially through movies such as *The Jazz Singer* (1927). But this burlesque also gave rise to an affinity with blacks unmatched by other ethnic groups. Thus Jews championed progressive labor and political movements and marched in solidarity with African Americans for civil rights (Rogin 1998: 251). The Irish and

Italians did not. I see contemporary Jewish t-shirts that draw on hip-hop as the latest voice in the ongoing dialogue between Jews and blacks over their kinship, differences, and roles in American society.

For example, YidGear offers a shirt with the catchphrase "Strictly Ghetto" (Figure 65). This design depicts not the rapper King Sun, who released a *Strictly Ghetto* album in 1994, but the silhouette of Hasidic Jews with long tzitzit fringes. The slippery semiotics of this t-shirt allows Jews, as in black-face, to borrow the "street cred" or cultural capital normally associated with African Americans. *We*, the shirt says, are as cool as *they*. Yet the design also reclaims the ghetto for Judaism—a word first used in reference to the Jewish quarter of sixteenth-century Venice. This shirt, then, portrays Jewishness in a fluid relationship with another ethnic identity.

Similarly, the "Too Cool For Shul" design by Jtshirt.com depicts a young man dressed in hip-hop garb, including Star of David bling. (*Shul* is Yiddish for synagogue.) They also offer a shirt with the phrase "True Jew!" tattooed, prison-style, on a man's knuckles. Cool Jewish Shirts sells "Jewboyz" and "Jewgirlz" (www.cooljewishtshirts.com). At KosherHam, one can purchase

**Figure 65**   Strictly Ghetto. Courtesy of Isaac Brynjegard-Bialik (www.YidGear.com).

"Jew-Tang" (a play on the rap group Wu-Tang Clan), "Jew Jitsu," and "Gin and Jews." The latter, which includes the silhouette of two Hasids holding a bottle, mimics Snoop Doggy Dogg's 1995 hit, "Gin and Juice." Shalom Shirts presents "Ninjew" and also, accompanied by a cartoon of an Asian man, "Fu Man Jew" (www.shalomshirts.com). All these designs, again, promote Judaism by blurring ethnic boundaries. They also reproduce lampoons of African Americans and Asian Americans that recall blackface minstrelsy and thus comment on, perhaps troublingly so, the place of Jews in the racial landscape of America.

YidGear plays with ethnic distinctions through its "The Notorious Y.I.D." shirt (Figure 66). This design uses the visage of the late Lubavitcher rebbe, Rabbi Menachem Schneerson, to spoof The Notorious B.I.G., the stage name of Christopher George Latore Wallace, a rapper murdered in a drive-by shooting in Los Angeles in 1997. Another shirt, "It's Gotta Be The Jewfro," likewise puns with African American identity (Figure 67). Yet this design also parodies a stereotypical 1970s Jewish male haircut. Rotem Gear similarly offers

**Figure 66** The Notorious Y.I.D. Courtesy of Isaac Brynjegard-Bialik (www.YidGear. com).

**Figure 67** It's Gotta Be the Jewfro! Courtesy of Isaac Brynjegard-Bialik (www. YidGear.com).

"Gotta love that Jewfro hairdo." These garments model Jewishness after African American culture—but also assert that African Americans usurped what was originally Jewish. *They*, in other words, are as cool as *us*. There is, I am proposing, no simple or singular way of reading these shirts or contemporary Jewish identity.

A t-shirt sold several years ago by MenschWear.com depicted chopsticks, a fortune cookie, and the iconic Chinese restaurant takeout box with the greeting "Merry Jewish Christmas."[6] This garment, like others, portrayed Jewish identity as an ethnic hybrid as well as an inside joke since many American Jews stereotypically "celebrate" Christmas by dining in Chinese restaurants. This shirt defined Jewishness as a non-Jewish culinary alternative to boredom on a Christian holiday.

Similarly, shirts from the Jewish Zodiac mirror the ubiquitous paper placemats in Chinese restaurants (http://jewzo.com). These slogans celebrate "Year of the Shmear," "Year of the Bagel," "Year of the Blintz," and so forth. Here, again, we see a blurring of ethnic boundaries and a humorous rendition of Jewishness that refers to a cultural practice rather than to a religious creed or to a canonical historical event. Jewish Fashion Conspiracy[7] also poked fun at Judaism while marking, or dissolving, the outer edges of ethnic Jewishness. They twist "Kiss Me I'm Irish" into "Bris me I'm Jewish." (*Bris* is the Yiddish term for ritual circumcision.) The shirt also included a green shamrock with a clipped leaf. MenschWear offered a comparable garment that showed a rabbi clutching a pair of large scissors while uttering "Just a little off the top." These shirts might appear as a sacrilegious assault on the covenantal rite, bestowed by God onto the biblical patriarch Abraham, that in many respects established Judaism and monotheism (see Silverman 2006, 2010). But circumcision has long been a staple of humor among Ashkenazi Jews, especially "*borscht* belt" comics who amused earlier generations of vacationers in the kosher resorts of the Catskill Mountains. Indeed, many shirts of the New Jew Cool actually recycle old—dare I say traditional?—Jewish comedy.

Many designs by Jean Roth's Rotem Gear combine "retro" motifs, a common theme in the genre, with witty phrases that often mock contemporary trends (www.rotemgear.com/). The "Better Living Through Kabbalah" and "Kaballywood" shirts spoof, of course, the pop culture stylishness of *faux* mysticism associated with the Kabbalah Center in Los Angeles, the pop star Madonna, and red-stringed bracelets that supposedly repel the Evil Eye. Rotem Gear often infuses multiculturalism into ethnic Jewishness. The slogan "My ancestors shlepped through Ellis Island and all I got was this lousy t-shirt!" could, except for the single Yiddish word, apply to many ethnic groups. Most significant, Rotem Gear affirms a Sephardi or Ladino identity, such as "it's not a party without a Sefardi" and "Sephardilicious" (Figure 68). Roth designed these shirts, she reported in a phone interview, to resist the dominance of Ashkenazi Jewry in defining Jewish authenticity and humor. In this sense, Rotem Gear fashions a doubled statement about modern Jewish identity such that Jews join wider conversations about diversity while also recognizing the often muted pluralism within Judaism.

Incidentally, the models who pose in many of the shirts marketed to New Jews are as likely to appear stereotypically Jewish—that is to say, Ashkenazi—as they are African American and Asian. This multiculturalism intentionally seeks to de-center the Eurocentrism of conventional Jewry, thus challenging the genealogical definition of who is, and is not, Jewish. In another flirtation with taboo, the models sometimes display Jewish-themed tattoos to contravene biblical law and Jewish tradition. Perhaps more scandalously, these tattoos conjure the branding of European Jewry during the Holocaust. This bodily decoration, like many t-shirt designs, pushes the appearance of Jewishness beyond any clear "fence," and tacks between Jewish specificity and the latest societal trend.

**Figure 68** Sephardilicious. Courtesy of R. Jean Roth; Rotem Gear.

Contemporary t-shirts, I proposed, represent Jewish identity in dialogue with other ethnicities. These garments reject the model of normative Jewry wherein an authoritative religious center defines valid Judaism by reigning in a potentially wayward and secular periphery. These shirts lend voice precisely to those outer edges. Likewise, the shirts echo the wider democratic impulse of modernity by investing any Jew with the legitimacy to sketch and smudge the contours of Jewish identity. Moreover, most contemporary t-shirt designs represent Jewishness as amusing, whimsical, and self-mocking—the very same tropes that animate much of the wider culture. We must therefore see these shirts as expressing enduring, if not ancient, tensions in the expression and attire of Jewish identity.

## UZI DOES IT

Consider the "SuperJew" shirt of *Heeb* magazine (Figure 69). This design, and many others like it, builds on the Jewish legacy of American superheroes.

**Figure 69**   SuperJew Courtesy of Heeb Media, LLC.

Superman, to cite a famous example, sprang from the pens of Jerry Siegel and Joe Shuster, two Jewish teenagers growing up in Cleveland, Ohio, in the 1930s. But neither Superman nor any other mainstream superhero ever self-identified as a Jew. They "passed" (see, for example, Fingeroth 2007). It is precisely this invisibility that *Heeb* contests with SuperJew.[8]

The superhero genre of New Jewish clothing also comments on gender. These designs generally defy the gentle, bookish image of Jewish manhood (see Brod 1995). Jewish masculinity today is complex and shifting (Brod and Zevit, eds. 2010). But "SuperJew" and other such garments seem content with mainly portraying Jewish men as singularly aggressive. Thus Judaica Heaven sells a post-9/11 shirt that depicts an Israeli F-16 fighter jet and the consoling phrase "America Don't Worry, Israel is Behind You" (www. judaicaheaven.com). Another shirt displays the famous Israeli machine gun and wryly exclaims, "Uzi Does It." Many Judaica shops, starting in the aftermath of the 1967 Six Day War, offer apparel decorated with emblems of the Israeli Defense Forces. KosherHam designed a "G.I. Jew" shirt.[9] These garments do more than merely communicate Jewish pride. They transform Jewish masculinity from an alternative form of manhood into just another variant of the "real man" image legitimated by the dominant culture (Boyarin 1997). These shirts dress Jewish acculturation in the garb of hypermasculinity.

Many shirts, too, represent Jewish manhood through an iconography of sexual prowess. Most Jews will undoubtedly recognize the OU or Ⓤ as the

imprimatur of the Orthodox Union that certifies foods as strictly kosher (www.
oukosher.org). This emblem stands for the scrupulous adherence to religious
tradition. However, the icon briefly appeared on a YidGear t-shirt accompanied
by the ribald phrase "Eat me—I'm kosher." YidGear promotes itself as "the
shirts your rabbi warned you about." Alas, those very same rabbis strenu-
ously objected to the provocation and especially the unauthorized reproduction of their copyrighted logo.[10] YidGear pulled the design. YidGear also offers
a drawing of tefillin with the naughty phrase "Get Laid" (Figure 70). This design presumes knowledge of the very Orthodoxy it offends, for only someone
familiar with traditional Judaism would know, as I discussed in Chapter 7,
that one "lays" tefillin. Despite this vulgarity, YidGear and all the garments
I review in this chapter never repudiate Judaism or advocate apostasy. Rather,
the garments seek only to rephrase Judaism.

Tough Jew Clothes sells a broad range of bawdy thongs, briefs, and boxer shorts
proclaiming "Temple Mount," "Spin My Dreidel," "Holy Land," and other soph-
omoric gags (www.cafepress.com/toughjew). LuckyJew.com offers a similar

**Figure 70**   Get Laid! Courtesy of Isaac Brynjegard-Bialik (www.YidGear.com).

repertoire, including "Blow Me" (accompanied by a drawing of a ram's horn or *shofar*), "Hebrew Hottie," and "Let's Get חי" (*chai*). Another LuckyJew shirt declares "I'm Jewish Wanna check," with an arrow pointing downward. This crude allusion to the circumcised body serves as an aggressively sexualized retort to the long-standing view of Jewish men as emasculated and thus illegitimately feminine (see Silverman 2006, chapters 8–9). In this interpretation, the shirt transforms male Jewish distinctiveness into just another wisecrack affirming the hegemony of non-Jewish gender norms. The message is, "See, Jewish men *are* circumcised. We *are* different. But this difference is less significant than the fact that we are just as virile and vulgar as everybody else." By resisting yet adopting the non-Jewish phallus, this shirt allows Jewish men to assert their Jewishness while "passing."

Many Jewish t-shirt designers borrow slogans from the 2003 film *The Hebrew Hammer*, directed by Jonathan Kesselman. The film parodied the so-called blaxploitation genre of the 1970s. At least two quips from *The Hebrew Hammer* now appear on garments, "Shabbat Shalom Motherfucker" and "Baadest Heeb this side of Tel Aviv." Likewise, a pair of phrases uttered by John Goodman in *The Big Lebowski*, the 1998 comedy written and directed by Joel and Ethan Coen, also make an appearance on contemporary shirts: "I don't roll [bowl] on Shabbos" and "Shomer fucking Shabbos"—the latter referring to Jews who strictly adhere to Sabbath strictures. In the film, Goodman plays the role of Walter Sobchak, a Vietnam War veteran and convert to Judaism who voices equal devotion to violence, bowling, and the Sabbath. Goodman's character would surely feel comfortable donning an "Uzi Does It!" shirt!

ShalomShirts sells an image of a man in a yarmulke holding a large pistol, taunting "Jew Talkin' to Me?" KosherShirts.com proclaimed "I have a Kosher Salami," "I hit a Homerun at Rachel's Bat Mitzvah," and "I ✿ Big Butts." Jtshirt.com offers "You Snooze, You Lose. . . To The Jews," "Sex with Me is 100% Kosher," "I hope you Jewish, Cause you Israeli Hot," "Don't Fuck with the Mossad," and "Jew so crazy." Cool Jewish Shirts prints "I ♥ Jewish Girls/ Boys," "100% Kosher Beef," "I have a Kosher Pickle," and "Nice Tallis, Want to F**k?" Likewise, KosherHam offers "Once you go Jew, nothing else will do," "I put the syn in synagogue," and, next to the face of Ron Jeremy, the Jewish porn star, "Ultimate Role Model." Another of KosherHam's shirts describes Staff Sergeant Donny Donowitz, Eli Roth's character in the Quentin Tarantino film *Inglourious Basterds* (2009), a "Hebrew School Hero." This character, states the KosherHam website, "represented two things: every Hebrew School kid's hero and not to fuck with the Yids."

Of course, the Yids or Yiddish culture generally admonished men to act like a *mensch*, which Leo Rosten defines in *The Joys of Yiddish* (1968) as "an upright, honorable, decent person." The *mensch*, in other words, is unlikely to wear a KosherHam t-shirt. But many contemporary Jewish t-shirt vendors apparently judge *menschlichkeit* to be too meekly Jewish and thus illegitimate—unless the *mensch*, as PopJudaica proclaimed on one rather funny shirt, is none other than Sammy Davis, Jr.!

"There's a movement," reported *The Jewish Daily Forward*, "inflected by hip-hop and queer liberation, of young Jews getting in touch with and celebrating their roots, rather than trying to 'pass.'"[11] But this movement, I suggest, especially in regard to masculinity, proclaims Jewishness through motifs and genres thoroughly rooted in the lexicon and mannerisms of the dominant culture. You might not "pass" in the synagogue. But you would surely "pass" on the street.

## "JEWISH GIRLS ARE HOT"

The "Jews Kick Ass" shirt (see Figure 62) I discussed earlier portrayed contemporary Jewish identity, however humorously, as exclusively masculine. To contest this androcentrism, many expressions of the New Jew Cool foreground femininity (see also Byers and Krieger 2007). Many designers, too, offer rejoinders to the passive image of Jewish women especially prominent, as Prell shows, in the clichés of the Jewish American Mother and Jewish American Princess (1999).

For example, Rotem Gear sells a "Jewtilicious" shirt (Figure 71) that encourages women to express their "Jewish bootiliciousness!" Likewise, a brand of clothing called Jew.Lo, which took its cue from J.Lo, or Jennifer Lopez, the fabulously successful Latina entertainer, promoted:

> the new Jewish female, bold, strong, invincible, and available. Jew.lo sees that Jew and cool are not incompatible . . . that the Jewish female has been underrepresented in the world of pop culture, or worse, hidden, and seeks to change that. . . Jew.Lo believes that sexuality and religion are not incompatible.

Marjorie Ingall, writing in *The Jewish Daily Forward*, confessed to finding Jew.Lo's "sassy, funky take on babe feminism appealing." To her, Jew.Lo hinted at resistance by young Jewish women to stereotypes of "selfless, guilt-provoking need and sexless, hostility-provoking greed" by modeling a new image that, however comedic, seemed "self-affirming, body-positive and fun." Jew.Lo, like Jewtilicious, mobilized humor to critique the absence or neglect of Jewish women in hip-hop, multiculturalism, and normative Judaism.[12]

After World War II, the Women's Zionist Organization of America, or Hadassah, staged fashion shows to prompt Jewish women to greater involvement in politics (Brautbar 2006: 13). The runway appealed to existing gender norms in the hopes of encouraging women to walk beyond traditional

**Figure 71**   Jewtilicious. Courtesy of R. Jean Roth; Rotem Gear.

femininity. Few members of Hadassah in the 1950s, I surmise, would have reached for Jew.Lo panties or tank tops. (Nor, for that matter, would Orthodox Jews, then or now, beholden as they are to the rules of tzniut or modesty.) And few young women of the New Jew Cool would affirm their identity with postwar knitted suits and evening gowns. But both groups of women dress for political change.

Rabbi's Daughters, another line of clothing and accessories, draws on the "expressiveness and humor" of Yiddish to combine "tradition and a fresh sense of style" (www.rabbisdaughters.com). Its slogans include "Goy Toy" (non-Jewish plaything), "Kvetch" (complain), "Yenta" (gossiper), and "Shiksa" (non-Jewish woman). It also prints the wise counsel offered by Rashi, the sev-enteenth-century sage, to "Receive with simplicity everything that happens to you." Rabbi's Daughters also sell a superhero shirt showing a masked, caped heroine socking a male villain who moans, while crumbling to the ground, "Oy!" (One wonders if this rogue received his thumping with any "simplicity."). On their panties, Rabbi's Daughters prints "Tush" (Figure 72) and "Kish Mir In Tuchas," the Yiddish equivalent of "Kiss My Ass," in pseudo-Hebrew font.

**Figure 72**  Tush. Courtesy of Rabbi's Daughters (www.rabbisdaughters.com).

The latter slogan acknowledges Jewish tradition while communicating the classic American value of unrestrained individualism.

Jewish Fashion Conspiracy ("putting the racy back into conspiracy") sold "Sexxxy men's briefs and hot ladies' low-rise panties . . . sweatshop free and positively smokin'!" One panty punned with the dreidel game played at Chanukah and proclaimed "a great miracle happened here!"—printed atop the crotch, of course. Jewish Fashion Conspiracy also offered a thong with the provocative label, "Chanukah bush." This garment intended to clothe, not unlike the KosherHam shirt that exclaims "Jewish Girls are Hot," contemporary Jewishness in a feminine sensibility, albeit in a style that many feminists might see as ultimately demeaning to women. The "Chanukah bush" shirt, too, played with the Jewish equivalent of the Christmas tree that is subject each December to considerable debate. Does this decoration promote an authentic Jewishness or subvert Judaism? It is a question that all these garments, in one form or another, pose—a question not easily answered.

A few years ago, Jewschool sold t-shirts and thongs that similarly commented on the relationship between tradition and taboo by printing the phrases "really not tznius" and "really, really, not tznius" on the crotches of women's thongs. A t-shirt shouted, "Tznius hos show me yer elbows." These garments assert a Jewish identity by obviously contravening rabbinic morality. Yet the latter slogan only makes sense, like the "Get Laid" design I discussed earlier, to readers familiar with Orthodox Judaism. Of course, this shirt also perpetuates misogyny by miming a slang locution for women popular in hip-hop and rap. Consequently, the garment both affirms and undermines, proclaims and ridicules, ethnic Jewishness.

"In the thick, messy context of contemporary American life," declares Jewcy, an online community:

> it's a remarkable moment to be a Jew. There is unparalleled opportunity for people hell-bent on making a meaningful difference with their lives, but also an unprecedented uncertainty about the relevance of old traditions and institutions (www.jewcy.com).

Jason Saft, one of the founders of Jewcy, reported to Rakoff (2003) about receiving "mail from teens who were picked on for being Jewish. They've bought the [Jewcy] T-shirt and worn it proudly to school. They're like, 'I'm Jewish. I'm Jewcy. Fuck you all.'" Fifty years ago, Rakoff correctly recognizes, "American Jews might not have felt so comfortable flipping off their tormentors" (2003). I agree. But while Jewcy and other t-shirts, briefs, and thongs take pride in Jewishness, they do so in ways that reveal the thorough embedding of Judaism in American society. Of course, devout Jews still dress apart. But Jewcy is not about religious Judaism, at least not in any conventional sense. Rather, Jewcy and other venues of the New Jew Cool aspire to a new form of Jewish identity that dresses ethnic particularism in the same cultural garb worn by everybody else.

## CONCLUSION

The New Jew Cool defiantly transgresses the authoritative vision of authentic Jewishness. Yet even ultra-Orthodox Jews enact religious disorder. The holiday of Purim raucously commemorates the postbiblical triumph of Persian Jewry over the archenemy Haman. In Europe, the festive license of Purim historically included drunkenness, masquerades, and cross-dressing (see, e.g., Belkin 2001). The centerpiece of this carnival was the *Purimspiel*, an irreverent reenactment of the Purim story that upended the categories and boundaries so vital to everyday Jewish life. The *Purimspiel* anticipated the New Jew Cool.

The most famous *Purimspiel* is still staged in the Bobov court of Hasidism (Epstein 1979; Troy 2002). In costume, Bobov men caricature hippies and African Americans, Arabs and soldiers, women and animals, even their own rebbe—everything Bobov rarely encounter, and never emulate, in everyday life. The Purim masquerade momentarily confounds the boundaries between men and women, Jew and Gentile, adult and child, human and beast, commoner and rebbe. Of course, at the end of the skit, all normative bound-aries are restored and renewed. Or so it seems.

Rabbis throughout history voiced unease with Purim antics, especially the cross-dressing (Horowitz 2006). But the folk hardly heeded. Purim lent ex-pression to muted discontent, illicit desire, and ambivalence. The Purim story also represented the unreal triumph of Jews over the dominant society. The so-called Purim Law enacted by Emperor Theodosius II in 408 specifically banned burning effigies of Haman since the figures resembled the Savior upon the Cross. The *Purimspiel* symbolically allowed everyday Jews to chal-lenge both Christianity and their own rabbis. Authorities persistently tried to curtail this ritual violence. But folk are not so easily contained.

Jews celebrate Purim by reciting the book of Esther, composed sometime in the third or fourth century B.C.E., inside the synagogue. Upon mention of the name Haman, the normally well-mannered congregation erupts into a cacophony of booing, hissing, stomping, clanking, thumping, and especially the twirling of *gragger* noisemakers. Even today, in this sense, Purim festivi-ties disrupt normative Judaism. The New Jew Cool builds on this tradition, if inadvertently. Contemporary t-shirts and thongs, however offensive to most religious Jews, nonetheless portray a common tradition of irony, wit, and co-medic renewal. The key difference between New Jews and traditionalists lies only in the tropes and tones of their respective dramas. I see the New Jew Cool as the most recent iteration of Jewish renewal, an age-old tradition, we might say, dressed in new clothing.

# Conclusion

> Jewish identity is authentic . . . and truthful . . . only when it assumes the instabil-
> ity of all identities.
>
> Stuart Charmé, *Jewish Social Studies* 2000

My concern in this book was not to document, like a laundry list, the specific items of apparel that clothed Jews over the centuries. I remain content to let others itemize the precise contents of various Jewish wardrobes. Rather, my interest lay in the effort to decode the symbolism of Jewish dress—to probe, in other words, meaning. Thus I interpreted Jewish clothing largely as a se-ries of conversations about gender, ethnicity, power, devotion, resistance, and tragedy. Some garments, we saw, especially ritual items, adorned only Jews. But other items, worn by Jew and non-Jew alike, appeared Jewish only in the sense that they conveyed aspects of Jewish experience. Often, I tacked be-tween how Jews dressed themselves and how they were ignobly dressed by others. Again and again, however, I returned to a single theme: Jewish cloth-ing throughout history materialized an ongoing, irresolvable debate over Jew-ish identity—a colloquy that continues, as we saw in the latter chapters, even today.

Generally speaking, I explored Jewish clothing from four perspectives. First, I showed that Jewish garments convey messages about the roles of men and women both sacred and mundane. In some contexts, Jews dress in accordance with rabbinic edicts that sustain this dichotomy or hierarchy; in other instances, Jews dress to challenge traditional or normative gender. Second, I demonstrated that Jews often subverted or outright ignored the de-risive dress codes imposed by European municipal and clerical authorities. Jewish clothing thereby coded for resistance as much as for submission to the dominant society. Third, I highlighted a similar tension between the rabbis and the folk—that is, conflict within the Jewish community itself. The rabbis, we saw, promoted stringent dress codes to symbolically enclose their com-munities within the Law. This fence also protected the rabbis' own vested interests. But many Jews more or less preferred to dress outside this vesti-mentary cloister. Last, I argued that Jewish clothing, especially after the rise of modernity, symbolized a wide-ranging tension between ethnic particularism and acculturation—between dressing like a Jew and dressing like an ordinary citizen defined largely by worldly success.

In the last chapter, I explored the sartorial slogans of the New Jew Cool. This style ranges from creative wit to tasteless irreverence and even, some might say, a certain self-hatred. But at a deeper level, this garb exemplifies the fluidity of ethnic identity in our postmodern moment. The designs and phrases, I showed, also seek to challenge the authority of traditional ethnic, religious, and institutional gatekeepers and to refashion Jewishness into an identity the entire society will recognize as not merely valid but also trendy and relevant. New Jews wear clothing that strives to reposition Jewishness at the center of contemporary culture, not at the periphery where Jews have long dwelled and dressed. But not all Jews are pleased, I noted, with this re-tailoring of Jewish identity and dress into a fashion statement. But fashion, in many transgressive respects, rules the day.

In 2003, American rapper Lil' Kim appeared in a diaphanous *burqa*, semi-naked, on the cover of the hip-hop magazine *Oneworld*. Muslims were out-raged.[1] Today, as we saw in Chapter 5, the West registers considerable moral qualms about *over*-dressed Muslim women. Nonetheless, the Western imagi-nation has long fantasized about *under*-dressed Arab women, especially, as Lil' Kim exemplified, seductive belly dancers and tempting harems (Jarmakani 2008). Christian bonnets and nun's habits are no less eroticized (Connerley 2006; Keenan 1999). But while popular culture often sexualizes Jewish women (Prell 1999), Jewish clothing rarely seems fetishized.

A rare and recent exception to the non-sexualization of Jewish garb comes into focus through the lens of Leonard Nimoy, the actor much beloved for his iconic role as Spock on *Star Trek*. In 2002, Nimoy published a collection of black-and-white photographs that portray alluring, often semi-dressed women as the *Shekhinah*, the feminine personification of God central to Jewish mysticism. Nimoy arranged his nudes as a meditation on cosmic femininity, eros, and generativity. His intent was far from pornographic.

Still, Nimoy's images evoke transgression as much as reverence. One set of photos features an unclothed woman draped in a tallit or prayer shawl, her arms raised in some unspoken entreaty, the fringes framing her naked breast. Another set depicts a female body, barely concealed in a gossamer robe, enwrapped in tefillin (Figure 73) Nimoy's artistry seems clearly moti-vated by genuine spirituality. But his photos are not likely to guarantee him any front row seats for the High Holidays in an Orthodox synagogue.

Nimoy's tableaus of the *Shekhinah* were widely noted in the secular and Jewish presses.[2] Yet his eroticization of men's ritual garments, draped on naked women, prompted relatively little controversy. Not so for the vestimen-tary transgressions of Jean-Paul Gaultier, the Jewish *enfant terrible* of French

**Figure 73**   Photograph by Leonard Nimoy of the *Shekhinah*, the feminine personification of God, enwrapped in tefillin. Courtesy of R. Michelson Galleries, Northampton,
Massachusetts.

fashion, in his fall 1993 "Hasidic" collection of *haute couture*. On the cat-
walk strutted women bedecked in fur caps, caftans, *faux* sidecurls, fringes,
yarmulkes, sashes, and dark colors—all evocative of the canonical attire of
Hasidic men.

The fashion industry applauded Gaultier's homage to Hasidic culture as
dignified, charming, and clever. The Jewish owner of an Upper West Side bou-
tique in New York City saw a powerful rejoinder to resurgent anti-Semitism in
Europe, while an art historian understood Gaultier to deconstruct gender and
diasporic identity (Nochlin 1996). *The New York Times* enjoyed the "campy
sendup: menorahs lined the runway; Maneschewitz wine was served; the invitations were lettered in Hebraic script."[3] Thus phrased, the designer's Hasidic
collection made Jewishness fashionable while challenging the second-class
status of women in traditional Judaism.

Yet some Jews viewed Gaultier's pastiche of Hasidism and *haute couture* with far less enthusiasm. When the French edition of *Vogue* staged a
photo shoot on the streets of Brooklyn, passing Hasidim voiced indignation

**Figure 74**   An outfit from Gunhyo Kim's "Il Galantuomo" line
of men's wear, inspired by Hasidic garb. Courtesy of firstVIEW.

(Nochlin 1996). In their religious eyes, the fashion designer's burlesque exceeded any legitimate claim to art or social commentary by crossing a taboo boundary between men and women. Gaultier dressed his models to insult, in their view, not to inspire.

Gaultier is not the only fashion designer enthralled by ultra-Orthodoxy. *The New York Times* reported that "a men's-wear collection by the Italian company Fabio Inghirami Studi . . . inspired by Hasidim drew some acidic letters after pictures appeared in the press."[4] At the 080 Barcelona Fashion show in 2008, a Korean-born graduate of Antwerp's Royal Academy of Arts, Gunhyo Kim, introduced his own take on Hasidic garb. Kim's "Il Galantuomo" line of men's wear included tasseled and striped shirts, fringed sashes and scarves, black hats, knee-high stockings, and long caftans (Figures 74–75).[5] Alexandre Herchcovitch, a Jewish fashion designer from Brazil, also draws on Orthodox styles—wide-brimmed hats,

**Figure 75**   Another outfit from Gunhyo Kim's "Il Galantuomo" line of men's wear, inspired by Hasidic garb. Courtesy of firstVIEW.

Star of David bling, fringes, long shirts recalling caftans, and black coats (Figures 76–77).[6]

Clothing designers like Gaultier, Kim, and Herchcovitch provocatively transform the tensions within modern Jewish identity into a fashion statement. They push Jewish attire, once seen as provincial and antiquated, to the forefront of contemporary culture. In so doing, they reshape ethnic identity into a garment, doffed and donned at will. These designers, too, for better or worse, violate the very canons of religious modesty they find so compelling.

In our current postmodern world, declared Stuart Charmé, an authentic Jewish identity—an identity truthful to the experiences of most Jews—is an *unstable* identity (2000). I agree. Contemporary Jewish t-shirts and thongs, like Hasidic *haute couture*, allow for little historical essentialism and no fixed canons of authenticity. They are, like so many linked websites, multiply positioned. And like cyberspace, too, contemporary Jewish identity, unlike the classic rabbinic fence, admits to no moral center.

**Figure 76**   An outfit from the Hasidic-inspired fashion in Alexandre Herchcovitch's 2007 fall fashion show. Getty Images.

Yet the postmodern Jewish wardrobe also, I suggested, speaks with contrary voices. Sarah Lefton, founder of Jewish Fashion Conspiracy, called her t-shirts a "counter-assimilation mechanism." And so they were. But this genre of Jewish garb also belies a thoroughly assimilated outlook, especially in regard to ribald verbal gags, belligerent gestures of masculinity, and in-your-face assertions of ethnic pride. These garments cast Jewishness as particularistic. Yet they represent Jewishness as wholly entangled with the dominant culture. And this tension, I showed, is a long-standing Jewish tradition. It is, in many respects, the very symbolic fibers woven into the history of Jewish dress.

New Jewish clothing, like biblical and medieval garb, communicates a variety of messages about home, diaspora, boundaries, authority, gender, commitment, and reverence—in a phrase, what it means to be a Jew. To critics,

**Figure 77** Another outfit from the Hasidic-inspired fashion in Alexandre Herchcovitch's 2007 fall fashion show. Getty Images.

exclamations of New Jewish identity might seem as flimsy as the cloth on which they are printed. But that, indeed, is the very message young Jews wish to convey: the fluidity and mutability of Jewishness. Jewish identity today is multiple and shifting—slipped on yet discarded like a fashion accessory, just another commodity, for good or bad, in the marketplace of self-invention. Many Jews surely feel uncomfortable with the messages printed on contemporary t-shirts and thongs, never mind quasi-Hasidic garb on fashion models and nudes enwrapped in tefillin. But these are just new voices, and new garments, in the age-old, ongoing, irresolvable debate over Jewish identity.

# Glossary

**Bar mitzvah** (male), **bat mitzvah** (female) (pl. **b'nai mitzvot**). Jewish coming of age rite, generally held at age thirteen, which in the twentieth century transformed into a major, often lavish ceremony.

**Bekishe**. Long black silk or polyester coat, worn by some Hasidic men, ornamented with subtle patterns.

**Chalitzah**. A special shoe used in a ritual to absolve a man of his biblical duty to wed the widow of his deceased, heirless brother (Deuteronomy 25:5–10).The ritual is still performed today in some Orthodox communities.

**Chilazon**. The marine animal that secreted the blue dye used to make *tekhelet* fringes.

**Conservative Judaism**. The religious denomination that fully accepts modern society yet strives to affirm fidelity to many aspects of traditional Jewish law; midway, in a sense, between Reform and Orthodox Judaism.

**Frum**. Yiddish word referring to a strictly observant person.

**Gartel**. Belt worn by Hasidic and other devout men during prayer; serves to divide a man's pure thoughts from the baser, lower organs of the body.

**Gematria**. Rabbinic numerology, based on the use of Hebrew letters as numerals, largely aimed at glimpsing hidden, mystical meanings in biblical words and phrases.

**Halacha**. Jewish law, formalized by the rabbis over the centuries, arising from the Mishnah but ultimately anchored to the Five Books of Moses or Torah. *Halacha* is best understood as the code of conduct for a religious lifestyle.

**Haredi** (pl. **Haredim**). The Hebrew umbrella term for ultra-Orthodox Jews, including Hasidim. Haredim generally shun modernity and modern dress.

**Haskalah**. The Jewish Enlightenment movement of the eighteenth and especially nineteenth centuries, based in Germany.

**Hasidic, Hasidim**. Devout traditionalist Jews, now a part of the Ultra-Orthodox or Haredi movement, who originally split from mainstream Jewry in the seventeenth century. Hasidim, organized into dynasties or courts, are known for their mystical inclinations, charismatic leaders, iconic fur hats, and stereotypically antiquated men's attire.

**Kabbalah**. Jewish mysticism, based on certain medieval texts, now widely popular in various "new age" configurations. Despite this, *kabbalah* remains a serious study to scholars and devout Jews.

**Kapoteh**. Long wool coat worn by some Hasidic men.

**Kittel**. Plain white robe worn by Orthodox Jewish men for certain rituals and in burial.

**Kippah**. (also sp. *kippa* and *kipa*). The Hebrew term for a small cap, or yarmulke, worn for prayer and generally associated with religious Jewish men.

**Maskilim**. Advocates of the Jewish Enlightenment movement or *Haskalah*.

**Mentsch**. The Yiddish word for a decent, upstanding, humble, and moral man.

**Midrash**. A rabbinic legend that seeks to explain some puzzle or enigma in the Hebrew Bible. In traditional Judaism, these exegetical tales have an authoritative status.

**Mishnah**. A series of early rabbinic conversations codified in the early third century that form the basis for subsequent Jewish law. The Mishnah, also known as the Oral Law, serves as a commentary on the laws in the Hebrew Bible, and thus provides the essential foundation for Orthodox Jewish scholarship.

**Mitnagdim**. The religious establishment that rejected the rise of Hasidim; the name means "opponents." Also known as the "Lithuanian school."

**Modern Orthodox**. Orthodox Jews who more or less dress in secular fashions; they participate in modern life to a much greater extent than ultra-Orthodox or Haredi Jews.

**Orthodox Judaism**. A broad category of strictly observant Jews, consisting of Modern Orthodox, traditional Orthodox or Lithuanians (see Haredim), and Hasidim.

**Purimshpeil**. A skit performed on the holiday of Purim that often inverts everyday norms of behavior.

**Rebbe.** The charismatic leader of a Hasidic court who, shaman-like, serves as an intermediary between humanity and God.

**Reform Judaism**. The Jewish denomination that arose in Germany in the latter nineteenth century that synthesizes Jewishness with modernity. The most assimilated of all Jewish religious groups.

**Rekel**. Long, dark wool coat worn by some Hasidic men.

**Responsum** (pl. **responsa**). A rabbinic legal decision offered in response to a question about how to apply divine law to a practical matter.

**Seder**. Ritual Passover feast.

**Sha'atnez**. A certain textile, understood to be a wool and linen blend, banned by biblical law (Deuteronomy 22:11; Leviticus 19:19).

**Shtetl**. The iconic Eastern European market town from which many Jews emigrated in the latter nineteenth century.

**Shtreimel**. Round, relatively squat fur hat worn by some Hasidic men.

**Shul.** Yiddish for synagogue.

**Sotah**. A biblical woman suspected of adultery by her husband; she underwent an infamous ordeal to determine her guilt or innocence, which included the public unfurling of her hair (Numbers 5:11–31).

**Spodik**. Tall fur hat worn by some Hasidic men.

**Tallit** (pl. **tallitot**). A fringed scarf or shawl traditionally worn by Jewish men during prayer and ritual. The garment is traced to Numbers 15:37–41 and Deuteronomy 22:12. Today, many women also wear *tallitot*. The fringed shawl or scarf is called a *tallit-gadol* (large tallit). A fringed undershirt worn by Orthodox Jewish men and boys—now, some women—is called a *tallit-katan* (small tallit) (see also tzitzit).

**Talmud**. The best-known compilation of classic rabbinic commentary, based on the Mishnah. There are two Talmuds, actually, the Palestinian or Jerusalem Talmud and the slightly later, larger, and more authoritative Babylonian Talmud. Both Talmuds were redacted in the fifth to sixth centuries.

**Tefillin**. Leather boxes, containing scriptural passages, affixed to leather straps and worn traditionally by religious men during morning prayers. One box is strapped around the forehead; the other is wound around the arm. The practice derives from Exodus 13:16 and Deuteronomy 6:8 and 11:18.

**Tekhelet**. A biblical blue dye, once used to color a single thread in the tzitzit fringes (Numbers 15:37–41; see also tallit). The color derived from a marine animal (*chilazon*) whose specific identity is the subject of ongoing controversy. The practice faded many centuries ago, but is now experiencing something of a revival.

**Torah**. The Hebrew word for the Five Books of Moses, consisting of Genesis (*Bereshit*), Exodus (*Shemot*), Leviticus (*Vayikra*), Numbers (*Bamidbar*), and Deuteronomy (*Devarim*). Also known as the Written Law.

**Totafot**. Some type of biblical headband, today understood to be part of the command for men to wear tefillin during morning prayers.

**Tzitzit**. Special fringes, consisting of set patterns of windings and knots, attached to prayer shawls and Orthodox undershirts (see also tallit).

**Tzniut**. The broad code of modesty governing Orthodox and ultra-Orthodox (Haredi) men and especially women. Tzniut is especially important for devout women's attire.

**Yarmulke**. The small, round cap worn by many Jewish men for prayer, ritual, and the study of sacred texts. Devout men—today, some women—wear a yarmulke at all times.

**Yeshiva**. A religious day school attended by Jewish boys.

# Notes

## INTRODUCTION

1. "The Day of Atonement," *The New York Times*, September 27, 1898, p. 6.
2. "Holiday Style: Mizrahi Dishes Do's and Don'ts," *Jewish Daily Forward*, September 12, 2006, http://www.forward.com/articles/3884/.
3. These abstinences were formalized in a third-century codification of Jewish law called, as I discuss later in this chapter, the Mishnah, specifically the section Yoma 8:1.
4. Another Yom Kippur tradition is for cantors or *kohanim* (priestly descendents) to remove their shoes before blessing their congregations. When the *kohanim* raise their arms for this benediction, they inevitably lift their hems. The absence of shoes spares congregations the insult of beholding potentially muddy footwear. Shoelessness, too, helps cantors avoid an even more awkward moment. Should a lace accidentally snap during the blessing, and a canter pause to tie it, his congregation might fear some dreadful unworthiness (B. Sotah 40a; see also Rabbi Mendel Weinbach, "Shoeless in the Synagogue," http://ohr.edu/yhiy/article.php/330).
5. See "Israel—Rabbi Elyashiv: No Crocs on Yom Kippur," Vos Iz Neias? (September 25, 2009), http://bit.ly/2XKXgX.
6. Benjamin Z. Kreitman and Joyce B. Kreitman, "Fashions for the Synagogue," *United Synagogue Review* 25 (1972): 14–15, 31.
7. I should also mention Ruth M. Green's *A Brief History of Jewish Dress* (2001, London: Safira)—notable for its illustrations, not for any sustained or scholarly insights. I note, too, the recent 2012 publication by Daisy Raccah-Djivre, *The Jewish Wardrobe: From the Collection of the Israel Museum, Jerusalem* (Milan, Italy: 5 Continents), and the forthcoming Berg Press title by Lynne Hume, *The Religious Life of Dress: Global Fashion and Faith*.
8. Following scholarly conventions, I abbreviate the Mishnah and Babylonian Talmud as M and B, followed by the name of a tractate and a folio page number. For the former, I consulted Herbert Danby's 1933 translation published by Oxford University Press, *The Mishnah: Translated from the Hebrew with Introduction and Brief Explanatory Notes*. My source for the Talmud was the twenty-seven-volume set published by Soncino Press, now available on a handy, searchable cd-rom.
9. But see, for example, Binyaminov (2002), Emelyanenko (1997), and Rubens (1967, chapter 2).

10. James Barron, "A Flight Is Diverted by a Prayer Seen as Ominous," *The New York Times*, January 21, 2010, http://www.nytimes.com/2010/01/22/nyregion/22airplane.html.

## CHAPTER 1 (UN)DRESSING THE ISRAELITES

1. Biblical texts refer to women as spinners and weavers (Exodus 35:25; Proverbs 31:13).
2. Sometimes the Torah mentions scarlet (*shani*) without the "worm" (e.g., Genesis 38:28), perhaps indicating a different, less opulent hue.
3. The Bible says little about children's clothing. But Job 38:9 may mention swaddling cloth (*chathullah*), and a young prophet in 1 Samuel 2:18 oddly wears a garment (*ephod*) normally associated with the High Priest.
4. Other references to biblical shoes include Carmichael (1977) and Nacht (1915–16). For the Cinderella tale cross-culturally, see Dundes (1989).
5. Eilberg-Schwartz discusses the controversial horn interpretation (1994: 143–45). For the iconography of Moses's veil in Christian art, see Britt (2003).
6. Centuries later, the redactors of the Hebrew Bible misunderstood Ham's glance (Bassett 1971). Taking it literally, they emended the tale so Ham's brothers walked backward into the tent to cover their father.
7. Other biblical instances of clothing and disguise include Joshua 9:4, 1 Samuel 28:8, and 2 Samuel 14:2.
8. For the High Priest's headdress in Jewish and Christian art, see Mellinkoff (1987).
9. In the tenth century, Jews started to drape ornaments on the Torah scrolls said to resemble the High Priest's adornments (Gutmann 1970).
10. The word *ephod* also suggests a divine image (Judges 17:5; 18:14).
11. In latter books of the Hebrew Bible, kings and prophets wear the same type of robe, in at least one instance woven from imported *bûs* linen (1 Chronicles 15:27).
12. Ordinary priests also dressed in a plain linen when ascending the altar to remove sacrificial ashes (Leviticus 6:10). Angels are similarly attired (e.g., Ezekiel 10:2).
13. This adage is variously traced to John Wesley's 1791 sermon "On Dress," Sir Francis Bacon's 1605 essay "Advancement of Learning," and the second-century rabbi Phineas ben Yair.
14. For the phallic symbolism of hair in the context of Jewish circumcision, see Bilu (2000), Silverman (2006, chapter 6), and, related, Leach (1970/2001).
15. Rachel Neiman, "A Sandal for All Occasions," *The Jerusalem Post*, May 15, 1996. The early Zionists also harnessed Yemenite jewelry and textiles to Jewish nationalism (Guilat 2006). Ironically, Israeli men often grew a hairstyle called a *blorit*, which the classic banned as idolatrous (Almog 2003).

## CHAPTER 2  THE FASHION OF THE RABBIS

1. The rabbis imaginatively elaborated on the divine source and symbolism of the outfits worn by Adam and the High Priest (e.g., Ricks 2000; Swartz 2002).

2. These solutions, with proper rabbinic references, appeared in "Weekly Halacha—Parshas Chayei Sara," Rabbi Doniel Neustadt Rav, Young Israel, Cleveland Heights, 2005, http://torahsearch.com/page.cfm/2079.

3. Here I draw on the footnoted commentary in the Soncino edition of the Talmud; see also Cohon (1987: 346).

4. My translation here is from http://www.chabad.org/library/article_cdo/aid/910314/jewish/Deot.htm.

5. The word "Sabbath" is the English rendition of the Hebrew "Shabbat." Yiddish speakers say "Shabbos."

6. The Talmud dressed menstruating women in old clothing (B. Kethuboth 64b–65b; see also Schwartz 2004: 132–33).

7. Camp S'dei Chemed, http://www.campsci.com/camp/next_summer/suggested_clothing_list.htm.

8. See Rabbi Gidon Rothstein's Halakhah in Brief #52, "Taering [*sic*] keriah for Jerusalem," http://www.rjconline.org/hib52.htm. On Passover, religious Jews enact a similar legal fiction. This holiday requires Jews to avoid eating and even owning *chametz*, that is, food containing any of five grains (wheat, rye, barley, oats, and spelt) that have been in contact with water for more than eighteen minutes prior to cooking (e.g., bread and pasta). Jews unwilling to dispose of so much food "sell" their *chametz* to non-Jews for a token fee, then repurchase the food after the holiday. Even modern Israel, through the Chief Rabbinate, sells state-owned *chametz* during the holiday.

9. A similar situation arises in Orthodox Jewry when a husband refuses to grant an estranged wife a Jewish divorce (*get*)—or is unable to do so, say, because he went missing in battle. The woman is henceforth called an *agunah* and unable to remarry. Any children she bears are not recognized as full Jews. No comparable scenario afflicts men. See the Organization for the Resolution of Agunot (http://www.getora.com) and the Jewish Orthodox Feminist Alliance (www.jofa.org).

10. See http://israel.usembassy.gov/consular/acs/marriage.html.

11. Aaron Moss, "Shoelaces," http://www.chabad.org/library/article_cdo/aid/398987/jewish/Shoelaces.htm.

## CHAPTER 3  BITTER BONNETS AND BADGES

1. Canon sixty-eight also forbade Jews from appearing in public for several days before Easter and especially on Good Friday. My translation is from *The Medieval Sourcebook*, http://www.fordham.edu/halsall/basis/lateran4.html.

2. Many Jewish communities in Europe once banned shoes from the synagogue to avoid soiling the building. Poor Jews walked to prayer in their
stockings, while the wealthy stored special footwear near the sanctuary
(Pollack 1971: 149–50).

3. The church also *un*-dressed Jews. In 1466, Pope Paul II added a novel
event to the Roman Carnival: footraces, including a contest by naked
Jews as witnessed in 1581 by essayist Michel de Montaigne, about
which he reported in his *Travel Journal* (1948: 946). Sometimes the unclothed Jewish runners were force-fed so they would collapse and vomit
(Wisch 2003: 152–53).

4. Among the many sources on the medieval Jewish patch are Rubens (1967:
82–88), *The Jewish Encyclopedia* entry on "Badge" and "Badge, Jewish" in
*Medieval Jewish Culture: An Encyclopedia*, N. Roth, ed., pp. 67–70, 2002,
New York: Routledge.

5. Neither the Torah nor early Jewish texts speak about the shape of the tablets. The profile we know today—tall, rectangular, rounded tops—emerged
in England in the thirteenth century (Mellinkoff 1974).

6. Of course, Cain's mark also served as a sign of divine protection (Genesis 4:15), a nuance often forgotten.

7. For a recent addition to the vast literature on non-Jewish medieval clothing, see Burns (2004).

8. Stein reports on the fascinating role of Jews in the international trade in
ostrich plumes, which lasted until 1914, when feathers turned unfashionable (2007).

9. On the role of the church and Christianity in shaping Nazism, see Ericksen and Heschel, eds. (1999) and Steigmann-Gall (2003).

10. For a translation of Weltsch's essay, see http://www1.yadvashem.org/
about_holocaust/documents/part1/doc14.html, or http://www.jewish-
virtuallibrary.org/jsource/Holocaust/badge.html.

11. The book is *The Yellow Star: The Legend of King Christian X of Denmark*,
authored by Carmen Agra Deedy, illustrated by Henri Sorensen (2000,
Peachtree Publishers).

12. See http://www.foreignaffairs.house.gov/archives/107/72977.pdf.

13. Jonathan Beck, "Auctioned Yellow Star Sparks Outrage," *The Jerusalem Post*,
December 31, 2007, http://www.jpost.com/Israel/Article.aspx?id=87202.

14. "The Gaza Withdrawal: The Evacuation; Tearfully but Forcefully, Israel
Removes Gaza Settlers," *The New York Times*, August 18, 2005; "Gaza
Settlers End Orange Star Distribution But Some Continue to Wear Them,"
*Israel Insider*, December 23, 2004, http://web.israelinsider.com/Articles/
Politics/4643.htm.

## CHAPTER 4  DRESSING FOR ENLIGHTENED CITIZENSHIP

1. As far back as the twelfth century, Jewish grooms furnished their brides
with new wardrobes (Pollack 1971: 35). Wedding gifts included shoes,

belts, cloaks, rings, veils, and diadems (Veselská 2004; Weinstein 2003).

2. The gift of French citizenship was perhaps aided by the payment of eighteen thousand pounds (Szajkowski 1955).

3. For an online translation, see "1804 Russian Set of Laws Concerning Jews" at http://www.jewishgen.org/belarus/1804_laws.htm.

4. A fascinating source is Vitaly Osipovich Levanda's 1874 book *The Complete Chronological Collection of Laws and Legal Positions Concerning the Jews: From the Legal Code of Czar Alexsei Mikailovich to the Present Time, 1649–1873* (*Polnyi khronologicheskii sbornik zakonov i polozhenii kasai-ushchikhsia Evreev: ot Ulozheniia Tsaria Aleksieia Mikhailovicha do nas-toiashchago vremeni, ot 1649–1873 g*), translated online at http://www.angelfire.com/ms2/belaroots/levanda.htm.

5. See Horowitz (1994) and Sinkoff (2004) for Jewish beards in the eighteenth century.

6. Ashkenazi Jews largely praised their new garments. But against the "coldness" of Western glitter, wrote a Sephardi memoirist, we "gathered tighter the folds of our homespun mantles . . . enjoying their softness and warmth" (Matza 1987).

7. See "Levi Strauss (1829–1902)," Jewish Virtual Library, http://www.jewishvirtuallibrary.org/jsource/biography/Strauss.html, and "For Students & Teachers" at the Levi Strauss & Co. website, http://www.levistrauss.com/heritage/.

8. See "Ida Rosenthal: Brassiere Tycoon," Who Made America?, http://www.pbs.org/wgbh/theymadeamerica/whomade/rosenthal_hi.html and "The Maidenform Story" at the company website, http://www.maidenform.com/custserv/custserv.jsp?sectionId=34.

9. See *The Rudi Gernreich Book*, Peggy Moffitt and William Claxton (1999, Taschen). Gernreich was also the subject of a 2001 retrospective by the Institute of Contemporary Art, University of Pennsylvania.

10. "New York's Petticoat Lane," *Puck*, February 27, 1884, p. 46.

11. "One of Every Four in Manhattan Borough A Jew," *Atlanta Constitution*, September 14, 1902, p. A3.

12. "Keeping in Style," *New York Tribune*, August 26, 1900.

13. "Well-dressed Women," *The New York Times*, October 28, 1925, p. 24.

14. "Women to Censor Window Displays," *The New York Times*, February 27, 1919, p. 12.

15. "Pastors Approve Ban on the Tango," *The New York Times*, January 5, 1914, p. 5; "Dr. Wise Attacks Fashion's Follies," *The New York Times*, January 2, 1922, p. 22; "Polish Rabbis Protest on Feminine Fashions," *The Washington Post*, August 11, 1924, p. 5.

16. "Ask Jews to Drop Yiddish and Wine," *The New York Times*, January 25, 1923, p. 10.

17. "Want Modest Garb for Women," *The New York Times*, October 27, 1925, p. 15.

18. "The Unpopularity of Jews," *The New York Times*, May 29, 1893, p. 5.

19. Emily Post, *Etiquette in Society, in Business, in Politics and at Home*, chapter 4, "Salutations of Courtesy: When a Gentleman Takes Off His Hat" (New York: Funk & Wagnalls, 1922), http://www.bartleby.com/95/4.html.

20. "Reform in Man's Dress," *The New York Times*, July 8, 1923.

21. A full run of *The American Jewess* is freely available online through the generosity of the Jewish Women's Archive, http://quod.lib.umich.edu/a/amjewess.

22. "Jewels No Longer Synonymous with Jewess," *The American Jewess*, vol. 9, is. 3, January 1899.

23. "Editorial," *The American Jewess*, vol. 2, is. 8, May 1896, pp. 438–40.

24. "A Plea for Simplicity," *The American Jewess*,' vol. 2, is. 8, May 1896, pp. 411–13.

25. "Gentle Manners," *The American Jewess*, vol. 9, is. 5, August 1899, p. 11.

26. "Mrs. Ruskay and Judaism," *The New York Times*, May 31, 1894, p. 1.

27. "Judaism and its Ceremonies," *The American Jewess*, vol. 4, is. 2, November 1896, pp. 78–81.

28. "Whole East Side Went Shopping Yesterday," *The New York Times*, December 24, 1900, p. 2.

## CHAPTER 5 FASHIONABLY MODEST OR MODESTLY UNFASHIONABLE?

1. "Rabbis: Modesty Slacking, Stand Guard" (November 19, 2006), http://www.ynetnews.com/articles/0.7340.L-3329995.00.html; "Operation 'Cover-Up,'" November 17, 2006, http://www.ynetnews.com/articles/0.7340.L-3329074.00.html.

2. The edict specifically forbids men from reciting a prayer called the *she'ma* in close proximity to female flesh or voices. This prayer, perhaps the liturgical centerpiece of Judaism, affirms, after Deuteronomy 6:4–9, the monotheistic existence of God.

3. "Basics of Tznius," http://www.davening.net/tznius.html.

4. Pamela McLoughlin, "BCA Skirts Guided by Religious Principles," *The New Haven Register*, February 4, 2007; for the team website, see http://www.schacademy.org/page.cfm?p=969.

5. Each month, Hasidic women re-trim their hair in preparation for a purifying bath (*mikvah*) necessary for resuming conjugal relations after a fourteen-day menstrual hiatus.

6. It is forbidden to wear a wig made from your own hair.

7. See http://www.hashkafah.com/lofiversion/index.php?t197.html. For yet another typology, see Heilman (1992: 121).

8. For an online source on the poster campaign, including unmoderated comments by readers, see http://www.crownheights.info/index.php?itemid=14326.

9. Neta Sela, "Haredi crusade against immodest clothing goes up in flames," *Israel Jewish Scene*, January 26, 2007, http://www.ynetnews.com/articles/0.7340.L-3357145.00.html.

10. Neta Sela, "'Modesty Patrol' Suspected of Spilling Acid on Teenage Girl," June 5, 2008, http://www.ynet.co.il/english/articles/0.7340.L-3552461.00.html.

11. "Married Yeshiva Students Warn Against Wives' Short Skirts, Tight Sweaters," November 9, 2006, http://www.jpost.com/JewishWorld/Judaism/Article.aspx?id=41834.

12. "Woman in Insular Hasidic Community Says Clothes Spurred Vandalism," September 7, 2007, http://wcbstv.com/topstories/orthodox.jew.vandalism.2.247104.html.

13. "Fashion Statement: Jewish Burqas," *The Jewish Daily Forward*, January 30, 2008, http://www.forward.com/articles/12558/.

14. Jonathan Lis, "5 Haredi Men Beat Woman Who Refused to Move to Back of Bus," October 21, 2007, http://www.haaretz.com/hasen/spages/915215.html; Aviram Zino, "High Court Slams 'Kosher' Bus Lines for Ultra-Orthodox," January 14, 2008, http://www.ynet.co.il/english/articles/0.7340,L-3494191.00.html.

15. A similar ruckus took to the skies in 2009 when Haredi Jews demanded that El Al, the national airline of Israel, institute "kosher" flights—no movies, no female attendants, mandatory segregated seating—during Passover. See Nathan Jeffay, "Haredi Jews Urged to Avoid El Al: 'Immodest' In-Flight Entertainment Is At Issue," *The Jewish Daily Forward*, March 20, 2009, http://www.forward.com/articles/104146/.

16. "Split Ends," *The Jewish Chronicle*, June 4, 2004, http://bit.ly/zvcA5l.

17. Thomas J. Luech, "Orthodox Jews in Brooklyn Burn Banned Wigs," *The New York Times*, May 17, 2004.

18. "Rabbis Issue Different Wig Rulings," *The Jewish Chronicle*, May 28, 2004, http://bit.ly/ychW9v.

19. See http://www.acewigs.com/shop/wigs/News/13485.php.

20. "IMC-USA expresses dismay over the public burning of wigs made of Hindu hair in New York City and Israel by Orthodox Jews," www.imc-usa.org/cgi-bin/cfm/PressRelease.cfm?PRID=80.

21. "Statement by The Bostoner Rebbe, Rabbi Levi Yitzchok Horowitz, Our Women of Valor be Praised, May 27, '04 / 7 Sivan 5764," *Israel National News*, http://www.savvysheitels.com/bostonerarticle.shtml.

22. Alan Scher Zagier, "Mennonites Leaving Mo. Over Photo Law," Associated Press. March 21, 2007, http://www.wwrn.org/article.php?idd=24583&sec=22&con=4.

23. Wendy Margolin, "Secretary Of State Approves Hats in License Photos," *Jewish United Fund News*, November 7, 2006, http://www.juf.org/news/local.aspx?id=10698.

24. Steve Lieberman, "Ramapo Arrest Controversy Sheds Light On How Police Deal With Religious Beliefs," *The Journal News*, July 6, 2008.

25. See, for example, Oren Dorell, "Effort to Accommodate Muslim Women's Modesty Spurs Debate," June 13, 2006, http://www.usatoday.com/news/nation/2006–06–13-muslim-modesty_x.htm; Elijah Jordan Tuner, "Alumni Pool Introduces Single-Sex Swim Hours," *The Tech*, March 21, 2008, http://tech.mit.edu/V128/N14/swimming.html.

26. Ingrid Peritz, "YMCA, Hasidic Jews at odds over exercise garb," November 21, 2006, http://www.scrippsnews.com/node/16131.

27. Turkey, a secular nation with a majority Muslim population, formally banned headscarves from universities in 1982. The ban was softened in the latter 1980s, then renewed in 1989 and, most recently, upheld by the European Human Rights Court in 2005. Amendments abolishing the ban in 2008 were annulled several months later by the Constitutional Court. This ongoing debate promises no resolution.

28. Jamey Keaten, "Sarkozy Says Burqas are 'Not welcome' in France," Associated Press, June 22, 2009, http://apne.ws/xv7gCq.

29. I gratefully acknowledge a personal communication from Mayanthi Fernando (June 2009) on French Jewish responses to *L'Affaire du Foulard*.

30. See Marc Perelman, "French Minister Unveils Plan to Fight Antisemitism, *The Jewish Daily Forward*, March 7, 2003, http://www.sisterhood.forward.com/articles/9398/.

31. Tzofia Hirschfeld, "Introducing 'Vogue' With Sleeves," Ynetnews.com, May 27, 2011, http://www.ynetnews.com/articles/0.7340.L-4070739.00.html.

32. Michal Lando, "'Shabbos Robe' Sellers Struggle," *The Jerusalem Post*, December 30, 2007, http://www.jpost.com/JewishWorld/JewishFeatures/Article.aspx?id=87126. See also Jonathan Mark, "Costume Jewry: For the Orthodox, there is no casual Friday or Saturday," *The New York Jewish Week*, November 29, 2002, p. 10.

33. In 2007, the scholarly journal *Fashion Theory* devoted a special double issue to Muslim fashion (Vol. 11, No. 2–3).

34. See Allan Salkin, "American Girl's Journey to the Lower East Side," *The New York Times*, May 22, 2009, http://nyti.ms/yGe9mn; Michael Paulson, "Meet Rebecca, Jewish American Girl doll," *The Boston Globe*, May 31, 2009, http://bo.st/Jvy8L.

35. See http://www.fulla.com/, http://www.noorart.com/ and Yaqin (2007).

36. In 2003, Saudi Arabia's Committee for the Propagation of Virtue and Prevention of Vice banned Barbie dolls because these "*Jewish* . . . dolls, with their revealing clothes and shameful postures . . . are a symbol of decadence." See "Barbie Deemed Threat to Saudi Morality," Associated Press, reprinted at USAToday.com, September 10, 2003, http://www.usatoday.com/news/offbeat/2003–09–10-barbie_x.htm.

37. Suzanne C. Ryan, "Suit Up, Boychik: It's Every Jewish Boy's Bad Dream: Going With Mom to Shop for a Bar Mitzvah Outfit," *The Boston Globe*, March 4, 1998.

38. Martha Mendelsohn, "All Dressed Up With 100 Bar/Bat Mitzvahs to Go," *The Jewish Week*, November 7, 2006, http://www.thejewishweek.com/bottom/specialcontent.php3?artid=1297.

39. Alex Witchel, "Needs Dress," *The New York Times*, February 23, 2003, p. 9.
40. Fishman seeks middle ground, excoriating the licentious excesses of secular culture and certain strands of feminism as well as berating reactionary Jewish Orthodoxy (2000).

## CHAPTER 6  BLACK HATS AND UNSUITABLE SUITS

1. "And You Thought Abercrombie & Fitch Was Pushing It?," Jaime Wolf, *The New York Times Magazine*, April 23, 2006.
2. See http://www.dovcharney.com/statement.html.
3. See, for example, Alan Duke, "American Apparel settles Woody Allen Suit for $5 million," May 18, 2009, http://bit.ly/nzC4m.
4. See http://www.ohelchabad.org/templates/articlecco_cdo/aid/78445.
5. See http://www.likelihoodofconfusion.com/?page_id=947, http://bit.ly/x8B9mL.
6. Yerachmiel Tilles, "Why the Long Black Coat?," http://www.chabad.org/library/article.asp?AID=3186.
7. *Gartels*, or *gartlach* in Yiddish, are sized according to width: six strings (one-half inch), eighteen strings (two inches), even forty-four strings or what ZionJudiaca.com calls the "Grand Rabbis' size."
8. "The Beard," Aron Moss, http://www.chabad.org/library/article_cdo/aid/160973/jewish/The-Beard.htm.
9. The feud erupted when the reigning rebbe, Yehoshua Moshe Hagar, took ill and his two sons, Yisrael and Menachem, vied for succession. See "Shtreimel vs. Shtreimel," June 30, 2008, http://www.ynetnews.com/articles/0.7340.L-3561961.00.html.
10. See, for example, "A Practical Guide to Keeping Your Clothes Kosher," Rabbi Shragga Simmons, Aish.com, http://www.aish.com/jl/m/48948976.html.
11. Among devout Jews, the acronym STaM (with a lowercase "a") refers to *Sifrei Torah*, *Tefillin*, *Mezuzot*, that is, the special calligraphy used in the writing of sacred texts.
12. My source here is an obscure publication, *The Talis in Jewish Life/The Mitzvah of Shaatnes*, by Shmuel L. Rubenstein (Bronx, 5724), available from the library of Hebrew Union College–Jewish Institute of Religion in Cincinnati.
13. "A Man of the Cloth," David Koeppel, *The New York Times*, July 22, 2001.
14. "Zara Apologizes for Mixing Materials in Man Suit," *European Jewish Press*, May 22, 2007, http://www.ejpress.org/article/news/western_europe/16970; "Zara Goes Kosher After Suit Offends Orthodox Jews," May 22, 2007, http://www.guardian.co.uk/world/2007/may/22/spain.israel.
15. Rabbi Gershon Tannenbaum, "Turkish Tallis Shatnez Crisis," *The Jewish Press*, February 25, 2009, http://www.thejewishpress.com/printArticle.cfm?contentid=38328.

## CHAPTER 7 STRAPS, FRINGES, SNAILS, AND SHAWLS

1. See http://www.stam.net/how_to_put_on_tefillin.aspx.
2. These cases are available online at www.ajudaica.com, www.jewish-source.com, and www.milechai.com.
3. Ken Lane, "Modern Day Dilemmas That Come While Wearing Tzitzit," March 17, 2009, http://www.frumsatire.net/2009/03/17/modern-day-dilemmas-that-come-while-wearing-tzitzit/.
4. For nine different tying techniques, see http://www.tekhelet.com/diagrams/TyingDiagramSeriesHomePage.htm.
5. The late French philosopher, Jacques Derrida, often meditated on the tallit (see Beal and Linafelt 2005).
6. I arrived at this sum by applying the Consumer Price Index in 2008 to Milgrom's (1983) earlier calculations.
7. See Akiva Herzfeld, "The Quest for the Holy Snail: The Story of *Tekhelet*," *The Commentator*, vol. 63, no. 5, Yeshiva University, http://commie.droryikra.com/v63i5/features/tekhelet.shtml; and "*Misnagdishe Techelet*: The work of *Amutat P'Til Tekhelet*," Beged Ivri, http://israelvisit.co.il/beged-ivri/techelet/misnagid.htm.
8. See, for example, Wertheim (1992: 120).
9. For background to Beged Ivri and Jewish fundamentalism more generally, see Gorenberg (2000).
10. See, for example, American Reform Responsa, 4. Woman Wearing a Talit (Vol. 80, 1970, pp. 55–56), http://data.ccarnet.org/cgi-bin/respdisp.pl?file=4&year=arr. See also Congregation and Tallit, New American Reform Responsa, Central Conference of American Rabbis, http://data.ccarnet.org/cgi-bin/respdisp.pl?file=9&year=narr.
11. See http://www.hasoferet.com/bar/barbie.shtml.
12. See http://sospire.blogspot.com/2004/03/who-knew-that-rosie-riveter-was-lefty.html.
13. See Friedman's statement on "Women's Tefillin" at Ritualwell.org (http://www.ritualwell.org/ritual/womens-tefillin) and her own website, www.yanafriedman.info/main.html.
14. See www.uscj.org/USCJ_Tallit_Order_Fo5975.html.
15. Nir Hasson and Liel Kyzer, "Police Arrest Woman for Wearing Prayer Shawl at Western Wall," November 18, 2009, http://www.haaretz.com/hasen/spages/1129040.html.
16. See "Woman Attacked for Tefillin Imprint," May 13, 2010, http://www.jta.org/news/article/2010/05/13/2394791/conservative-woman-attacked-for-tefillin-imprint.
17. For the controversy, see Robert Mackey, "An 'Israeli Remix' of a Palestinian Scarf," *The New York Times*, February 8, 2010, http://thelede.blogs.nytimes.com/2010/02/08/a-new-israeli-remix-of-a-palestinian-scarf/.
18. "Talit HaKatan Shel Shabbatai Tzvi," http://danielsieradski.com/2005/04/4040/talit-hakatan-shel-shabbatai-tzvi/.

## CHAPTER 8 I ♥ YARMULKE DAY

1. See http://www.chabadtalk.com/go/ph/ph-7.htm. Another Lubavitcher source on the yarmulke is http://www.chabad.org/library/article_cdo/aid/110370/jewish/The-Skullcap.htm.

2. "Waste Materials. On Old Used Leather," *The New York Times*, June 28, 1874, p. 3.

3. See *Reform Judaism in the Large Cities*, Union of American Hebrew Congregation, 1931, and *The Voice Of The Jewish Laity: A Survey Of The Jewish Layman's Religious Attitudes And Practices*, Arthur L. Reinhart, National Committee on Religious Propaganda, the National Federation of Temple Brotherhoods, 1928.

4. *Catalogue of Anglo-Jewish Historical Exhibition, 1887. Royal Albert Hall. And of Supplementary Exhibitions Held at the Public Record Office, British Museum, South Kensington Museum*. London: William Clowes and Sons, 1887.

5. "Yom Kippur Worship (Orthodox)," *The American Jewess*, Vol. 2, is. 1, p. 10.

6. See Jonathan Mark, "Costume Jewry: For the Orthodox, There is No Casual Friday or Saturday," *The New York Jewish Week*, November 29, 2002, http://www.thejewishweek.com/news/newscontent.php3?artid=7045&print=yes.

7. In one folktale, yarmulkes allowed devout Victorian Jews to tip their top hats in accordance with secular etiquette while remaining covered before God (see Zimmer 1992: 337).

8. "'Stalling' on Jews Charged by Mayor," *The New York Times*, September 16, 1946.

9. The Na Nachs maintain several websites (e.g., http://www.nanach.net/ and http://www.nanach.org/) on which they post YouTube videos of their music and dancing. See also Adam Molner, "Rolling With the *Na Nachs*, the Most High-Spirited and Newest Hasidic Sect," July 29, 2008, http://www.haaretz.com/hasen/spages/984972.html.

10. For a nice, concise summary of this controversy, see a 1999 essay by Samuel G. Freedman, "The Battle Over Reform Judaism," online at *Salon Magazine*, http://www.salon.com/news/feature/1999/05/01/jews/index.html.

11. See http://www.chabad.org/library/article_cdo/aid/160972/jewish/Whats-Up-With-the-Kipah.htm.

12. My source here is my own father, Philip Silverman.

13. For a cute essay on this topic, see Joshua Hammerman's "The Yarmulke Bin," *The Jewish Week*, September 7, 2007.

14. For the actual article, published on September 23, 1990, click on the "media" link at the webpage for J. Levine, http://levinejudaica.com.

15. The Union of American Hebrew Congregations published a forty-six-page guidebook, "Sweatshops: Raising Awareness in Congregations,"

http://rac.org/_kd/Items/actions.cfm?action=Show&item_id=979&destination=ShowItem; see also Anat Tamir, "Kosher Clothing," posted on the website ClickonJudaism, hosted by the Commission on Outreach and Synagogue Community, Union for Reform Judaism, http://clickonjudaism.org/pages/contemporary_issues.html.

16. For an English translation of the original Yiddish editorial of April 3, 1911, see "Jews and Birds," *Forest and Stream*, April 22, 1911, p. 614.
17. The Obama-kah was not officially linked to the campaign, http://jewsforobama.blogspot.com. I assume likewise for the other yarmulkes. Voters could purchase the McCippah, and another Obama-kah, at PopJudaica.com.
18. The Goldman case is widely discussed (e.g., Levine 2010). For other U.S. cases involving yarmulkes, see http://www.jlaw.com/Summary/yarmulke.html.
19. Copies of the Supreme Court decision are easily located on the Internet (e.g., http://caselaw.lp.findlaw.com).
20. See Steve Barnes, "District Settles Suit Over Muslim Head Scarf," Steve Barnes, *The New York Times*, May 20, 2004, http://bit.ly/zYsjJB.
21. See "Jewish Parents Sue Alabama School System For Persecuting Their Children," http://www.aclu.org/news/n081497b.html.
22. See, e.g., American Civil Liberties Union, "Sikh Religious Musicians Settle with US Airways After Wrongful Removal From Flight," December 14, 2009, http://bit.ly/8zFe2X; "Sikh Woman Sues IRS after Losing Job Over Religious Knife," *Houston Chronicle*, January 8, 2009, http://www.chron.com/disp/story.mpl/front/6200755.html; and Gohil and Sidhu (2008).
23. On sensitive pates, metal yarmulke clips may cause autoimmune hair loss (Yosefy, Ronnen, and Edelstein 2003). Similarly, some Jews have allergic reactions to tefillin leather (Feit 2004). Jewish summer camps may periodically remove yarmulke bins to stem the spread of head lice (Sales and Saxe 2004: 53). A less severe consequence of the yarmulke is a hot and sweaty scalp in warm weather. To alleviate this discomfort, Belle Kipa stitches a looser yarmulke than the normal, tightly woven "Israeli style" (http://bellekipa.com). Several "customers have told me their heads feel cooler."
24. Sarah Kershaw, "A Sign of Judaism Gets a Swoosh; Commercial or Trendy Skullcaps Add Fad to a Ritual," *The New York Times*, April 19, 2000, pg. B1.
25. Nathan Jeffay, "Criminals Slammed for 'Using' Religion," *The Jewish Daily Forward*, October 17, 2008, http://www.forward.com/articles/14358/.
26. "The Case of the Koufax Kipa," New Jersey News On-Line, December 6, 2007, http://www.njjewishnews.com/njjn.com/120607/sptsTheCase.html. See also "Koufax in Dispute With Collectibles Dealer," *The New York Times*, May 14, 1995.
27. See http://www.gottahaverockandroll.com/LotDetail.aspx?lotid=6605.

28. See http://www.myspace.com/yarmulkeday; and "Yarmulke Day Stresses Tolerance; Student Started Tradition As a 'Joke'" Alice Hunt, *Poughkeepsie Journal*, December 19, 2006.
29. For the discontinued *bramulke* (formerly www.bramulke.com), see http://www.dailyjews.com/articles/69_wear_a_bra_on_your_h.htm. The *Yarmulkebra* website is up and running.


## CHAPTER 9  JEWTILICIOUS

1. The shirt originally appeared at http://www.cafepress.com/jewschool; a similar shirt can be seen at http://www.nyfirepolice.com/go_ahead_make_my_shabbos_t-shirt.asp.
2. The "If I am not . . ." aphorism, attributed to Rabbi Hillel, appears in the tractate of the Mishnah called *Pirkei Avot* (1:14), or "Sayings of the Fathers." The latter slogan, in a curious case of invented tradition, is widely attributed to the Talmud but actually derives from a misattribution by Anaïs Nin's 1961 novel *Seduction of the Minotaur* (Crane and Kadane 2008).
3. Online peddlers of edgy Christian garb include Divine Cotton, Christian Swag, Gospel Garments, A Different Direction, Second Coming Clothing, ChristianTz.com, Fear God shirts, and Alleluia Wear. For Islamic t-shirts, see www.islamicteeshop.com, MuslimGear.com, KhalifahKlothing.com, and MuslimHipHopShop.com.
4. See The Anti-Defamation League, "Heeb Magazine's 'Crimes of Passion' Issue Offensive and Blasphemous," March 1, 2004, http://www.adl.org/PresRele/Mise_00/4460_00.htm.
5. You can readily find Sandler performing his Chanukkah Songs on YouTube. For the so-called December Dilemma, see Shandler and Weintraub (2007) and Ron Gompertz's 2006 pop culture book, *Chrismukkah: Everything You Need To Know to Celebrate the Hybrid Holiday* (New York: Stewart, Tabori and Chang). The affiliated website sells yarmulkes in the Noël colors of green and red (www.chrismukkah.com).
6. MenschWear.com and many other t-shirt vendors use the services of Café Press (www.cafepress.com), a popular online company for user-designed, print-on-demand products. MenschWear.com no longer exists.
7. Sarah Lefton, founder of the Jewish Fashion Conspiracy, has moved on to an online animated Torah (http://www.g-dcast.com).
8. That said, two current Jewish-themed comics are the Jewish Hero Corps (www.jewishsupers.com) and Shaloman (Mark 1 Comics, P.O. Box 5097, Philadelphia, PA 19111, USA).
9. An online community of Jews in the U.S. military (www.jewsingreen.com/) sells t-shirts that say, among other things, "G.I. Jews," "Aim Chai," and "Jews in Green."
10. See Adam Wills, "OU: 'Kosher' Thong Is Wrong," JewishJournal.com, September 16, 2004, http://www.jewishjournal.com/up_front/article/ou_kosher_thong_is_wrong_20040917.

11. Marjorie Ingall, "Yidishe Hotties, Unite!" *The Jewish Daily Forward*, May 23, 2003, http://www.forward.com/articles/8883/.

12. Jew.Lo no longer exists.

## CONCLUSION

1. Ali Asadullah, "Rap Music Mogul Disrespects Muslims with Magazine Cover," Islam Online, December 23, 2002, http://www.islamonline.net/ English/news/2002–12/23/article12.shtml.

2. See, for example, Abby Ellin, "Girth and Nudity, a Pictorial Mission," *The New York Times*, May 13, 2007, http://www.nytimes.com/2007/05/13/ fashion/13nimoy.html; "Leonard Nimoy: In Search of Shekhina," *Moment*, February 2004, http://momentmag.com/Exclusive/2004/200402-Leonard-Nimoy.html.

3. Amy M. Spindler, "Gaultier Hits Home," *The New York Times*, March 16, 1993. See also Amy M. Spindler, "Piety on Parade: Fashion Seeks Inspiration," *The New York Times*, September 5, 1993.

4. See note 63, "Gaultier Hits Home." The designer was Quirino Conti; see Alessandra Ilari, "The Multicultural World of Quirino Conti," *Daily News Record*, January 3, 1994, pp. 24, 26.

5. Photos of *Il Galantuomo* are posted at the Fashion From Spain website (www.fashionfromspain.com/icex/cda/controller/pageGen/0,3346, 1549487_5857806_5857485_4076987_0,00.html) and Diane Pernet's blog *A Shaded View of Fashion* (http://dianepernet.typepad.com/diane/ 2008/03/barcelona-fashi.html).

6. Alana Newhouse, "Shmatte Chic: The Rise—finally!—Of Jewish Fashion," Slate.com, March 2, 2007, http://www.slate.com/id/2160971/. For further photos, see Herchcovitch's website (http://herchcovitch.uol.com.br/#).

# Bibliography

Abrahams, Israel. 1969. *Jewish Life in the Middle Ages*. New York: Atheneum (Orig. 1896).

Abrahams, Israel. 1891. Jewish Ethical Wills. *The Jewish Quarterly Review* 3: 436–84.

Almog, Oz. 2003. From Blorit to Ponytail: Israeli Culture Reflected in Popular Hairstyles. *Israel Studies* 8: 82–117.

Alvi, Sajida, Homa Hoodfar, and Sheila McDonough, eds. 2003. *Muslim Veil in North America: Issues and Debates*. Toronto: Women's Press.

Antin, Mary. *The Promised Land*. New York: Houghton Mifflin.

Aran, Gideon. 2006. Denial Does Not Make The Haredi Body Go Away: Ethnography of a Disappearing (?) Jewish Phenomenon. *Contemporary Jewry* 26: 75–113.

Auslander, Leora. 2000. Bavarian Crucifixes and French Headscarves: Religious Signs and the Postmodern European State. *Cultural Dynamics* 12: 283–309.

Aviv, Caryn and David Shneer. 2005. *New Jews: The End of the Jewish Diaspora*. New York: New York University Press.

Avrutin, Eugene M. 2005. The Politics of Jewish Legibility: Documentation Practices and Reform During the Reign of Nicholas I. *Jewish Social Studies* 11: 136–69.

Avrutin, Eugene M., et al. 2009. *Photographing the Jewish Nation: Pictures from S. An-Sky's Ethnographic Expeditions*. Waltham: Brandeis University Press and Hanover: University Press of New England.

Baizerman, Suzanne. 1992. The Jewish *Kippa Sruga* and the Social Construction of Gender in Israel. In *Dress and Gender: Making and Meaning in Cultural Contexts*. R. Barnes and J. B. Eicher, eds. Pp. 93–105. Oxford: Berg.

Bakhtin, Mikhail. 1984. *Rabelais and His World*. Bloomington: Indiana University Press.

Banerjee, Mukulika and Daniel Miller. 2008. *The Sari*. Oxford: Berg.

Barnes, Ruth and Joanne B. Eicher, eds. 1993. *Dress and Gender: Making and Meaning in Cultural Contexts*. Oxford: Berg.

Baskind, Samantha. 2007. Distinguishing the Distinction: Picturing Ashkenazi and Sephardic Jews in Seventeenth- and Eighteenth-Century Amsterdam. *Journal for the Study of Sephardic & Mizrahi Jewry*, February, pp. 1–13. Online at http://sephardic.fiu.edu/journal/SamanthaBaskind.pdf.

Bassett, F. W. 1971. Noah's Nakedness and the Curse of Canaan: A Case of Incest? *Vetus Testamentum* 21: 232–37.

Bauer, Jules. 1880. Le chapeau janune chez les juifs comtadins. *Revue des etudes juives* 36: 53–56.

Beal, Timothy K. and Tod Linafelt. 2005. To Love the Tallith more than God. In *Derrida and Religion: Other Testaments*. Y. Sherwood and K. Hart, eds. Pp. 175–88. London: Routledge.

Behrman, S. N. 1954. *The Worcester Account*. New York: Random House.

Belasco, Daniel. 2009. *Reinventing Ritual: Contemporary Art and Design for Jewish Life*. New Haven: Yale University Press.

Belkin, Ahuva. 2001. The Scarf and the Toothache: Cross-dressing in the Jewish Folk Theatre. In *Masquerade and Identity: Essays on Gender, Sexuality and Marginality*. E. Tseëlon, ed. Pp. 101–13. London: Routledge.

Ben-Meir, Orna. 2008. The Israeli Shoe: Biblical Sandals and Native Israeli Identity. In *Jews and Shoes*. E. Nahshon, ed. Pp. 77–89. Oxford: Berg.

Ben-Zvi, Avi Nilsson. 1982. The Caftan of the "Jerusalem Costume." *Israel Museum Journal* 1: 55–62.

Berger, Aliza. 1998. Wrapped Attention: May Women Wear *Tefillin*? In *Jewish Legal Writings by Women*. M. D. Halpern and C. Safrai, eds. Pp. 75–118. Jerusalem: Urim Publications.

Berkovic, Sally. 1999. *Straight Talk: My Dilemma as a Modern Orthodox Jewish Woman*. Hoboken: Ktav.

Berkovitz, Jay R. 2001. Social and Religious Controls in Pre-Revolutionary France: Rethinking the Beginnings of Modernity. *Jewish History* 45: 1–40.

Berkowitz, Michael. 1993. *Zionist Culture and West European Jewry before the First World War*. Cambridge: Cambridge University Press.

Bilu, Yoram. 2000. Circumcision, the First Haircut and the Torah: Ritual and Male Identity Among the Ultraorthodox Community of Contemporary Israel. In *Imagined Masculinities: Male Identity and Culture in the Modern Middle East*. M. Ghoussoub and E. Sinclair-Webb, eds. Pp. 33–63. Saqi Books.

Binyaminov, Anatoly. 2002. Dress and Jewelry. In *Mountain Jews: Customs and Daily Life in the Caucasus*. L. Mikdash-Shamailov, ed. Pp. 135–49. Jerusalem: Israel Museum.

Bleich, Chaya Devora. 2003. The Woman's *Yarmulke*. In *Hide and Seek: Jewish Women and Hair Covering*. L. Schreiber, ed. Pp. 134–37. New York: Urim.

Bokser, Ben Zion. 1963. The Thread of Blue. *Proceedings of the American Academy for Jewish Research* 31: 1–32.

Bonfil, Robert. 1994. *Jewish Life in Renaissance Italy*. Trans. Anthony Oldcorn. Berkeley: University of California Press. (Orig. Italian 1991).

Boyarin, Daniel. 1993. *Carnal Israel: Reading Sex in Talmudic Culture*. Berkeley: University of California Press.

Boyarin, Daniel. 1994. *A Radical Jew: Paul and the Politics of Identity*. Berkeley: University of California Press.

Boyarin, Daniel. 1997. *Unheroic Conduct: The Rise of Heterosexuality and the Invention of the Jewish Man*. Berkeley: University of California Press.

Boyarin, Daniel and Jonathan Boyarin. 1993. Diaspora: Generation and Ground of Jewish Identity. *Critical Inquiry* 19: 693–725.

Boyarin, Jonathan and Daniel Boyarin. 1995. Self-exposure as Theory: The Double Mark of the Male Jew." In *Rhetorics of Self-Making*. D. Battaglia, ed. Pp. 16–42. Berkeley: University of California Press.

Brautbar, Shirli. 2006. Fashioning Gender and Jewishness: Hadassah, Fashion Shows, and Beauty Culture in the Post-World War II Era. *Dress* 33: 11–29.

Bridgeman, Jane. 1987. Purple Dye in Late Antiquity and Byzantium. In *The Royal Purple and the Biblical Blue: Argaman and Tekhelet: The Study of Chief Rabbi Dr. Isaac Herzog on the Dye Industries in Ancient Israel and Recent Scientific Contributions*. E. Spanier, ed. Pp. 159–65. Jerusalem: Keter Publishing House.

Brilliant, Richard. 1997. Portraits as Silent Claimants: Jewish Class Aspirations and Representational Strategies in Colonial and Federal America. In *Facing the New World: Jewish Portraits in Colonial and Federal America*. R. Brilliant, ed. Pp. 1–8. New York: Prestel.

Britt, Brian. 2003. Concealment, Revelation, and Gender: The Veil of Moses in the Bible and in Christian Art. *Religion and the Arts* 7 (3): 227–73.

Brod, Harry. 1995. Of Mice and Supermen: Images of Jewish Masculinity. In *Gender and Judaism: The Transformation of Tradition*, T.M. Rudavsky, ed. Pp. 279–93. New York: New York University Press.

Brod, Harry and Rabbi Shawn Israel Zevit, eds. 2010. *Brother Keepers: New Perspectives on Jewish Masculinity*. Harriman, TN: Men's Studies Press.

Bronner, Leila Leah. 1993. From Veil to Wig: Jewish Women's Hair Covering. *Judaism* 42: 465–77.

Brown, Erica. 2003. "A Crown of Thorns": Orthodox Women Who Chose Not to Cover Their Hair. In *Hide and Seek: Jewish Women and Hair Covering*. L. Schreiber, ed. Pp. 178–95. New York: Urim.

Broyde, Rabbi Michael J. 1991. Tradition, Modesty and America: Married Women Covering Their Hair. *Judaism* 40: 79–87.

Broyde, Rabbi Michael J. 1997. Shaving on the Intermediate Days of the Festivals. *Journal of Halacha* 33: 71–94.

Burns, E. Jane, ed. 2004. *Medieval Fabrications: Dress, Textiles, Cloth Work, and Other Cultural Imaginings*. New York: Palgrave Macmillan.

Byers, Michele and Rosalin Krieger. 2007. From Ugly Duckling to Cool Fashion Icon: Sarah Jessica Parker's Blonde Ambitions. *Shofar* 25: 43–63.

Cahan, Abraham. 1917. *The Rise of David Levinsky*. New York: Harper & Brothers. (My copy is the 1969 edition published by Peter Smith, Gloucester, Massachusetts.)

Carmichael, Calum M. 1977. A Ceremonial Crux: Removing a Man's Sandal as a Female Gesture of Contempt. *Journal of Biblical Literature* 96: 321–36.

Carrel, Barbara Goldman. 1999. Hasidic Women's Head Coverings: A Feminized System of Hasidic Distinction. In *Religion, Dress, and the Body*. L.B. Arthur, ed. Pp. 163–79. Oxford: Berg.

Cassen Flora. 2011. The Jewish Badge in Fifteenth- and Sixteenth-Century Italy: The Iconic O, the Yellow Hat, and the Paradoxes of Distinctive Sign Legislation. Paper delivered at The Twenty-Fourth Annual Klutznick-Harris Symposium, "Fashioning Jews: Clothing, Culture and Commerce," Creighton University, Omaha, NE, October 23–24, 2011.

Cayam, Aviva. 1998. Fringe Benefits: Women and *Tzitzit*. In *Jewish Legal Writings by Women*. M.D. Halpern and C. Safrai, eds. Pp. 119–42. Jerusalem: Urim Publications.

Charmé, Stuart. 2000. Varieties of Authenticity in Contemporary Jewish Identity. *Jewish Social Studies* 6: 133–55.

Chesler, Phyllis and Rivka Haut, eds. 2002. *Women of the Wall: Claiming Sacred Ground at Judaism's Holy Site*. Woodstock, VT: Jewish Lights.

Chinitz, Jacob. 2007. The Role of the Shoe in the Bible. *Jewish Bible Quarterly* 35: 41–46.

Clifford, James. 1997. *Routes: Travel and Translation in the Late Twentieth Century*. Cambridge, MA: Harvard University Press.

Cohen, Rabbi Alfred, ed. 1996. *Tekhelet: The Renaissance of a Mitzvah*. New York: Yeshiva University Press.

Cohen, Israel. 1914. *Jewish Life in Modern Times*. New York: Dodd, Mead and Company.

Cohen, Judah. 2009. Hip-Hop Judaica: The Politics of Representin' Heebster Heritage. *Popular Music* 28: 1–18.

Cohen, Mark R. 1994. *Under Crescent and Cross: The Jews in the Middle Ages*. Princeton: Princeton University Press.

Cohen, Mark R. 2005. Feeding the Poor and Clothing the Naked: The Cairo Geniza. *Journal of Interdisciplinary History* 35: 407–21.

Cohen, Richard I. 1998. *Jewish Icons: Art and Society in Modern Europe*. Berkeley: University of California Press.

Cohen, Shaye J.D. 1993. "Those Who Say They Are Jews And Are Not: How Do You Know A Jew In Antiquity When You See One?" In *Diasporas in Antiquity*. S.J.D. Cohen and E. S. Frerichs, eds. Pp. 1–45. Atlanta: Scholars Press.

Cohen, Steven M. and Ari. Y. Kelman. 2005. *Cultural Events and Jewish Identities: Young Adult Jews in New York*. New York: The National Foundation for Jewish Culture, UJA-Federation of New York, Commission on Jewish Identity and Renewal. Online at http://bjpa.org/Publications/details.cfm?PublicationID=2911.

Cohen, Stuart A. 2007. Tensions Between Military Service and Jewish Orthodoxy in Israel: Implications Imagined and Real. *Israel Studies* 12: 103–26.

Cohn, Yehudah. 2008. *Tangled Up In Text: Tefillin and the Ancient World*. Providence: Brown University Press.

Cohon, Samuel S. 1987. *Essays in Jewish Theology*. Cincinnati: Hebrew Union College Press.

Connerley, Jennifer L. 2006. Quaker Bonnets and the Erotic Feminine in American Popular Culture. *Material Religion* 2: 174–203.

Crane, Jonathan Kadane and Joseph Born Kadane. 2008. Seeing Things: The Internet, The Talmud and Anais Nin. *Review of Rabbinic Judaism* 11: 342–45.

Cutler, Allan. 1970. Innocent III and the Distinctive Clothing of Jews and Muslims. *Studies in Medieval Culture* 3: 92–116.

Dan, Joseph. 1996. Hasidism—the Third Century. In *Hasidism Reappraised*. A. Rappoport-Albert, ed. Pp. 425–26. London: Littman Library of Jewish Civilization.

Davis, Eli and Elise Davis. 1983. *Hats and Caps of the Jews*. Jerusalem: Massad Ltd., Publishers.

Daxelmüller, Christoph. 1995. Organizational Forms of Jewish Popular Culture since the Middle Ages. In *In and Out of the Ghetto: Jewish-Gentile Relations in Late Medieval and Early Modern Germany*. R. Po-Chai Hsia and H. Lehmann, eds. Pp. 29–48. Cambridge: Cambridge University Press.

Douglas, Mary. 1966. *Purity and Danger: An Analysis of Concepts of Pollution and Taboo*. London: Routledge.

Duker, Abraham G. 1949–50. Emerging Culture Patterns in American Jewish Life. *Publications of the American Jewish Historical Society* 39 (104): 351–88.

Dundes, Alan, ed. 1989. *Cinderella: A Casebook*. Madison: University of Wisconsin Press (Orig. 1982).

Dundes, Alan, ed. 2002. *The Shabbat Elevator and Other Subterfuges: An Unorthodox Essay on Circumventing Custom and Jewish Character*. Lanham: Rowman & Littlefield.

Duschinsky, Charles. 1918. The Rabbinate of the Great Synagogue, London, from 1756–1842. *The Jewish Quarterly Review* 9: 103–37.

Dynner, Glenn. 2006. *Men of Silk: The Hasidic Conquest of Polish Jewish Society*. Oxford: Oxford University Press.

Edwards, David W. 1982. Nicholas I and Jewish Education. *History of Education Quarterly* 22: 45–53.

Edwards, Douglas R. 1994. The Social, Religious, and Political Aspects of Costume in Josephus. In *The World of Roman Costume*. J. L. Sebesta and L. Bonfante, eds. Pp. 153–59. Madison: University of Wisconsin Press.

Eicher, Joanne B. 2000. The Anthropology of Dress. *Dress* 27: 59–70.

Eicher, Joanne B. ed. 1999. *Dress and Ethnicity: Change Across Space and Time*. Oxford: Berg.

Eilberg-Schwartz, Howard. 1994. *God's Phallus, And Other Problems for Men and Monotheism*. Boston: Beacon.

Ellinson, Rabbi Getsel. 1992. *Women and the Mitzvot. Vol. 2. The Modest Way*. New York: Feldheim.

Elon, Menachem. 1994. *Jewish Law: History, Sources, Principles*. Translated from the Hebrew by B. Auerbach and M. J. Sykes. 4 vols. Philadelphia: Jewish Publication Society.

Emanuel, Rabbi Moshe Shlomo. 1995. *Tefillin: The Inside Story*. New York: Feldheim.

Emelyanenko, Tatjana. 1997. Central Asian Jewish Costume. In *Facing West: Oriental Jews of Central Asia and the Caucasus*. W. Uitgevers Zwolle, ed. Pp. 33–62. Zwolle, Netherlands: Waanders Publishers;

Emmett, Ayala. 2007. A Ritual Garment, The Synagogue, and Gender Questions. *Material Religion* 3 (1): 76–87.

Epstein, Shifra. 1979. *The Celebration of a Contemporary Purim in the Bobover Hasidic Community*. Unpublished PhD Thesis. University of Texas at Austin.

Ericksen, Robert P. and Susannah Heschel, eds. 1999. *Betrayal: German Churches and the Holocaust*. Minneapolis: Augsburg Fortress.

Fader, Ayala. 2009. *Mitzvah Girls: Bringing up the Next Generation of Hasidic Jews in Brooklyn*. Princeton: Princeton University Press.

Falk, Pesach Eliyahu. 1998. *Modesty: An Adornment for Life*. New York: Feldheim.

Feit, Neal E. 2004. Cutaneous Disease and Religious Practice: Case of Allergic Contact Dermatitis to Tefillin and Review of the Literature. *International Journal of Dermatology* 43: 886–88.

Feldman, Jan. 2003. *Lubavitchers as Citizens: A Paradox of Liberal Democracy*. Ithaca: Cornell University Press.

Feldman, Jeffrey. 2008. The Holocaust Shoe: Untying Memory: Shoes as Holocaust Memorial Experiences. In *Jews and Shoes*. E. Nahshon, ed. Pp. 119–30. Oxford: Berg.

Fingeroth, Danny. 2007. *Disguised As Clark Kent: Jews, Comics, And the Creation of the Superhero*. New York and London: Continuum.

Finkel, Avraham Yaakov. 1990. *The Responsa Anthology*. Northvale: Jason Aronson.

Fishkoff, Sue. 2004. New Jew Cool. *Reform Judaism* 33, online at http://reformjudaismmag.net/04fall/fishkoff.shtml.

Fishman, Sylvia Barack. 2000. Modesty and the Modern Jewish Woman. *Jewish Orthodox Feminist Alliance Journal*, 2000, online at http://www.jofa.org/social_htm.php?bib_id=789.

Frankel, Giza. 1980. Notes on the Costume of the Jewish Woman in Eastern Europe. *Journal of Jewish Art* 7: 50–57.

Friedman, Lee M. 1948–49. Mrs. Child's Visit to a New York Synagogue in 1841. *Publications of the American Jewish Historical Society* 38 (1–4): 173–84.

Friedman, Philip. 1955. The Jewish Badge and the Yellow Star in the Nazi Era. *Historia Judaica* 17: 41–70.

Friedman, Richard Elliot. 1987. *Who Wrote the Bible?* New York: Summit Books.

Gandz, Solomon. 1930. The Knot in Hebrew Literature, or from the Knot to the Alphabet. *Isis* 14: 189–214.

Gay, Ruth. 1996. *Unfinished People: Eastern European Jews Encounter America*. New York: W.W. Norton.

Geertz, Clifford. 1973. Deep Play: Notes on the Balinese Cockfight. In *The Interpretation of Cultures: Selected Essays*. Pp. 412–53. New York: Basic Books.

Gilman, Sander L. 2006. *Multiculturalism and the Jews*. New York: Routledge.

Glenn, Susan A. 2002. In the Blood? Consent, Descent, and the Ironies of Jewish Identity. *Jewish Social Studies* 8: 139–52.

Gohil, Neha Singh and Dawinder S. Sidhu. 2008. The Sikh Turban: Post-9/11 Challenges to the Article of Faith. *Rutgers Journal of Law and Religion* 9 (2): 1–60.

Gold, David L. 1987. The Etymology of the English Noun *yarmlke* "Jewish skullcap" and the Obsolescent Hebrew Noun *yarmulka* "idem" (With An Addendum on Judezmo Words for "Jewish Skullcap"). *Jewish Language Review* 7: 180–99.

Gorenberg, Gershom. 2000. *The End of Days: Fundamentalism and the Struggle for the Temple Mount*. Oxford: Oxford University Press.

Grossman, Lawrence. 2010. The Kippah Comes to America. In *Continuity and Change: A Festschrift in Honor of Irving Greenberg's 75th Birthday*. S. T. Katz and S. Bayme, eds. Pp. 129–49. Lanham: University Press of America.

Grossmark, Tziona. 2005. Laws Regarding Idolatry in Jewelry as a Mirror Image of Jewish-Gentile Relations in the Land of Israel during Mishnaic and Talmudic Times. *Jewish Studies Quarterly* 12: 213–226.

Guenther. Irene. 2004. *Nazi Chic? Fashioning Women in the Third Reich*. Oxford: Berg.

Gruenwald, Ithamar. 1993. Midrash & the "Midrashic Condition": Preliminary Considerations. In *The Midrashic Imagination: Jewish Exegesis, Thought, and History*. M. Fishbane, ed. Pp. 6–22. Albany: State University of New York Press.

Guilat, Yael. 2006. Between Lulu and Penina: The Yemenite Woman, Her Jewelry, and Her Embroidery in the New Hebrew Culture. *Nashim: A Journal of Jewish Women's Studies & Gender Issues* 11: 198–223.

Gutmann, Joseph. 1970. Torah Ornaments, Priestly Vestments, and the King James Bible. In *Beauty in Holiness: Studies in Jewish Customs and Ceremonial Art*, pp. 122–24. Hoboken, NJ: Ktav.

Halter, Marilyn. 2000. *Shopping for Identity: The Marketing of Ethnicity.* New York: Schocken Books.

Hamel, Gildas. 2001. Sacred and Profane Clothing in Ancient Israel: *Sha'atnez*. In *The World of Religions: Essays on Historical and Contemporary Issues in Honour of Professor Noel Quinton King for His Eightieth Birthday.* G. W. Trompf and G. Hamel, eds. Pp. 29–42. Delhi: ISPCK.

Hansen, Karen Tranberg. 2004. The World in Dress: Anthropological Perspectives on Clothing, Fashion, and Culture. *Annual Review of Anthropology* 33: 369–92.

Hapgood, Hutchins. 1965. *The Spirit of the Ghetto: Studies in the Jewish Quarter of New York.* With Drawings from Life by Jacob Epstein. Preface and Notes by Harry Golden. New York: Funk & Wagnalls (Orig. 1902).

Haran, Menahem. 1978. *Temples and Temple-Service in Ancient Israel: An Inquiry into the Character of Cult Phenomena and the Historical Setting of the Priestly School.* Oxford: Clarendon Press.

Harris, Leon. 1979. *Merchant Princes: An Intimate History of Jewish Families Who Built Great Department Stores.* New York: Harper & Row.

Harvey, Warren Zev. 1986. The Pupil, the Harlot and the Fringe Benefits. *Prooftexts* 6: 259–64.

Heilman, Samuel. 1976. *Synagogue Life: A Study in Symbolic Interaction.* Chicago: University of Chicago Press.

Heilman, Samuel. 1992. *Defenders of the Faith: Inside Ultra-Orthodox Jewry.* New York: Schocken Books.

Hellman, Samuel. 2001. *When a Jew Dies: The Ethnography of a Bereaved Son.* Berkeley: University of California Press.

Heinze, Andrew R. 1990. *Adapting to Abundance: Jewish Immigrants, Mass Consumption, and the Search for American Identity.* New York: Columbia University Press.

Helman, Anat. 2008. Kibbutz Dress in the 1950s: Utopian Equality, Anti-Fashion, and Change. *Fashion Theory* 12: 313–39.

Helmreich, William B. 1982. *The World of The Yeshiva: An Intimate Portrait of Orthodox Jewry.* New York: Free Press.

Henkin, Rabbi Yehuda. 2003a. Contemporary Tseni'ut. *Tradition* 37: 1–48.

Henkin, Rabbi Yehuda. 2003b. More on Women's Hair Covering. *Tradition* 37: 148–51.

Henkin, Rabbi Yehuda, ed. 2003c. Talit for Women. In *Responsa on Contemporary Jewish Women's Issues.* Pp. 32–33. Hoboken, NJ: Ktav.

Herz, Rebecca Shulman. 2003. The Transformation of Tallitot: How Jewish Prayer Shawls Have Changed Since Women Began Wearing Them. *Women In Judaism* 3 (3), online at http://www.utoronto.ca/wjudaism/contemporary/contemp_index1.html.

von Hesse-Wartegg, Ernst. 1882, *Tunis, the Land and the People.* New York: Dodd, Mean, and Company.

Hezser, Catherine. 2008. The Halitzah Shoe: Between Female Subjugation and Symbolic Emasculation. In *Jews and Shoes.* E. Nahshon, ed. Pp. 47–63. Oxford: Berg.

Horn, P. 1968. Textiles in Biblical times. *Ciba Review* 1968, No. 2: 1–37.

Horowitz, Bethamie. 2003. *Connections and Journeys: Assessing Critical Opportunities for Enhancing Jewish Identity.* Revised edition. UJA-Federation of Jewish Philanthropies of New York. (Orig. 2000). Online at http://www.jewishdatabank.org/Reports/Connections_And_Journeys_2003rev.pdf.

Horowitz, Elliott. 1994. The Early Eighteenth Century Confronts the Beard: Kabbalah and Jewish Self-Fashioning. *Jewish History* 8: 95–115.

Horowitz, Elliott. 2006. *Reckless Rites: Purim and the Legacy of Jewish Violence.* Princeton: Princeton University Press.

Huddlestun, John R. 2001. Unveiling the Versions: The Tactics of Tamar in Genesis 38:15. *The Journal of Hebrew Scriptures* 3, Article 7, online journal at http://www.arts.ualberta.ca/JHS/Articles/article_19.pdf (accessed December 7, 2005).

Huddlestun, John R. 2002. Divestiture, Deception, and Demotion: The Garment Motif in Genesis 37–39. *Journal for the Study of the Old Testament* 98: 47–62.

Hughes, Diane Owen. 1983. Sumptuary Law and Social Relations in Renaissance Italy. In *Disputes and Settlements: Law and Human Relations in the West.* J. Bossy, ed. Pp. 69–99. Cambridge: Cambridge University Press.

Hughes, Diane Owen. 1986. Distinguishing Signs: Ear-Rings, Jews and Franciscan Rhetoric in the Italian Renaissance City. *Past and Present* 111: 3–59.

Hughes, Lindsey. 1988. *Russia in the Age of Peter the Great.* New Haven: Yale University Press.

Hunt, Alan. 1996. The Governance of Consumption: Sumptuary Laws and Shifting Forms of Regulation. *Economy and Society* 25: 410–27.

Hyman, Paula. 1991. Gender and the Immigrant Jewish Experience in the United States. In *Jewish Women in Historical Perspective.* Judith Baskin, ed. Pp. 312–36. Detroit: Wayne State University Press.

Jacobson, Howard. 2002. Shoes and Jews. *Revue des Etudes juives* 161: 233.

Jarmakani, Amira. 2008. *Imagining Arab Womanhood: The Cultural Mythology of Veils, Harems, and Belly Dancers in the U.S.* New York: Palgrave Macmillan.

*Jewish Encyclopedia.* 1901–1906. Funk & Wagnalls. Online at http://www.jewishencyclopedia.com.

Johnson, Robert. 1815. *Travels Through Part of the Russian Empire and the Country of Poland; Along the Southern Shores of the Baltic.* London: J.J. Stockdale.

Jolly, Penny Howell. 2002. Marked Difference: Earrings and "The Other" in Fifteenth-Century Flemish Art. In *Encountering Medieval Textiles and Dress: Objects, Texts, Images.* D.G. Koslin and J.E. Snyder, eds. Pp. 195–207. New York: Palgrave Macmillan.

Joselit, Jenna Weissman. 1994. *The Wonders of America: Reinventing Jewish Culture, 1880–1950.* New York: Henry Holt.

Joselit, Jenna Weissman. 2001. *A Perfect Fit: Clothes, Character, and the Promise of America.* New York: Henry Holt.

Kaplan, Aryeh. 1975. *Tefillin*. New York: National Conference of Synagogue Youth/ Union of Orthodox Jewish Congregations of America.

Kaplan, Marion A. 1991. *The Making of the Jewish Middle Class: Women, Family, and Identity in Imperial Germany*. Oxford: Oxford University Press.

Kaplan, Marion A. 2005. As Germans and as Jews in Imperial Germany. In *Jewish Daily Life in Germany, 1618–1945*. M.A., Kaplan, ed. Pp. 173–251. Oxford: Oxford University Press.

Keenan, William. 1999. From Friars to Fornicators: The Eroticization of Sacred Dress. *Fashion Theory* 3: 389–409.

Kellner, Alison Bender. 2004. What Do Girls at Metro Schechter High School Think About Females Wearing *tallit* or tefillin? *Gleanings: A Digest of Jewish Educational Thought and Practice* 7 (1), originally online at http://www.jtsa.edu/davidson/ melton/gleanings/v7n1.shtml#harvest1.

Kennedy, Randall. 2002. *Nigger: The Strange Career of a Troublesome Word*. New York: Pantheon Books.

Kidwell, Claudia B. and Margaret C. Christman. 1974. *Suiting Everyone: The Democratization of Clothing in America*. Washington, DC: Smithsonian Institution Press.

Killerby, Catherine Kovesi. 1994. Practical Problems in the Enforcement of Italian Sumptuary Law, 1200–1500. In *Crime, Society, and the Law in Renaissance Italy*, T. Dean and K.J.P. Lowe, eds. Pp. 99–120. Cambridge: Cambridge University Press.

Kirshenblatt-Gimblett, Barbara. 2005. The "New Jews": Reflections on Emerging Cultural Practices. Paper delivered at Re-thinking Jewish Communities and Networks in an Age of Looser Connections, Wurzweiler School of Social Work, Yeshiva University, and Institute for Advanced Studies, Hebrew University. December 6–7, 2005. New York City. Online at http://www.nyu.edu/classes/bkg/ web/yeshiva.pdf.

Kisch, Guido. 1942. The Yellow Badge in History. *Historia Judaica* 4: 95–127.

Kister, M. J. 1989. "'Do Not Assimilate Yourselves…' Lā tashabbahū…" *Jerusalem Studies in Arabic and Islam* 12: 321–53.

Kitov, Rabbi Eliyahu. 1968. *The Book of Our Heritage: The Jewish Year and Its Days of Significance. Volume 1: Tishrei-Shevat*. New York: Feldheim.

Klaff, Vivian. 2006. Defining American Jewry From Religions and Ethnic Perspectives: The Transitions to Greater Heterogeneity. *Sociology of Religion* 67: 415–38.

Knowles, Michael P. 2004. What Was the Victim Wearing? Literary, Economic, and Social Contexts for the Parable of the Good Samaritan. *Biblical Interpretation* 12: 145–74.

Kollontai, Pauline. 2004. Messianic Jews and Jewish Identity. *Journal of Modern Jewish Studies* 3: 195–205.

Kotik, Yekhezkel and David Assaf. 2002. *Journey to a Nineteenth-Century Shtetl: The Memoirs of Yekhezkel Kotik*. Detroit: Wayne State University Press.

Kranzler, George. 1995. *Hasidic Williamsburg: A Contemporary American Hasidic Community*. Northvale, NJ: Jason Aronson.

Krauss, Samuel. 1970. The Jewish Rite of Covering the Head. In *Beauty and Holiness: Studies in Jewish Customs and Ceremonial Art*. J. Gutmann, ed.

Pp. 420–67. New York: Ktav. (Reprinted from *Hebrew Union College Annual* 19, 1945–46, 121–68).

Kreitman, Benjamin Z. and Joyce B. Kreitman. 1972. Fashions for the Synagogue. *United Synagogue Review* 25: 14–15, 31.

Kremer, Roberta S., ed. 2007. *Broken Threads: The Destruction of The Jewish Fashion Industry in Germany and Austria*. Oxford: Berg.

Kruger, Paul A. 1984. The Hem of the Garment in Marriage: The Meaning of the Symbolic Gesture in Ruth 3:9 and Ezek 16:8. *Journal of Northwest Semitic Languages* 12: 79–86.

Kruger, Paul A. 1988. The Symbolic Significance of the Hem (KāNāF) in 1 Samuel 15.27. In *Text and Context: Old Testament and Semitic Studies for F.C. Fensham*. W. Claassen, ed. Pp. 105–16. Sheffield: JSOT Press.

Kuchta, David. 2002. *The Three-Piece Suit and Modern Masculinity: England, 1550–1850*. Berkeley: University of California Press.

Landau, David. 1992. *Piety and Power: The World of Jewish Fundamentalism*. New York: Hill and Wang.

Landau, Melanie. 2008. Re-Covering Woman as Religious Subject: Reflections On Jewish Women and Hair-Covering. *The Australian Journal of Jewish Studies* 22: 52–74.

Lauterbach, Jacob Z. 1928. Should One Cover the Head When Participating in Divine Worship? *Central Conference of American Rabbis Year Book* 38: 589–603. Reprinted in *Studies in Jewish Law, Custom and Folklore*. Pp. 225–39. New York: KTAV.

Lea, Henry Charles. 1906. *A History of the Inquisition of Spain*. Vol. 1. New York: Macmillan.

Leach, Edmund. 2001. Biblical Hair. In *The Essential Edmund Leach: Volume 2: Culture and Human Nature*. S. Hugh-Jones and J. Laidlaw, eds. Pp. 201–26. New Haven: Yale University Press (Orig. unpub. 1970).

Leach, William. 1984. Transformation in a Culture of Consumption: Women and Department Stores, 1890–1925. *The Journal of American History* 71: 319–42.

Levine, Louis D., ed. 2002. *Lives Remembered: A Shtetl Through a Photographer's Eye*. New York: Museum of Jewish Heritage.

Levine, Samuel J. 2010. Goldman vs. Weinberger: Religious Freedom Confronts Military Conformity. In *Law and Religion: Cases in Context*. Leslie C. Griffin, ed. Pp. 71–84. New York: Aspen Publishers.

Levine, Stephanie Wellen. 2003. *Mystics, Mavericks, and Merrymakers: An Intimate Journey Among Hasidic Girls.* New York: New York University Press.

Lichtenstadter, Ilsa. 1943. The Distinctive Dress of Non-Muslims in Islamic Countries. *Historia Judaica* 5: 35–52.

Lipset, David and Eric K. Silverman. 2005. Dialogics of the Body: The Moral and the Grotesque in Two Sepik River Societies. *Journal of Ritual Studies* 19: 17–52.

Lipton, Sara. 1999. *Images of Intolerance: The Representation of Jews and Judaism in the Bible moralisée*. Berkeley: University of California Press.

Lipton, Sara. 2008. Where Are the Gothic Jewish Women? On the Non-iconography of the Jewess in the *Cantigas de Santa Maria. Jewish History* 22: 139–77.

Llewellyn-Jones, Lloyd. 2005. The Fashioning of Delilah: Costume Design, Histori-
cism and Fantasy in Cecil B. DeMille's *Samson and Delilah* (1949). In *The Clothed
Body in the Ancient World*. Liza Cleland, Mary Harlow, and Lloyd Llewellyn-Jones,
eds. Pp. 14–29. Oxford: Oxbow Books.

Loeb, Laurence D. 1977. *Outcaste: Jewish Life in Southern Iran*. London: Gordon and
Breach.

Lowenstein, Steven M. 2005. The Beginning of Integration, 1780–1870. In *Jewish
Daily Life in Germany, 1618–1945*. M.A., Kaplan, ed. Pp. 93–171. Oxford: Oxford
University Press.

Mahler, Raphael. 1985. *Hasidism and the Jewish Enlightenment: Their Confrontation
in Galicia and Poland in the First Half of the Nineteenth Century*. Philadelphia:
Jewish Publication Society.

Makela, Maria. 2000. The Rise and Fall of the Flapper Dress: Nationalism and the
Anti-Semitism in Early-Twentieth-Century Discourses on German Fashion. *Journal
of Popular Culture* 34: 183–208.

Marmorstein, Emile. 1954. The Veil in Judaism and Islam. *Journal of Jewish Studies*
5: 1–11.

Manolson, Gila. 1997. *Outside/Inside: A Fresh Look at Tzniut*. Southfield, MI: Targum.

Marcus, Jacob Rader. 1999. *The Jew in the Medieval World: A Source Book:
315–1791*. Revised edition with an introduction and updated bibliography by
Marc Saperstein. Cincinnati: Hebrew Union College Press (Orig. 1938).

Margalit, Natan. 1995. Hair in *TaNaKh*: The Symbolism of Gender and Control.
*Journal of the Association of Graduates in Near Eastern Studies* 5 (2): 43–52.

Margalit, Natan. 2004. Priestly Men and Invisible Women: Male Appropriate of the
Feminine and the Exemption of Women from Positive Time-Bound Commandments. *AJS Review* 28 (2): 297–316.

Matthews, Victor H. 1995. The Anthropology of Clothing in the Joseph Narrative.
*Journal for the Study of the Old Testament* 65: 25–36.

Matza, Diane. 1987. Jewish Immigrant Autobiography: The Anomaly of a Sephardic
Example. *MELUS* 14 (1): 33–41.

McCloud, Aminah B. 1995–1996. American Muslim Women and U.S. Society. *Journal of Law and Religion* 12 (1): 51–59.

McGoldrick, Dominic. 2006. *Human Rights and Religion: The Islamic Headscarf Debate in Europe*. Portland, OR: Hart Publishing.

McGovern, P.E. and R.H. Michel. 1987. Has Authentic Tekĕlēt Been Identified?
*Bulletin of the American Schools of Oriental Research* 265: 81–83

McKay, Heather A. 1996. Gendering the Discourse of Display in the Hebrew Bible.
In *On Reading Prophetic Texts: Gender Specific and Related Studies in Mem-
ory of Fokkelien van Dijk-Hemmes*. Bob Becking and Meindert Dijkstra, eds.
Pp. 169–99. Leiden: Brill.

Mellinkoff, Ruth. 1973. The Round, Cap-Shaped Hats Depicted on Jews in BM Cotton
Claudius B. iv. In *Anglo-Saxon England 2*. P. Clemoes ed. Pp. 155–65. Cambridge:
Cambridge University Press.

Mellinkoff, Ruth. 1974. The Round-topped Tablets of the Law: Sacred Symbol and Emblem of Evil. *Journal of Jewish Art* 1: 28–43.

Mellinkoff, Ruth. 1981. *The Mark of Cain*. Berkeley: University of California Press.

Mellinkoff, Ruth. 1987. Christian and Jewish Mitres: A Paradox. In *Florilegium in Honorem Carl Nordenfalk Octogenarii Contextum*. P. Bjurström, N.-G. Hökby, and F. Mütherich, eds. Pp. 145–58. Stockholm: Nationalmuseum Stockholm.

Mellinkoff, Ruth. 1993. *Outcasts: Signs of Otherness in Northern European Art of the Late Middle Ages*. Vols. 1, 2. Berkeley: University of California Press.

Merback, Mitchell B. 1998. *The Thief, the Cross and the Wheel: Pain and the Spectacle of Punishment in Medieval and Renaissance Europe*. Chicago: University of Chicago Press.

Metzger, Thérèse and Mendel Metzger. 1982. *Jewish Life in the Middle Ages: Illuminated Hebrew Manuscripts of the Thirteenth to the Sixteenth Centuries*. New York: Alpine Fine Arts.

Meyer, Michael A. 1988. *Response to Modernity: A History of the Reform Movement in Judaism*. Oxford: Oxford University Press.

Milgrom, Jacob. 1983. Of Hems and Tassels. *Biblical Archaeology Review* 9 (3): 61–65.

Mintz, Jerome R. 1992. *Hasidic People: A Place in the New World*. Cambridge, MA: Harvard University Press.

Montaigne, Michel de. 1948. *Complete Works: Essays, Travel Journal, Letters*. Trans. By Donald M. Frame. Stanford: Stanford University Press.

Moore, Kathleen M. 2007. Visible through the Veil: The Regulation of Islam in American Law. *Sociology of Religion* 68: 237–51.

Morris, Rabbi Henoch. 2006. Yarmulkas and Hats: Societal Custom or *Halachic* Imperative? *Journal of Halacha and Contemporary Society* 52: 5–36.

Nacht, Jacob. 1915–16. The Symbolism of the Shoe with Special Reference to Jewish Sources. *The Jewish Quarterly Review* 6: 1–22.

Nadler, Steven. 2003. *Rembrandt's Jews*. Chicago: University of Chicago Press.

Navon, Mois. 2003/2004. False Tekhelet. www.tekhelet.com (accessed April 2006).

Navon, Mois. 2004. *Beged* or *Simlah*—Is There a Difference? *Jewish Bible Quarterly* 32: 266–69.

Needham, Rodney. 1967. Percussion and Transition. *Man* 2: 606–14.

Ner-David, Haviva. 2002. *Tzitzit* and Tefillin at the Kotel. In *Women of the Wall: Claiming Sacred Ground at Judaism's Holy Site*. P. Chesler and R. Haut, eds. Pp. 63–93. Woodstock, VT: Jewish Lights.

Niditch, Susan. 2008. *"My Brother Esau Is a Hairy Man": Hair and Identity in Ancient Israel*. Oxford: Oxford University Press.

Nochlin, Linda. 1996. Foreword: The Couturier and the Hasid. In *Too Jewish? Challenging Traditional Identities*. N. L. Kleeblatt, ed. Pp. xvii–xx. New York: The Jewish Museum and New Brunswick: Rutgers University Press.

Ochs, Vanessa L. 2002. Women and Ritual Artifacts. In *Women of the Wall: Claiming Sacred Ground at Judaism's Holy Site*. P. Chesler and R. Haut, eds. Pp. 310–34. Woodstock, VT: Jewish Lights.

Oden, Robert A., Jr. 1987. Grace or Status? Yahweh's Clothing of the First Humans. In *Bible Without Theology: The Theological Tradition and Alternatives to It*. Pp. 92–105. San Francisco: Harper & Row.

Oegema, Gergern S. 1996. *The History of the Shield of David: The Birth of a Symbol*. Frankfurt: Peter Lang.

Oz, Almog. 2000. *The Sabra: The Creation of the New Jew*. Berkeley: University of California Press.

Palmer, Christine. 2011. The "Disinherited" Priesthood: A Look into Biblical Israel's Unshod Priest. Paper delivered at The Twenty-Fourth Annual Klutznick-Harris Symposium, "Fashioning Jews: Clothing, Culture and Commerce," Creighton University, Omaha, NE, October 23–24, 2011.

Patai, Raphael. 1959. *Sex and Family in the Bible and the Middle East*. Garden City, NY: Doubleday.

Paul, Robert A. 1985. David and Saul at En Gedi. *Raritan* 4: 110–32.

Peiss, Kathy. 1986. *Cheap Amusements: Working Women and Leisure in Turn-of-the-Century New York*. Philadelphia: Temple University Press.

Platt, Elizabeth Ellen. 1979. Jewelry of Bible Times and the Catalog of Isa 3:18–23. Parts I and II. *Andrew University Seminary Studies* 17 (1): 71–84; (2): 189–201.

Plaut, Gunther. 1955. The Origin of the Word "Yarmulke." *Hebrew Union College Annual* 26: 567–70.

Poll, Solomon. 1962. *The Hasidic Community of Williamsburg*. Glencoe: The Free Press.

Pollack, Herman. 1971. *Jewish Folkways in Germanic Lands (1648–1806)*. Cambridge, MA: MIT Press.

Prell, Riv-Ellen. 1999. *Fighting to Become Americans: Assimilation and the Trouble between Jewish Women and Jewish Men*. Boston: Beacon.

Propp, William H. 1987. The Skin of Moses' Face—Transfigured or Disfigured? *Catholic Biblical Quarterly* 49: 375–86.

Prouser, Ora Horn. 1996. Suited to the Throne: The Symbolic Use of Clothing in the David and Saul Narratives. *Journal for the Study of the Old Testament* 71: 27–37.

Prouser, Ora Horn. 2008. The Biblical Shoe: Eschewing Footwear: The Call of Moses as Biblical Archetype. In *Jews and Shoes*, E. Nahshon, ed. Pp. 39–45. Oxford: Berg.

Putik, Alexandr. 1993. The Origin of the Symbols of the Prague Jewish Town: The Banner of the Old-New Synagogue: David's Shield and the "Swedish" Hat. *Judaica Bohemiae* 29: 4–37.

Rabinowitz, Dan. 2007. Yarmulke: A Historical Cover-up? *Hakira: The Flatbush Journal of Jewish Law and Thought* 4: 221–38.

Rakoff, Joanna Smith. 2003. The New Super Jew. *Time Out New York*, 427 (December 4–11): 13–14, 16, 18.

Rapoport, Chaim. 2000. Why Women are Exempt from positive time-bound commandments: Is there a true Torah view? *Le'ela* (December): 53–64. Online at http://www.jofa.org/social.php/ritual/dailypractic/timeboundcom.

Ravid, Benjamin. 1992. From Yellow to Red: On the Distinguishing Head-covering of the Jews of Venice. *Journal Jewish History* 6: 179–210.

Raz, Ayala. 1999. Fashion in Eretz-Israel: What We Were Wearing in the Early Days of this Century. Israel Review of Arts and Letters. Online at http://www.mfa.gov.il/MFA/MFAArchive/1990_1999/1999/1/Ayala%20Raz%20-%20Fashion%20in%20Eretz-Israel.

Raz, Ayala. 2008. The Equalizing Shoe: Shoes as a Symbol of Equality in the Jewish Society in Palestine during the First half of the Twentieth Century. In *Jews and Shoes*. E. Nahshon, ed. Pp. 149–58. Oxford: Berg.

Renteln, Alison Dundes. 2004. Visual Religious Symbols and the Law. *American Behavioral Scientist* 47 (12): 1573–96.

Ricks, Stephen D. 2000. The Garment of Adam in Jewish, Muslim, and Christian Tradition. In *Judaism and Islam: Boundaries, Communication and Interaction: Essays in Honor of William M. Brinner*. B.H. Hary, J.L. Hayes and F. Astren, eds. Pp. 705–39. Leiden: Brill.

Rieber, Moti. 2005. Simplicity as a Jewish Value: Reclaiming and Reconstructing Sumptuary Legislation. *Reconstructionist*, Spring: 41–48.

Robinson, Chase F. 2005. Neck-Sealing in Early Islam. *Journal of the Economic and Social History of the Orient* 48: 401–41.

Rogin, Michael. 1998. *Blackface, White Noise: Jewish Immigrants in the Hollywood Melting Pot*. Berkeley: University of California Press.

Rosenthal, Richard. 2001. Halakhah, Minhag and Gender. In *Gender Issues in Jewish Law: Essays and Responses*. J. Walter and M. Zemer, eds. Pp. 107–29. New York: Berghahn Books.

Rosman, Moshe. 1996. *Founder of Hasidism: A Quest for the Historical Ba'al Shem Tov*. Berkeley: University of California Press.

Ross, Tamar. 2004. *Expanding the Palace of Torah: Orthodoxy and Feminism*. Waltham: Brandeis University Press.

Roth, Cecil. 1928. Sumptuary Laws of the Community of Carpentras. *Jewish Quarterly Review* 28: 357–83.

Roth, Norman. 2003. Clothing. In *Medieval Jewish History: An Encyclopedia*. Pp. 172–76. New York: Routledge.

Roth, Norman. 2005. *Daily Life of the Jews of the Middle Ages*. Westport, CT: Greenwood.

Roussin, Lucille A. 1994. Costume in Roman Palestine: Archaeological Remains and the Evidence of the Mishnah. In *The World of Roman Costume*. J.L. Sebesta and L. Bonfante, eds. Pp. 182–90. Madison: University of Wisconsin Press.

Ruane, Christine. 2002. Subjects Into Citizens: The Politics of Clothing in Imperial Russia. In *Fashioning the Body Politic: Dress, Gender, Citizenship*. W. Parkins, ed. Pp. 49–70. Oxford: Berg.

Rubens, Alfred. 1967. *A History of Jewish Costume*. New York: Crown.

Rubin, Israel. 1972. *Satmar: An Island In The City*. Chicago: Quadrangle.

Safran, Rabbi Eliyahu. 2007. *Sometimes You Are What You Wear! An Argument for Tzniut—Modesty*. Bloomington, IN: Xlibris.

Salah, Asher. 2011. How a Rabbi Should Be Dressed: The Question of Cassock and Clerical Clothing among Italian Rabbis from the Renaissance to Contemporary Times. Paper delivered at The Twenty-Fourth Annual Klutznick-Harris

Symposium, "Fashioning Jews: Clothing, Culture and Commerce," Creighton University, Omaha, NE, October 23–24, 2011.

Sales, Amy L. and Leonard Saxe. 2004. *"How Goodly Are Thy Tents": Summer Camps as Jewish Socializing Experiences.* Hanover, NH: Brandeis University Press/University Press of New England.

Saperstein, Marc. 1989. *Jewish Preaching, 1200–1800: An Anthology*. New Haven: Yale University Press.

Sarna, Jonathan D. 1982. *People Walk on their Heads: Moses Weinberger's Jews and Judaism in New York*. Translated from the Hebrew and edited. New York: Holmes and Meier. 1982.

Sarna, Jonathan D. 2006. "Facing the New World:" What Portraits of Early American Jews Reveal and What They Obscure. In *Writing a Modern Jewish History: Essays in Honor of Salo W. Baron*. B. Kirshenblatt-Gimblett, ed. Pp. 27–33. New York: The Jewish Museum, and New Haven: Yale University Press.

Satlow, Michael L. 1995. *Tasting the Dish: Rabbinic Rhetorics of Sexuality*. Atlanta: Scholars Press.

Satlow, Michael L. 1997. Jewish Constructions of Nakedness in Late Antiquity. *Journal of Biblical Literature* 116: 429–54.

Schnur, Rabbi Susan and Anna Schnur-Fishman. 2006. How Do Women Define the Sacred? *Lilith* 31 (3): 20–27.

Schoener, Allon, ed. 1967. *Portal to America: The Lower East Side 1870–1925*. New York: Holt, Rhinehart and Winston.

Schram, Steven. 2002. Tefillin: An Ancient Acupuncture Point Prescription For Mental Clarity. *Journal of Chinese Medicine* 70: 5–8.

Schreiber, Lynne, ed. 2003. *Hide and Seek: Jewish Women and Hair Covering*. New York: Urim.

Schreier, Barbara A. 1994. *Becoming American Women: Clothing and the Jewish Immigrant Experience, 1880–1920.* Chicago: Chicago Historical Society.

Schwartz, Joshua. 2004. Material Culture in the Land of Israel: Monks and Rabbis on Clothing and Dress in the Byzantine Period. In *Saints and Role Models in Judaism and Christianity*. M. Poorthuis and J. Schwartz, eds. Pp. 121–37. Leiden: Brill.

Scott, Joan Wallach. 2007. *The Politics of the Veil*. Princeton: Princeton University Press.

Shandler, Jeffrey and Aviva Weintraub. 2007. "Santa, Shmanta": Greeting Cards for the December Dilemma. *Material Religion* 3: 380–403.

Shapero, Miriam. 1987. *The Dress System of Traditional Jewry*. Unpublished rabbinic thesis, Hebrew Union College-Jewish Institute of Religion, Graduate Rabbinic Program, New York, New York.

Shapiro, Marc. 1990. Another Example of "Minhag America." *Judaism* 39: 148–54.

Shinar, Pessah. 2000. Some Remarks Regarding The Colours Of Male Jewish Dress In North Africa And Their Arab- Islamic Context. *Jerusalem Studies in Arabic and Islam* 24: 380–95.

Sholem, Gershom. 1949. The Curious History of the Six-Pointed Star: How the "Magen David" Became the Jewish Symbol. *Commentary* 8: 243–51.

Siebert-Hommes, Jopie C. 2002. "On the Third Day Esther Put on Her Queen's Robes" (Esther 5:1): The Symbolic Function of Clothing in the Book of Esther.

*Lectio difficilior* 1, online at http://www.lectio.unibe.ch/02_1/siebert.htm (accessed July 26, 2005).

Silverman, Eric Kline. 2001. *Masculinity, Motherhood, and Mockery: Psychoanalyzing Culture and the Iatmul Naven Rite in New Guinea*. Ann Arbor: University of Michigan Press.

Silverman, Eric Kline. 2006. *From Abraham to America: A History of Jewish Circumcision*. Lanham, MD: Rowman & Littlefield.

Silverman, Eric Kline. 2010. Circumcision and Masculinity: Motherly Men or Brutal Patriarchs? In *Brother Keepers: New Perspectives on Jewish Masculinity*, H. Brod and Rabbi S.I. Zevit, eds. Pp. 34–56. Harriman, TN: Men's Studies Press.

Singer, Mendel E. 2001. Understanding the Criteria for the *Chilazon*. *Journal of Halacha and Contemporary Society* 42: 5–29.

Sinkoff, Nancy. 2004. *Out of the Shtetl: Making Jews Modern in the Polish Borderlands*. Atlanta, GA: Society of Biblical Literature.

Smith, Debra W., ed. 2005. *Every Tallit Tells a Tale*. Randolph, NJ: Stella Hart, Inc.

Smith, Ellen. 2001. Greetings from Faith: Early-Twentieth-Century American Jewish New Year Postcards. In *Visual Culture of American Religions*. D. Morgan and S. Promey, eds. Pp. 229–48. Berkeley: University of California Press.

Spanier, Ehud, ed. 1987. The Royal Purple and the Biblical Blue: *Argaman* and *Tekhelet*: The Study of Chief Rabbi Dr. Isaac Herzog on the Dye Industries in Ancient Israel and Recent Scientific Contributions. Jerusalem: Keter Publishing House.

Speiser, E.A. 1957. TWTPT. *Jewish Quarterly Review* 48: 208–17.

Stanislawski, Michael. 1983. *Tsar Nicholas I and the Jews: The Transformation of Jewish Society in Russia, 1825–1855*. Philadelphia: Jewish Publication Society.

Steigmann-Gall, Richard. 2003. *The Holy Reich: Nazi Conceptions of Christianity, 1919–1945*. Cambridge: Cambridge University Press.

Stein, Sarah Abrevaya. 2007. Mediterranean Jewries and Global Commerce in the Modern Period: On the Trail of the Jewish Feather Trade. *Jewish Social Studies* 13: 1–39.

Steinhauer, Harry. 1990. Holy Headgear. *Antioch Review*, Winter: 4–26.

Stephens, Ferris J. 1931. The Ancient Significance of *Sisith*. *Journal of Biblical Literature* 50: 59–70.

Sterman, Baruch. 1999. The Meaning of Tekhelet. *B'or Ha'Torah* 11: 185–95. Reprinted online at http://sterman.freehostia.com/MeaningOfTekhelet.htm (accessed December 22, 2009).

Sterman, Baruch. 2002. A Response to Dr. Singer's Review of *Murex trunculus* as the Source of Tekhelet. *Journal of Halacha and Contemporary Society* 43. Reprinted online at www.tekhelet.com/ResponseJHCS.htm (accessed November 2005).

Stern, Menahem. 1974–1984. *Greek and Latin Authors on Jews and Judaism. Vols. 1-3. Edited with Introductions, Translations, and Commentary.* Jerusalem: The Israel Academy of Sciences and Humanities.

Stern, Sacha. 1994. *Jewish Identity in Early Rabbinic Writings*. Leiden: E.J. Brill.

Stillman, Yedida K. 1974. "The Wardrobe of a Jewish Bride in Medieval Egypt." In *Studies in Marriage Customs*. I. Ben-Ami and D. Noy, eds. Pp 297–304. Folklore Research Center Studies IV. Jerusalem: Magnes.

Stillman, Yedida K. 1976. The Importance of the Cairo Genizah Manuscripts for the History of Medieval Female Attire. *International Journal of Middle East Studies* 7: 579–89.

Stillman, Yedida K. 2003. *Arab Dress: A Short History: From the Dawn of Islam to Modern Times*. Leiden: Brill.

Straus, Raphael. 1942. The "Jewish Hat" as an Aspect of Social History. *Jewish Social Studies* 4: 59–72.

Strickland, Debra Higgs. 2003. *Saracens, Demons, & Jews: Making Monsters in Medieval Art*. Princeton: Princeton University Press.

Stubbs, Katherine. 1998. Reading Material: Contextualizing Clothing in the Work of Anzia Yezierska. *MELUS* 23 (2): 157–72.

Summers, Leigh. 2001. *Bound to Please: A History of the Victorian Corset*. Oxford: Berg.

Swartz, Michael D. 2002. The Semiotics of the Priestly Vestments in Ancient Judaism. In *Sacrifice in Religious Experience*. A.I. Baumgarten, ed. Pp. 57–80. Leiden: Brill.

Szajkowski, Zosa. 1955. The Comtadin Jews and the Annexation of the Papal Province by France, 1789–1791. *Jewish Quarterly Review* 46: 181–93.

Thompson, Cynthia L. 1988. Hairstyles, Head-coverings, and St. Paul: Portraits from Roman Corinth. *Biblical Archaeologist* 51: 99–115.

Tigay, Jeffrey H. 1982. On the Meaning of TWTPT. *Journal of Biblical Literature* 101: 321–31.

Tigchelaar, Eibert J.C. 2003. The White Dress of the Essenes and the Pythagoreans. In *Jerusalem, Alexandria, Rome. Studies in Ancient Cultural Interaction in Honour of A. Hilhorst*. F.G. Martínez and G.P. Luttikhuizen, eds. Pp. 301–21. Leiden, Boston: Brill.

Tobenkin, Elias. 1925. *God of Might*. New York: Minton, Balch & Company.

van der Toorn, Karel. 1995. The Significance of the Veil in the Ancient Near East. In *Pomegranates and Golden Bells: Studies in Biblical, Jewish, and Near Eastern Ritual, Law, and Literature in Honor of Jacob Milgrom*. David P. Wright, David Noel Freedman, and Avi Hurvitz, eds. Pp. 327–39. Winona Lake: Eisenbrauns.

Trachtenberg, Joshua. 1939. *Jewish Magic and Superstition: A Study in Folk Religion*. New York: Behrman's Jewish Book House.

Trachtenberg, Joshua. 1943. *The Devil and the Jews: The Medieval Conception of the Jew and its Relation to Modern Antisemitism*. New Haven: Yale University Press.

Troy, Shari. 2002. *On the Play and Playing: Theatricality as Leitmotif in the Purimshpil of the Bobover Hasidim*. PhD Thesis. Dept of Theater, City University of New York.

Turnau, Irena. 1990. The Dress of the Polish Jews in the 17th and 18th Centuries. In *Proceedings of the Tenth World Congress of Jewish Studies*, Div D, Vol. II. Pp. 111–14. Jerusalem: World Union of Jewish Studies.

Van Dam, Cornelis. 1997. *The Urim and Thummim: A Means of Revelation in Ancient Israel*. Winona Lake, ID: Eisenbrauns.

Vedeler, Harold Torger. 2008. Reconstructing Meaning in Deuteronomy 22:5: Gender, Society, and Transvestitism in Israel and the Ancient Near East. *Journal of Biblical Literature* 127: 459–76.

Veselská, Dana. 2004. "And She Took Her Veil, and Covered Herself" (Genesis 24:65) 'Bridal Head Coverings' from the Collections of the Jewish Museum in Prague. *Judaica Bohemiae* 40: 93–103.

Vilhjálmsson, Vilhjálmur Örn. 2003. The King and the Star. In *Denmark and the Jews*. M. B. Jensen and Steven L. B. Jensen, eds. Pp. 102–17. Copenhagen: Institute for International Studies, Department for Holocaust and Genocide Studies.

Vincent, Nicholas. 1994/96. Two Papal Letters on the Wearing of the Jewish Badge, 1221 and 1229. *Jewish Historical Studies: Transactions of The Jewish Historical Society of England* 34: 209–24.

Wages, Emily. 2001. You Wear a Kippah? In *Yentl's Revenge: The Next Wave of Jewish Feminism*. D. Ruttenberg, ed. Pp. 161–67. Seattle: Seal Press.

Wallach, Kerry. 2011. Weimar Jewish Chic from Wigs to Furs: Jewish Women and Fashion in 1920s Germany. Paper delivered at The Twenty-Fourth Annual Klutznick-Harris Symposium, "Fashioning Jews: Clothing, Culture and Commerce," Creighton University, Omaha, NE, October 23–24, 2011.

Weiner, Jason. 2005a. Tzitzit—In or Out? *The Journal of Halacha and Contemporary Society* 49: 81–104.

Weiner, Jason. 2005b. On the Halakhic Basis for Wearing Black Hats. In *Milin Havivin (Beloved Words): An Annual Devoted to Torah, Society and the Rabbinate*, Vol. 1. Pp. 127–37, published by Yeshivat Chovevei Torah Rabbinical School.

Weinstein, Roni. 2003. *Marriage Rituals Italian Style: A Historical Anthropological Perspective on Early Modern Italian Jews*, 2003, Leiden: Brill.

Weiss, Susan. 2009. Under Cover: Demystificaiton of Women's Head Covering in Jewish Law. *Nashim: A Journal of Jewish Women's Studies & Gender Issues* 17: 89–115.

Welch, John W. and Claire Foley. 1996. Gammadia on Early Jewish and Christian Garments. *BYU Studies* 36: 252–58.

Wengeroff, Pauline. 2000. *Rememberings: The World of a Russian-Jewish Woman in the Nineteenth Century*. Translation by Henny Wenkart. Bethesda: University Press of Maryland.

Were, Graeme and Susanne Küchler, eds. 2005. *The Art of Clothing: A Pacific Experience.* London: UCL Press.

Wertheim, Aaron. 1992. *Law and Custom in Hasidism*. Translated by S. Himelstein. Hoboken, NJ: Ktav.

Wiesberg, Dvora E. 1992. On Wearing *Tallit* and Tefillin. In *Daughters of the King: Women and the Synagogue*. Susan Grossman and Rivka Haut, eds. Pp. 282–84. Philadelphia: The Jewish Publication Society.

Winston, Hella. 2005. *Unchosen: The Hidden Lives of Hasidic Rebels.* Boston: Beacon Books.

Wisch, Barbara. 2003. Vested Interest: Redressing Jews on Michelangelo's Sistine Ceiling. *Artibus et Historiae* 24: 143–72.

Wolfson, Elliot R. 2004. Flesh Become Word: Textual Embodiment and Poetic Incarnation. In *Language, Eros, Being: Kabbalistic Hermeneutics and Poetic Imagination*. Pp. 190–260. New York: Fordam University Press.

Woolf, Jeffrey R. 2000–1. Between Law and Society: Mahariq's Responsum on the "Ways of the Gentiles" (Huqqot Ha-'Akkum). *AJS Review* 25: 45–69.

Yaqin, Amina. 2007. Islamic Barbie: The Politics and Gender of Performativity. *Fashion Theory* 11: 173–88.

Ye'or, Bat. 1985. *The Dhimmi: Jews and Christians under Islam*. Translated by D. Maisel, P. Fenton, and D. Littman. Rutherford, NJ: Fairleigh Dickinson University Press (Orig. French 1980).

Yerushalmi, Yosef Hayim. 2005. *Haggadah and History: A Panorama in Facsimile of Five Centuries of the Printed Haggadah*. Philadelphia: Jewish Publication Society.

Yitzhak, Rabbi Hertzel Hillel. 2006. *Tzitzit, A Comprehensive Halachic Guide to the Ritual four-Cornered Garments According to Sephardic Tradition: Tzel Heharim Series*. Jerusalem/New York: Feldheim.

Yosefy, Chaim, Meir Ronnen, and Dennis Edelstein. 2003. Pseudo Alopecia Areata Caused by Skull-caps with Metal Pin Fasteners Used by Orthodox Jews in Israel. *Clinical & Developmental Immunology* 10 (2–4): 193–95.

Zborowski, Mark and Elizabeth Herzog. 1952. *Life Is With People: The Jewish Little-Town of Eastern Europe*. New York: International Universities Press.

Zenner, Walter P. 1985. Jewishness in America: Ascription and Choice. *Ethnic and Racial Studies* 8: 117–33.

Ziderman, Irving. 2008. The Biblical Dye Tekhelet and its Use in Jewish Textiles. *Dyes in History and Archaeology* 21: 36–44.

Zimmer, Eric. 1992. Men's Headcovering: The Metamorphosis of This Practice. In *Reverence, Righteousness, and Rahamanut: Essays in Memory of Rabbi Dr. Leo Jung*. J. J. Schacter, ed. Pp. 325–52. Northvale: Jason Aronson.

# Index